CHANGING RELATIONS: ACHIEVING INTIMACY IN A TIME OF SOCIAL TRANSITION

In a fast-changing world, what impact does social change have on our everyday relationships? How do modernisation processes influence our broader values, and how might these then affect our desires to marry, have a family, and develop our social networks? And how do sudden events in a society – invasions, civil conflict, terrorist attacks, collapse of a political system – influence our relationship decisions and processes?

In this book, Robin Goodwin critically reviews the literature on modernisation and contemporary relationships, challenging simplistic conclusions about the end of intimacy and the inevitable decline of personal commitment. Reviewing work from across the globe, he also contends that adaptation to rapid change is moderated by individual, social class, and cultural variations, with consequently differing impacts on everyday relations. In doing so, he brings together contemporary debates in psychology, sociology, and the political sciences on coping with social change and its impact on personal relations.

Robin Goodwin is professor of social psychology at Brunel University, West London. A winner of the New Faculty (Steve Duck) Prize from the International Society for the Study of Personal Relationships, he is an Associate Fellow of the British Psychological Society, associate editor at the *Journal of Social and Personal Relationships,* and past chair of the publications committee for the International Network on Personal Relationships.

ADVANCES IN PERSONAL RELATIONSHIPS

HARRY T. REIS
University of Rochester

MARY ANNE FITZPATRICK
University of South Carolina

ANITA L. VANGELISTI
University of Texas, Austin

Although scholars from a variety of disciplines have written and conversed about the importance of personal relationships for decades, the emergence of personal relationships as a field of study is relatively recent. *Advances in Personal Relationships* represents the culmination of years of multidisciplinary and interdisciplinary work on personal relationships. Sponsored by the International Association for Relationship Research, the series offers readers cutting-edge research and theory in the field. Contributing authors are internationally known scholars from a variety of disciplines, including social psychology, clinical psychology, communication, history, sociology, gerontology, and family studies. Volumes include integrative reviews, conceptual pieces, summaries of research programs, and major theoretical works. *Advances in Personal Relationships* presents first-rate scholarship that is both provocative and theoretically grounded. The theoretical and empirical work described by authors will stimulate readers and advance the field by offering new ideas and retooling old ones. The series will be of interest to upper division undergraduate students, graduate students, researchers, and practitioners.

OTHER BOOKS IN THE SERIES

Attribution, Communication Behavior, and Close Relationships
  Valerie Manusov and John H. Harvey
Communicating Affection: Interpersonal Behavior and Social Context
  Kory Floyd
Communicating Social Support
  Daena J. Goldsmith

Continued after the Index

Changing Relations: Achieving Intimacy in a Time of Social Transition

ROBIN GOODWIN

Brunel University

CAMBRIDGE
UNIVERSITY PRESS

CAMBRIDGE UNIVERSITY PRESS
Cambridge, New York, Melbourne, Madrid, Cape Town, Singapore, São Paulo, Delhi

Cambridge University Press
32 Avenue of the Americas, New York NY 10013-2473, USA

www.cambridge.org
Information on this title: www.cambridge.org/9780521842044

First published 2009

Printed in the United States of America

A catalogue record for this publication is available from the British Library.

Library of Congress Cataloguing in Publication data
Goodwin, Robin, 1964–
   Changing relations : achieving intimacy in a time of
   social transition / Robin Goodwin.
      p. cm.
   Includes bibliographical references and index.
   ISBN 978-0-521-84204-4 (hardback)
   1. Interpersonal relations.   2. Intimacy (Psychology)   3. Social networks.
   4. Social change.   I. Title.
   HM1106.G667 2009
   302.3′4–dc22   2008032134

ISBN 978-0-521-84204-4 hardback

To Kinga
Whose Love, Wisdom, and Beauty have changed my life

Contents

Foreword

As author Robin Goodwin writes, "This book is an attempt to deal with one big question: what happens to people's everyday relationships when there are significant changes in their society?" This is a very important question because relationships have differed substantially across both time and cultures. Take love. Members of many contemporary societies value love, consider it the basis for marriage, think it should be sexual, and seek opposite sex romantic partners. This hasn't always and everywhere been the case. In ancient Greece, for example, members of that society valued platonic forms of love. In their milieu, love wasn't linked with marriage, an institution that was then typically motivated by economic and political reasons. The ultimate in relationships for early Athenians was the nonsexual adoration of another, best exemplified in the bonds between two men. More recently, societies such as China have seen dramatic changes in the bases on which marriages are formed, going from predominantly arranged marriages to love matches. With shifts such as this occurring, it is crucial to know how sociocultural contexts and changes in societies affect the way we relate to others.

Research on relationships has thrived in the past 25 to 30 years. But research on how societal change influences relationships has not been a major focus. A few writers (e.g., Beck and Beck-Gernsheim, 2002), often from a sociological perspective, have written on this. Their analyses are largely scattered in diverse publications and have been neither integrated nor compared. The current volume fills a gap by bringing together this line of scholarship.

STRENGTHS OF THE VOLUME

Goodwin addresses in a superb way the intertwined nature of personal relationships and societal change. A few of his strengths as an author are that

- he writes in an engaging manner that I think you will enjoy reading;
- he offers a rich mosaic of ideas – asking and insightfully elaborating crucial questions;
- he brings a good appreciation of conceptual views on social change, succinctly explaining them, critically evaluating them, and showing their similarities and differences;
- he articulates his own fresh model of change that helps organise the book;
- he has a wealth of information about both (a) how relationships have varied across time and culture and (b) the social changes associated with those variations.

I have studied relationships throughout my professional career. Robin Goodwin's book has given me a world tour that has taught me new information and expanded my thinking. He has answered numerous questions, often in a more complex way that befits the complexity of social reality. I am grateful to him.

INTERNATIONAL ASSOCIATION FOR RELATIONSHIP RESEARCH SPONSORSHIP

This volume is sponsored by the International Association for Relationship Research. It is an exemplary addition to their *Advances in Personal Relationship Series*. The series includes integrative reviews and conceptual pieces. This volume is an integrative review but with a fresh conceptual framework. It admirably achieves the standards and orientation of the series in presenting

first-rate scholarship that is both provocative and theoretically grounded. The theoretical and empirical work described by authors will stimulate readers and advance the field by offering new ideas and retooling old ones. The series will be of interest to upper division undergraduate students, graduate students, researchers, and practitioners.

TWO IMPLICATIONS OF STUDYING SOCIAL
CHANGE FOR THE STUDY OF RELATIONSHIPS
AS A FIELD

Goodwin's key lesson that relationships aren't always the same across time and culture is related to a couple of issues for the study of relationships as a field. First, most knowledge about relationships comes from specific disciplines. The field as a whole has been described as multidisciplinary in the sense that scholars from psychology, sociology, communication, and other disciplines study relationships and are interested in one another's work. Nonetheless, research is still done largely from each investigator's own intellectual tradition. Investigators typically don't go beyond the classes of variables of concern to their discipline. Researchers working within their own discipline may briefly acknowledge the need to test their ideas cross-culturally, but for the most part principles are offered without careful identification of macro conditions when they don't hold. By showing the variety and plasticity of the forms that relationships take, Goodwin is issuing a strong reminder that we must attend to how principles studied by many relationship scholars may not be universal. All scholars, especially those examining the individual and interpersonal aspects of relationships, need to strive even more arduously to determine when phenomena can be found and when principles do and don't operate.

The second issue for the field that Goodwin's focus raises is related to the first. If many of the principles identified by relationship researchers are historically and/or culturally bound, can there be a science of relationships? Does the study of relationships become an historical and/or ethnographic activity without the rigor of a true science? My answer is that, despite historical and cultural variability, the study of relationships can qualify as a science. If there is cultural and historical variability, what I think is necessary for a science is that higher-order principles can be articulated about how basic principles may vary. For example, one belief found in societies such as England and the United States is that the more partners love each other, the more likely they are to marry. In collectivist societies this belief is much less prevalent (Levine, Sato, Hashimoto, & Verma, 1995). Thus scholars initially working in the West might advance the basic principle that love increases the likelihood of marriage, and later scholars with a broader scope might advance the meta-principle that the degree of collectivism-individualism in a society will alter the association between love and the likelihood of marriage. In this volume, Goodwin is taking steps to understand the principles underling how social change may alter relationship principles initially obtained in a given time and place. He is creatively advancing a path that others should extend and that would qualify the study of relationships as a science despite variability in findings.

A PREVIEW OF THE BOOK'S CONTENTS

The book has seven chapters. Chapters 1, 2, and 7 are at a broader conceptual level while the middle four chapters deal with particular aspects of relationships.

In Chapter 1, Goodwin defines social change ("any substantial shift in a political, economic, or social system") and discusses theoretical views of change. These theories deal with the various forms that social change takes and the causes or factors that shape social change. Goodwin notes that some see change as a linear progression with contemporary societies having achieved the highest level, whereas others see change as a more cyclical process of ups and downs. He describes a chicken-and-egg problem facing scholars of social change: which comes first, changes in people's ideas and values or changes in the social structure? He notes that change often involves both movement and resistance. Finally, he advances his own model of change, dividing it into two types: gradual, indirect change such as industrialisation, which occurs over a protracted time frame vs. rapid, direct change such as China's introduction of the one-child policy that had an immediate, abrupt impact. Goodwin's model takes into consideration the factors that mediate and moderate change. Illustrative of mediation, gradual social changes often lead to changes in general beliefs and values (an intervening process or mediator) that then lead to changes in relationships. Illustrative of moderators are factors (e.g., individual, group, or cultural) that influence the extent to which social change leads to transformation of relationships.

I especially admire three aspects of this model. First, the model illuminates different types of change. Second, I appreciate the analysis of mediating and moderating factors. This focuses attention on processes involved in change and times when change is or is not likely. The concern with how social change impacts relationships and the identification of various mediating and moderating factors lead to my third kudo. Social change is a decidedly macro level variable. Yet the model incorporates variables across a spectrum of levels from individual difference factors through group and cultural forces. It gives a more complete picture.

Chapter 2 deals with views of modernisation. Writers concerned with modernisation generally believe that industrialisation is associated with cultural values and leads to predictable social and cultural consequences. Linked to modernisation are the notions of globalisation of industries, markets, communication, values, and so on – and of people being individualistically (rather than more collectively) oriented. Goodwin first describes views of modernisation including modernisation's presumed consequences for personal relationships. He next discusses individualisation and globalisation. He then critiques views of modernisation asking such questions as "Is industrialisation really producing homogeneity around the world?" and "Is a dichotomous view of a traditional vs. a modern world too simplistic?"

With Chapter 3, Goodwin begins his treatment of specific aspects of relationships. In this chapter he addresses issues of whether people get attached to a partner and, if and when they do so, how partners are selected and how intimacy is achieved. He notes a trend away from marriages arranged by elders toward individuals selecting their own partners. Goodwin describes the role of new technologies, especially the Internet, in relationship formation and the ways these technologies influence the role social networks (e.g., individuals and the social ties between them) play in the development of long-term relationships. His answer here may surprise some readers. Implicit at multiple points in this chapter is a question asked by many: Is the current nature of society undermining people's capacity to form and/or sustain intimate bonds?

In Chapter 4, Goodwin turns to friendships and the interrelated concepts of social networks, social capital, and social support (the resources others provide to us). Social capital is anchored in one's social network but the notion of social capital is broader than just the idea of a social network of relationships. Social capital implies we get resources from our networks, that we experience interpersonal trust, and that our social relationships involve normative regulation. This chapter begins with the debate between those arguing that the "modern world" undermines friendships vs. those who posit that friendships and social networks assume new importance as the role of the family fades and the challenges of daily life mount. A major section of the chapter deals with the thesis, advanced by Robert Putnam and others, that social capital and trust are declining. They depict this as being largely due to the detriment of society. In considering social support, Goodwin looks at factors that enhance or diminish the amount of support provided. The chapter ends with discussion of the social support and social capital among immigrants (again with a focus on what enhances or diminishes these) and finally, based on theories and some of Goodwin's own research, how terrorist attacks might influence support.

Next up is sex (Chapter 5) – how social change is influencing sexual standards (e.g., premarital sexual relations), homosexuality, contraception/abortion, and the transmission of sexual diseases. Many see a general loosening of sexual conduct. Although evidence of this can be found, Goodwin also notes some of the resistance to such a trend and qualifications that should be added to such a simple, broad generalisation.

In the book's longest chapter, Chapter 6, Goodwin addresses marriage and the family. In rough terms, this chapter is divided into an initial section dealing mostly with gradual change, a second section dealing with rapid change, and a shorter final section on adaptation. The first part of the chapter looks at ways the family might be changing along several dimensions (e.g., extended vs. nuclear composition, the role of the family in elder care, family size, parental roles, parent-child relations, childcare, division of labor, gender roles, cohabitation, single parenthood, the importance assigned to marriage). Underlying this depiction is the question: has the family declined? The second section of the chapter looks at rapid change in three regions of the world (Eastern Europe, Asia, and the Middle East) and the impact of two major events (war and immigration). In the third section, Goodwin reviews evidence on the variability in the adaptations to social change. He cites authors calling into question modernisation theory's view that workplace modernisation will inevitably lead to a corresponding linear type modernisation of family behavior. Goodwin discusses an alternative ecocultural model of change. In this model, people adapt to their ecological situation. In one version of this model, ecological conditions influence family structure and values, which, in turn, have an effect on family interaction and socialisation patterns, which, in turn, impact on children's development of self and their relations with others.

In the final chapter, Goodwin briefly summarises a few of the key conclusions of the volume. He then presents an analysis of the extent to which social change might impact on eight classes of variables that in turn influence relationships. In this framework, social change is apt to have little or no impact on evolutionary and physiological variables, a small to moderate influence on individual values and personality, and a moderate to large impact on role relationships and work structure. Goodwin ends his volume using his analysis to reflect on prospects for personal relationships in the future.

CONCLUSIONS

Throughout the literature on relationships and social change, as well as throughout this book, there is an underlying question of whether contemporary societies are undermining relationships. Some authors see contemporary society as enhancing relationships. What seems to be a more widespread worry is that contemporary social change is causing a decline in social life. Still other scholars such as Roy Baumeister and Mark Leary (1995) claimed that humans have a fundamental need to belong, perhaps implying that regardless of the social system people will seek ways to satisfy their need for interpersonal connection.

Goodwin's analysis leads him to conclude, "It is too simple to portray social change and its implications for close relationships as simply positive or negative. Change is likely to have differential impacts on different individuals, groups and cultures." His analysis and marshalling of evidence in getting to this conclusion is a major accomplishment of his book. To Professor Goodwin I say "Bravo!" To you as a reader I say "If you are interested in how social changes are associated with people's everyday relationships, read this book." Like me, you will be glad you did.

Daniel Perlman
University of North Carolina at Greensboro
Publication Committee Chair, International Association
for Relationship Research, 2006–08

REFERENCES

Baumeister, R. F., & Leary, M. R. (1995). The need to belong: Desire for interpersonal attachments as a fundamental human motivation. *Psychological Bulletin, 117,* 497–529.

Beck, U., & Beck-Gernsheim, E. (2002). *Individualization: Institutionized individualism and its social and political consequences.* Sage: London.

Levine, R., Sato, S., Hashimoto, T., & Verma, J. (1995). Love and marriage in eleven cultures. *Journal of Cross-Cultural Psychology, 26,* 554–571.

Acknowledgements

I owe a huge thank-you to a number of people who helped me with this book. My research collaborators in Georgia, Russia, Ukraine, Hong Kong, Poland, and Hungary generously provided me with personal accounts of their own experiences during a time of transition. These were invaluable when developing my arguments for this book. I also received useful feedback and support from Elaine Hatfield and members of the cross-cultural discussion group during my sabbatical in Hawaii in 2005. As the book neared completion, my colleagues at Brunel – Kinga Goodwin, Miriam Park, and John Roberts – gave me detailed feedback on draft materials, although, of course, I take full responsibility for any errors in the text. My publisher, Cambridge University Press – in particular, Philip Laughlin, Eric Schwartz, and Simina Calin – showed extreme patience in a lengthening deadline. (I will never again criticise my students for overdue submissions.) Finally, Daniel Perlman, as Chair of the Publication Committee of the International Association for Relationship Research, gave me great support during the final phase of the writing and kindly consented to write the Foreword to this text.

CHAPTER 1

The Nature of Social Change

INTRODUCTION

This book attempts to deal with one big question: What happens to people's everyday relationships when there are significant changes in their society? These changes can be dramatic, such as a war or an invasion or the sudden collapse of a political social system, as in Eastern Europe in the late 1980s. These changes can also be the result of the fears that accompany new terrorism threats or the anxieties that can follow a planned handover of a people's authority to a new governmental system (as in the transitions of Macao and Hong Kong to the Chinese mainland in the late 1990s). Changes can also be more subtle, but no less significant, such as when significant populations are on the move. Such a movement may impact significantly on both the migrating groups and their new host societies.

According to Lauer, "Social change is normal and continual, but in various directions, at various rates, and at multiple levels of social life" (Lauer, 1977, p. 6), and some argue that change may be one of the most constant parts of our environment (Segall et al., 1990). Yet, while every society is undoubtedly in some state of flux all the time, most of these changes are relatively small and gradual: There are no wars at home, little dramatic shift in political systems, and only small changes in migration patterns. What I will focus on for much of this book is the large and relatively rapid changes: the overnight overthrow of a government or the rapid collapse of a regime (such as in South Africa after apartheid), civil war, or an unexpected terrorist attack. Rapid changes such as these often leave substantial numbers of people with little opportunity to adapt their everyday lives, and this rapid change can be very stressful. Toffler (1970) famously coined the phrase "future shock" when discussing multiple rapid changes. During such sudden transitions, important aspects of a society may shift, and these shifts can have important impacts on people's everyday interactions with one another – be that at work, in the family, or when involved with leisure activities. Of course, not everyone is equally affected – indeed, one of the key themes of this book is that these changes have uneven effects on different groups of people. However, this book is about changes that have an impact on the daily lives of a large percentage of a population – not the twenty thousand civil servants who suffer a pay cut as a result of a policy shift but the twenty million who find that, overnight, their whole economic system has been replaced by one that is ideologically very different. Of key concern is the way in which people cope with an often confusing new world or lifestyle and how this impacts on their personal relationships.

DEFINING AND MEASURING SOCIAL CHANGE

The study of social change originated back to at least by the time of the ancient Greeks. Aristotle was fascinated by change and its relation to organic growth, and he was among the first to make a scientific study of change (Nisbet, 1969). Although the study of social change has formed a key mission for sociological research (Gillies & Edwards, 2005), defining social change has been far from easy (Berry, 1980). Indeed, social change has become rather a catchall term referring to just about anything in a state of flux.

Ibn Khaldun, a fourteenth-century Arab scholar, stressed the historical method in understanding change and pointed to the multiple factors that needed to be accounted for to understand any change. These included the physical environment, the social structure, and the different personalities involved. Consistent with this, definitions of change have typically included alterations in social actions and interactions, human relationships, and attitudes (Lauer, 1977). Lauer himself defines social change as "alterations in social phenomena at various levels of human life from the individual to the global" (p. 4). Such levels range from individual attitudes and interactions to organisational, institutional, community, and societal changes and cultural, civilization, and global transitions. Boudon similarly refers to social change as an "inclusive concept that refers to alterations in social phenomena at various levels from the individual to the global" (Boudon, 1986, p. 112). Giddens (1989) notes that while "there is a sense in which everything changes, all of the time" (p. 43), significant change means "modification of *basic institutions* during a specific period" (p. 45). This has to be set against a baseline of that which remains stable during this time. Some of the difficulties here are summarised by Etzioni and Etzioni (1964):

Social change ... may originate in any institutional area, bringing about changes in other areas, which in turn make for further adaptations in the initial sphere of change. Technological, economic, political, religious, ideological, demographic, and stratificational factors are all viewed as potentially independent variables which influence each other as well as the course of society (p. 7).

In practice, the ways in which social scientists have defined social change have closely reflected the methods they have used to study such change and the topics that have attracted their attention. Much sociological and political work has been very broad-brush, employing large-scale surveys. Such work has attempted to capture large historical phases (such as industrialisation) and, more recently, postindustrialisation (Gillies & Edwards, 2005). As studies of post-industrialisation have become more common, there has been a keen interest in the study of disintegration, a theme that I will return to several times in this book. Such work often had an interest in the state of alienation that such change precipitated and frequently an explicit interest in the development and actions of different social classes. Here the analysis has been primarily at the structural/institutional level; entire societies, or at least complete social classes, have been studied. More-microanalytic studies, such as the classic study of Young and Willmott (1957) of Bethnal Green in East London, have focused on everyday lives and interactions, while maintaining a strong interest in social class. In contrast, psychologists have been more interested in identifying and reacting to changes in terms of coping strategies, values, and beliefs, whether precipitated by events within or outside of society. In this book, I define social change as "any substantial shift in a political, economic, or social system. This may be identified through economic or political indicators, population movements, changes in legal statuses, or the widespread and rapid adoption of a new technology that significantly impacts on the everyday lives of large proportions of a population." In this definition, the emphasis is on change from "above" rather than a slower evolution within a society. This is then separated from the *impact* of this change, which can occur at a number of levels, both societal and within the group or individual.

THEORIES OF CHANGE

When considering how social change influences relationships, it is useful first to consider how some of the major theorists of social change have approached the issue of social transformation. Identifying these perspectives allows us to understand some of the ideological viewpoints inherent in the research on social change that I will review throughout this book.

There are a number of different ways of classifying theories of social change. Berry (1980) distinguishes between accounts that separate sociocultural, institutional, and individual change and between change that is internal and that which is instigated from without. Boudon (1986) compares broad theories that consider general (and generally irreversible) trends with others that claim that if certain conditions allow (for example, industrialisation), something else will happen. An example of the latter is provided by Parsons (1966), who suggests that the family undergoes nucleation following industrialisation. For some, it is the *form* of the change that is important, whilst for others *causes* or *factors of change* are important, such as the psychological values that individuals hold that lead to particular social processes. We can also consider levels of abstraction (Is the whole society under consideration or just part of it?) and the degree of plasticity a theory permits human behaviour. Therefore, some theories are rather deterministic, allowing for only limited control over our action, although few completely limit a human's freedom of action. Other accounts permit individual variations and smaller group pressures to help act as determinants of action.

In the following review, I compare broad theories that point either to a simple developmental path or imply an evolution of societies to theories that are more cyclical in nature. I also consider functionalist theories (that generally emphasise a gradual process of change) to those that stress ideas and social psychological processes as drivers of change. Finally, I consider some of the factors that may lead people to resist change. This notion of *resilience* to change will reappear several times later in the book, as I consider how rapid social changes have impacted on communities, families, and individuals.

Development and Evolution

Developmental and evolutionary theories envisage a sense of progress and hold a linear view that tends to see only the most recent societies as having achieved the highest level. Change is viewed as having four characteristics: It is natural, inevitable, and continuous and moves in a particular direction (Nisbet, 1969). Change is also seen as necessary, just as Darwin explains development following on from natural selection. Change can proceed from natural causes (such as in Herbert Spencer's theory of fixed stages; Spencer, 1897) or may follow contradictions within a society (in the works of Hegel or Marx). Whilst this notion of societal progression dates back to Aristotle, a concern with intellectual and cultural progress was a driving force behind the developmental theories of key thinkers in the nineteenth and early twentieth centuries.

Social evolutionists compare modernity with a more "primitive" and "traditional" way of life. They are often critical of the traditional mode of living, seeing it as marred by being hierarchical and trapped within its local and rural setting. For Spencer, societies are becoming more complex and increasingly coherent and heterogeneous: "up from the simple tribe, alike in all its part, to the civilized nation, full of structural and functional unalikeness" (1892, p. 585). Parsons (1966) similarly sees social evolution as a movement to increasingly complex social institutions. In his *Evolutionary and Comparative Perspectives*, he divided history into an early "primitive" phase, succeeded by an "intermediate" phase, finally culminating in a "modern or industrialised" society. Comte, who coined the term "sociology," saw progress in societies occurring through reason. "The experience of the past proves ... that the progressive march of civilization follows a natural and unavoidable course" (1887, p. 555). This path moves from the theological (dominated by a belief in the supernatural) through a transitional metaphysical/juridical stage (which emphasises the role of nature) to a final scientific/positive phase. This scientific/positive stage is an ideal state, characterised by reasoning, where "observation dominates over imagination" (p. 573). Such ideal societies, of course, are usually modern and Western. Focusing on the institution of marriage, Westermarck (1922) sees marriage, too, as evolving from primitive promiscuity to group marriage, polygamy, polyandry, and finally monogamy.

Noticeably, however, not all theorists of societal development were so optimistic. In his theory of *Gemeinschaft* and *Gesellschaft*, Tönnies traced the development of society from a tradition-based, collective *Gemeinschaft* society, where folk life and culture persisted, to a freer and less traditional state of *Gesellschaft*. As with the other theorists described above, this latter stage is marked by rational will and a development to a "civilized" state that is a linear and irreversible process (Tönnies, 1957). However, Tönnies is far less certain about the benefits of this change. Instead, he sees these developments as also encouraging alienation and atomisation, as the whole world becomes one anonymous city. Family life in particular is often negatively influenced by such change. In a similar vein, Durkheim (1951) suggested a two-stage theory of evolution of social change: from undifferentiated peoples who live in "mechanical solidarity" to a more differentiated society, where there are sharp divisions between societal members. This new society is less homogeneous and emphasises differences between peoples. This leads to a lack of integration of society demonstrated, famously, in his discussion of increased suicide rates. I will argue that this pessimism about societal atomisation is still evident in many contemporary theories of family change.

Closely related to evolutionary accounts of social change are those of geographic determinism. Huntingdon (1924) examined the rise and fall of civilisation, locating many of these changes in terms of the geographic differences between societies. The notion of change as environmentally driven can also be found in Steward's *Theory of Culture Change: The Methodology of Multilinear Evolution* (1955). From Steward's perspective, cultural change results from adaptation to the environment – something he calls "cultural ecology." As we will see, however, while such a theme is also present in modern-day cross-cultural psychological accounts of cultural differentiation (for example, in Van de Vliert, 2006), it has also gathered considerable criticism over the years. As LaPiere (1965) observes:

A verdant piece of land may afford human beings an opportunity to maintain thereon an agricultural society; but the existence of a verdant piece of land does not ensure its being inhabited or ... [that] it will be used for agriculture (p. 213). It is men ... who determine what uses they make of the environments that are offered to them (p. 214).

For such critics, particular restrictions in a physical environment may be important for some aspects of societal organisation, but the environment interacts with many other physical, biological, and demographic factors.

A competing account of progression was offered by Karl Marx. Famously, he claimed, "The history of all hitherto existing society is the history of class struggles" (Marx & Engels, 1932, p. 9). For Marx, historical imperatives would lead to the development of class consciousness and the inevitable "victory of the proletariat" (p. 21). His is a theory of progress, even if this progress is not simple. Instead, there are a series of "dialetical conflicts" that will eventually lead to the liquidation of the exploiting class and the establishment of a classless society. Change is not evolutionary but revolutionary, with contradictions in society the key to these changes. Material conditions determine social and political life and, as a result, social relationships.

The notion that new technology leads directly to social changes can also be related to ideas of evolution and change. Economic theories of social change view technology as influencing economics, which then in turn can influence the family (Rothenbacher, 1998). Many have noted how transportation has affected the ways in which people communicate and meet with each other. For some, the invention of the steam engine and the development of roads and other transport systems have been seen as leading to a weakening in kinship ties (see, for example, Ogburn & Nimkoff, 1955). In his study of the Tanala of Madagascar, Linton (1939) claimed that the irrigation of crops meant that joint families no longer needed to irrigate the fields. The unavailability of land for wet rice cultivation led to mobility and the development of new villages, so that the joint families became scattered, only meeting for religious ceremonies or similar occasions. Another frequently cited example is that of the contraceptive pill. The introduction of this pill seemed to allow women a much greater control over their sexual behaviour, and it coincided with the much-touted "sexual revolution" of the 1960s and 1970s in Western Europe and North America.

However, the impact of new technology is probably often overstated, and, as I will argue throughout this book, the exact effects of any technological changes are often hard to fathom. Changes in societies attributed to technological revolutions may come from a range of political and societal factors in a society that might only be partially related to technology. Technological change is frequently short-lived and may affect only some parts of the social system and some populations (LaPiere, 1965). As Giddens notes, technology does things only in the sense that human beings act on it; it does not drive social change without the actions of individuals. So, while information technology may be important in influencing the global economy, this has to be viewed alongside other social systems associated with capitalism and industrialisation (Giddens & Pierson, 1998). Furthermore, particular opinion leaders (important individuals, but also the news media and other sources of influence) may be crucial in technology take-up. Thus, the introduction of the contraceptive bill in the 1960s probably advanced sexual liberation, but it was only widely distributed within certain cultures. The same technology can lead to several outcomes and can be applied differently in different societies. Automobiles may take people out of a community, but they can also help people maintain otherwise distant social ties or allow for the development of new relationships that might otherwise have been impractical. The growth of less costly international airfares makes relationships between people living in geographically distant places economically more viable, but it can also make working apart from family members a more feasible option. Duffield, Gavin, and Scott (2004) studied close relationships initiated through internet dating. In their analysis of more than two hundred members of an internet UK dating site who met their partners online, it was face-to-face interaction – or the relatively "old" technology of the telephone – that was the key determinant of whether or not the couple continued to meet, not the simple use of internet technology.

A core assumption made in many of these ideas of societal development is that all societies are converging into one Western model. Many of these convergence theories are based on the premise that certain technical skills are demanded by an industrial world, and this leads to homogenisation (Giddens, 1989). Whilst such accounts can provide a useful explanation for some rapidly changing societies, they also allowed an intellectual elite to justify conflicts as inevitable and natural and failed to allow for a more complex cultural evolution that took a number of different paths. Instead, there may be different types of developments in different societies (Giddens, 1989). Because much of this is key to current debates about the ideal nature of relationships and how societal development has influenced them, I will discuss this further in my consideration of modernisation and Westernisation theories in the next chapter.

Cyclical Change and the Functionalist Perspective

Not all theorists see societies as on a progressive trend. For others, societies go through a series of ups and downs, often described in terms of life cycles (for example, Spengler, 1926). Such cyclical theories may be relatively optimistic (Toynbee & Caplan, 1972) or more pessimistic (Spengler, 1926) about the standing of modern Western societies. Some of these approaches also embrace the notion of adaptation, which is also discussed by evolutionary theorists. For example, in general systems theory (Etzioni, 1968), social systems go through ongoing changes in order to meet individual needs. These then provide feedback that allows adaptation to the environment, permitting these systems to continuously change. In studying cultural phenomena, such as art forms and music, Sorokin (1998) noted how systems fluctuate between times of concern for the public good (which he termed "ideational") and more selfish (or "sensate") times, when individual welfare comes first. Whilst Sorokin describes a movement from the ideational of the Middle Ages towards the sensate and then the ideational again, different aspects of society may have different priorities at the same time. This reinforces the important observation that change can occur at different levels and in different ways within a single society (LaPiere, 1965).

The adaptive significance of change is stressed by the *structural functional theorists*. Functionalists try to understand problems of change processes in the context of a stable system. Theorists here see change as slow and societies as interrelated parts, with cause and effect having a reciprocal impact on one another. Change often occurs from within the group as is often resisted (Durkheim, 1982; Nisbet, 1969). In a similar vein, *systems theorists* see disturbance in any part of a system as leading to a strong desire for reassurance and equilibrium (Wapner & Craig-Bray, 1992). Functionalists frequently describe changes in the roles and functions of the family. The modernisation process is often seen as having led to a homogenisation of households, with each member having very different and clear functions (Rothenbacher, 1998). A large change in a family member's occupational prospects following a major societal transition in society can certainly lead to problematic issues within the family regarding this individual's legitimate position. This may lead to some reassignment of roles and duties. However, over time there is adaptation – what Parsons refers to as an evolutionary "upgrading." Families may adapt by adopting "pseudo-kin" when faced with the need for additional workers to contribute to a family enterprise, a pattern often evident following migration (Lau, 1981). Similarly, technological changes may lead to some changes in family structures, but the family also adapts to these over time. For example, the introduction of power looms in the 1820s led to pressures on the traditional family labour pattern, as well as differentiation between work roles and other family functions. This produced widespread dissatisfaction that culminated in strikes and riots. However, new initiatives, such as the cooperative movement, and some flexibility in factory processes led to new family structures that were better able to deal with the new work patterns (Smelser, 1959).

Ideas and the Social Psychological Approach

For centuries, social scientists have been struggling with the problem of which came first: the economic system, which then led to changes in ideas, values, and political institutions, or particular political and cultural values, which then drove the economic system (Diez-Nicolas, 2003). Marxists, for example, argue that ideas are important, but material (economic) factors are ultimately more significant. In contrast, idealists emphasise the role of ideas, ideologies, or values in effecting change (Lauer, 1977). For example, ideological factors of culture and ideas can be seen as leading to behavioural changes, which then influence the family (Rothenbacher, 1998). Weber (1958) saw the development of capitalism as helped by a particular version of Protestant thought, which shaped the personalities of key entrepreneurs. Whilst Weber suggested a sense of cultural development (over time, societies tend to become more rational and coherent, similar to those theorists of progress I described above), different religious beliefs may lead to different social movements, with different outcomes in diverse cultures (Lauer, 1977). Although it is easy to exaggerate the tension, there are important differences between those who stress the importance of social structures in forming an individual's values and those who tend to emphasise the role of values in forming the social structure. My position is to agree with Boudon and to stress the interaction between the material and the ideal. In his words:

According to circumstances, values may or may not be a variable that it is important to take into account. Depending on the situation, they may be seen as primary or secondary, or it may be impossible to decide which they are (Boudon 1986, p. 182).

This view is taken by many contemporary psychologists studying social change who have striven to identify which individual characteristics can lead to, or result from, social change (for example, Georgas, Berry, Shaw, Christakopoulou, Mylonas, 1996). In a similar vein, Berry (1980) argues that particular psychological characteristics may be antecedents to change, others consequences of change, while yet others combine both.

To effect ideational change, certain key figures might be particularly important in a society (Giddens, 1989). These include religious and intellectual figures, political elites, and opinion leaders in a particular generation. Kennedy and Kirwil (2004) argue that the sociology of elites is vital for understanding transition cultures, such as the social transitions that have occurred in Poland since the end of communism. Martindale (1962) argues that intellectuals are major movers of change. Inkeles and Smith (1974) find education to be a key predictor of modern lifestyles and attitudes, followed by exposure to mass media and occupation as important predicting variables. Certainly, education can have a radicalising effect, with the more educated people often having new opportunities following large-scale upheavals. For example, in China at the start of the twentieth century, the young opposed anything that appeared reactionary, while students played an important part in the May Fourth Movement of 1919, which led to the birth of modern China. However, it must be remembered that those who lead modernising trends in a society might be quite dissimilar from those who traditionally led a society, with different interests and motives in their leadership.

Parenting behaviour may be important in producing the kinds of values that lead to psychological change. McClelland (1961) speaks of "modern man," where the desire for achievement leads to an entrepreneurial spirit and rapid economic development. Here it is the parent's warmth and encouragement that lead to a need for achievement, although the parent–child interaction is also important. Kahl (1968), working in the United States, Brazil, and Mexico, identifies seven core areas that contribute to activism in modern society: activism, low integration with relatives, preference for urban living, individualism, low community stratification, participation in mass media, and low stratification of life chances. I return to these concepts of modernity in more detail in the next chapter.

By stressing the importance of individual psychological factors, social psychological theories are often challenged to explain the widespread presence of a particular value or attribute (such as the need for achievement). But at the same time, it is also clear that different people react to changes in different ways, sometimes in manners that might not have been expected. Hence, some embrace a change as an opportunity, while others see it as a threat, with much depending on the local situation as well as the coping skills of the individual (Lazarus & Folkman, 1984). The impact of rapid social change on personal relationships is often complex: For example, greater social fluidity in wartime allows for previous forbidden matches, and widespread societal uncertainty leads to the persistence of some relationships that might otherwise have drifted apart. Many have pointed out that social constraints only act in terms of actors' interests or motivations; it is individuals who are the true agents of actions (Giddens & Pierson, 1998). An ideational account reminds us to consider the importance of taking into account the meaning for the individual or his or her group of any social change. A change in social structure does not instantly lead to major changes in behaviours, although it may motivate some actions. Ideational accounts also challenge us to ask how particular changes are *comprehensible* (Boudon, 1986; Weber, 1921). I return to the significance of this appraisal process below.

STRESS AND RESISTANCE TO CHANGE

A number of authors have also considered the stresses involved in social change. The aftermath of any radical societal upheaval is likely to be greater stress than before, although situations differ greatly in the time it takes for the situation to return to prerevolutionary level. As I will argue throughout this book, every significant social change is also potentially dysfunctional in some respects, and over the long run some may have dysfunctional by-products. In LaPiere's words, "Any change always involves considerable stress, both individual and collective. . . . [I]n the process of being accomplished, the change produces its own stress and strains – discontents, frustrations, dissensions, and disappointments" (1965, p. 478). Unsurprisingly, therefore, just as change is constantly occurring, resistance is also continuous (Lauer, 1977).

Most studies of change focus on resistance to top-down events, such as the imposition of a dress code on women or limitations on fertility. Some also consider how individuals or groups may confront the introduction of new technologies or other innovations. Unfortunately, organisational and ideological changes are frequently hard to assess unambiguously, so that individuals often resist quite functional innovations as well as productive ones (LaPiere, 1965). A wide range of groups or individuals within a society might resist change, especially when the change is not clearly understood or is seen as threatening (Spicer, 1952). Military establishments may promote radical internal change – such as in a coup – but they are usually amongst those most opposed to change. Established religious groups may also be seen as resistant to change – for example, when the Catholic Church has challenged some aspects of birth control. Those living in rigidly or clearly defined social groups might also be less liable to accept change. And, of course, those with a vested interest in maintaining the status quo are likely to resist change, including not only those who were wealthy or powerful under the old regime or social system, but also those who have skills and knowledge that are now redundant or who see values such as basic loyalty under threat. Even those whose daily routines now need major change may feel disquietude following new structural changes. Writing in the 1960s, LaPiere described the disruptive effects of the arrival of supermarkets in town for many housewives. The new establishments did not permit these women their familiar casual conversations with the shop staff (LaPiere, 1965).

The persistence of certain structural factors in a society may also encourage the continuity of particular traditions or encourage a more subtle form of resistance. In highly rule-bound societies, where there is selective application of those rules, personal relationships become highly important and social networks prime (Hofstede, 2001). Frequently, the flouting of regulations is permitted through the existence of well-placed personal contacts that allow for this (Fukuyama, 1995). More than a decade after the end of communism in the Soviet Union, the continuation of collectivistic activities in schools meant that particular styles of child upbringing persisted. Similarly, small-business developments in the 1990s still depended on relatives and friends as functional aids when bank loans and other financial guarantors were unreliable. I return to this when I consider friendships and social networks in more detail in Chapter 4.

If there is one simple message from the different theorists cited above, it is that social change is an extremely complex phenomenon and that there are few simple rules that apply readily to all situations (Altman, 1992). Grand theories are rarely testable or appropriate everywhere. Whilst we might be able to count the number of televisions (or, indeed, divorces) in a society, it is much more difficult to designate a "Stage Two" society, or even a "postindustrial" one, without creating serious questions about the permanence of change, what identifies one particular phase, and so on (LaPiere, 1965). Few people can claim to have seen the simple "growth of a civilisation"; instead, we see only a mixture of the old persistence and new phenomena (Nisbet, 1969).

Rather than asking whether there are simple causes and effects in the study of social change, it is probably more fruitful to try to explain why some causes lead to quite different effects in different situations (Boudon, 1986). As a result, Boudon concludes, theories can only be locally and partly valid and "scientific." "[T]he only *scientific* theories of social change are *partial* and *local* ones" (p. 208).

To constitute a socially significant change, the new needs to be not only adopted by many, but thoroughly incorporated into a social system (LaPiere, 1965). In reality, of course, most radical social change is unexpected, and it is hard to see in advance the extent to which it will be truly adopted or personalised into everyday life. Change should also be transmitted between groups (usually between generations) before it can be seen as truly enduring, and this, of course, takes time (Inglehart, 2003). Finally, societal change occurs alongside other, more naturally occurring life changes that may interact with or be exacerbated by the societal trauma around them. Thus, the social roles adopted by a new parent will continue even during revolutions, as will the status changes accompanying the loss of employment, even if that employment is a direct result of broader societal change (Wapner & Craig-Bray, 1992).

As I will discuss throughout this book, the study of social change is often heavily influenced by the value judgements of observers and the levels of analysis at which *they* think change is occurring. For example, when we look at broad social change across countries, as do researchers investigating the move from industrial to postindustrial societies, we are likely to make significant value judgements about the impact of politics, economics, religion, and the like in trying to explain cultural variations. Focusing on a particular society – such as the United States following the Second World War – we may attribute a rapid increase in the birthrate to greater economic affluence or a rise in hedonism following the jubilation of victory (LaPiere, 1965). A decline in social networks might be interpreted as a decline in this jubilation, a rise of particular individualistic values, or the outcome of new, distracting technologies, such as television (Putnam, 2000). The interpersonal *outcomes* of social change are sometimes even more difficult to determine. Huston (2000) identifies three levels of analysis when considering the ecological niches in which couples operate: the individual, the relational (in particular, the dynamics of a marital couple), and the societal. Shared beliefs and value systems provide an important backdrop for everyday marital interactions; changes in work structures influence time management within a couple; and environmental stressors can be "brought home" and exacerbate couple interactions. The ultimate implications of this, however, may be hard to predict, as the correlation between marital satisfaction and divorce is often not strong, particularly in many non-Western societies. As Johnson notes, spouses decide to stay together, not only because of *personal commitments*, but because of moral obligations (which may reflect their religion or wider social or cultural norms) as well as legal and financial restraints (*structural commitments*). As a result, couples may remain together in stressful situations because of their financial situation, the lack of competing alternative relationships, or fears of wider societal sanctions (Johnson, Caughlin, & Huston, 1999).

A FRAMEWORK

Throughout this book, I will encapsulate some of the above work on social change into a general framework that examines both rapid and direct societal transformations and more gradual, indirect processes and their impacts on personal relationships. This framework is presented below.

The basic principle I suggest here is not a new one: As societies change, people are motivated to adapt their lives to fit in with the new changes in their daily lives. Much of this adaptation is pragmatic – for instance, if traveling in a car with a member of the opposite sex could lead to arrest and internment, then such a behaviour is likely to decrease. Other adaptations are more long-term; preferences, values, and behaviours evolve to meet the biological necessities of food, shelter,

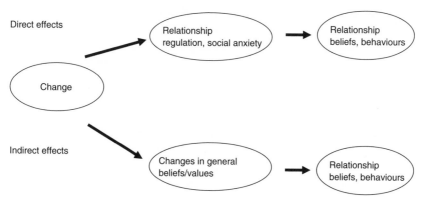

Figure 1.1. Modelling change.

safety, and reproduction within a particular environmental niche. This at its simplest is a functionalist account, one that rejects the notion that societal change either is inevitable or is moving towards any particular end. Indeed, in my next chapter on modernisation I will argue that such a notion of progression is likely to be regressive for the study of relationships and change. At the same time, I will also argue, in line with many of the critics of functionalism, that the impacts of societal changes are often more a story of dissonance than simple adaptation, particularly when these changes are imposed upon unwilling populaces. I divide the impact of social changes on personal relationships into two main types: rapid and direct and slower and more indirect. All of these changes have to be understood within a network of other moderating and mediating factors, which I discuss below.

Rapid, Direct Change

Some social changes have a direct impact on those who live in a particular society. In most cases, these direct impacts can be seen as introducing new relationship constraints or regulations. The effects of these changes will then have further impacts on individuals' relationships and may in themselves go on to stimulate demands for new social change (Rothenbacher, 1998). As examples of such legislation, the one-child policy, introduced in China in 1979, aimed to restrict the number of children a couple could have; bigamy became illegal under the Chinese Marriage Law (1980) and in India under the Hindu Marriage Act of 1955, with the latter act also prohibiting child marriage in India; and moral codes introduced by the Taliban in Afghanistan after they came to power in 1996 forbade women from leaving home wearing attractive clothes or from being on the streets not wearing a burka. Indeed, sexual behaviour has often been subject to strict regulation, such as when in 1966 Nicolae Ceauşescu abolished abortions in Romanian state hospitals. The Chernobyl disaster led to many couples in the Ukraine becoming reluctant to have children for fear of birth defects (Panok, Pavlenko, & Korallo, 2006). In Eastern Germany, following the end of communism and then unification, school curricula required the development of new personal skills and the adaptive behaviours appropriate for the new economic and political climate (Elder, 1998; Silbereisen & Wiesner, 2002). In Russia, mothers have gone to great lengths to avoid having their sons being drafted into the Chechen conflict, even to the extent of getting legally divorced but remaining in the same house so that their sons can claim they are the family's sole supporters (Turiel, 2002). War or other continuing conflicts can lead to serious family stresses and new adaptation. More than a century ago, Durkheim suggested that suicide rates decrease during times of national crisis, as social integration rises during this time (Durkheim, 1951). More recently, similar declines in divorce have been noted following terrorist attacks (Nakoney, Reddick, & Rodgers, 2004). In a study conducted in the United Kingdom after the 9/11, 2001 attacks, we found that those who anticipated a higher probability of future attacks were the most likely to increase contact with their families and friends shortly after 9/11 (Goodwin, Willson, & Gaines, 2005). Following that event, longer-term restrictions on travel had further consequences for the development of transnational relationships, with the fear of terrorism likely to have had a negative impact on broader intergroup contacts (Greenberg, Solomon, & Pyszczynski, 1997).

In other cases, it is rapid changes in economic circumstances that lead to changes in personal relationship. Such material challenges include a widespread loss of jobs, a reconfiguration of social roles following a political or economic change, or forced migration to find work as a result of war or political turmoil. In these cases, individuals may try to cope by adopting new family members into a household to help deal economically with their migration or by reformulating social networks to deal with urgent personal or family needs. Famine may also directly influence the kinds of work performed by a family: In such situations, women may defy traditional expectations to seek work in government programmes if their men are unable to feed their families. Similarly, the pauperisation of a particular group might increase the likelihood of prostitution and sex trafficking. Recurrent plagues in the Middle Ages helped break down class barriers and weakened the bonds of family and community (LaPiere, 1965). This led to a challenging of established beliefs about established social order, giving rise to new opportunities for social mobility. Even the *anticipation* of social transitions or major disruptive events can have direct effects on relationships. An example is the impact of the social changes following the handover of the sovereignty of Hong Kong from the UK to China. Here, changes in mobility opportunities were anticipated to lead to direct effects on employment and the political system. This was accompanied by a general anxiety that accompanied the handover (DeGolyer, 1995; Ho & Chau, 1995; Schwarzer & Chung, 1995). Our data showed that those who were most anxious were more likely to report changes in their relationships (Goodwin & Tang, 1998).

Often, of course, the effects of a social change may be far-reaching and not necessarily those intended by the instigators of the social change: The one-child policy in China had a subsequent impact on further child rearing, as children became spoilt and boys in particular treated as "little emperors." The construction of a dam can lead to mass relocation and the breaking up of intergenerational relationships. In other cases, because these changes are usually about structures (such as the number of children) or rules of behaviour (for example, when women are forbidden to be seen alone in public with men), it is of course possible that the changes may not necessarily have *direct* effects on emotions or beliefs about relationships. So, for example, individuals may appear to embrace a new religious regime by wearing only permitted clothing, but they may maintain their older, less religious values. I discuss this possibility when looking ahead in the final part of this book.

Indirect, Gradual Change

Much of the social science literature about relationships has speculated about the impact on relationships of more subtle, longer-term changes in societies. Here the emphasis is more on changes in beliefs and values and the manner in which gradual transitions in a society are filtered through these beliefs/values. Some of this value change might occur through the influence of powerful groups or opinion leaders, or it might be associated with the development of new technologies or industrial practices. As a result, these changes fit in more closely with the psychological/ideational factors in social change discussed above.

One important debate in social science over the last five decades has been about the impact of modernisation on family relationships. Modernisation theorists argue that industrialised values become incorporated into the personal value system: "Value changes are caused by adaptation to structural changes in the value-forming institutions of society that accompany industrialization, employment in service occupations, increased education, spreading communications, and so forth" (Schwartz & Sagie, 2000, p. 489ff). Modernisation can be seen primarily as a gradual process of adaptation that may take place over generations, with its impact on relationships less direct than changes in some legal structures (Inglehart, 2003). Indeed, relationship changes are largely seen as a secondary consequence of the values adopted in a modernising society. Modernisation is a core theme in the study of social change, and the theory – and its limitations – are discussed in more detail in Chapter 2.

One indirect impact of social change is the gradual change in beliefs and values that can occur amongst migrant groups over time (Feldman & Rosenthal, 1991). Whilst direct relationship changes may occur as a result of forced migrations (as a result of either economic or political pressures), over time migrant families, and particularly the offspring of these families, are also likely to change their values to fit those of a new culture (Phalet & Schönpflug, 2001). Industrialisation may also introduce new working habits and practices that then influence family activities (Coontz, 2000). For example, Turkish migrants in Germany placed great emphasis on conformity and tradition, particularly for their sons, as they were seen as future providers and family caretakers. However, while there was a continuing commitment to family values amongst this younger generation, new autonomy values also entered through education in the new culture. The extent of these value changes does partially depend, however, on the extent to which the migrating groups want to have contact with their new society, as well as the degree to which the host society accepts this contact (Berry, 1997).

Technological changes can, in principle, have both rapid and more gradual impacts on relationship practices. Previously, I discussed the example of the introduction of the first steam train, then the car and the aeroplane, for the development of distal networks. Similarly, the development of internet dating may have changed the range of perceived (if not immediately available) others over a relatively short time. This may be important, as there is evidence to suggest that the perception of available alternative partners is an important indicator of relationship satisfaction (Udry, 1981). Other technologies (such as the introduction of television to a society) may work more incrementally through the familiarisation of an audience with alternative lifestyles. Important here is the idea that these technological changes, whilst important, are likely to impact on individuals' relationships mainly as a result of complex interactions with existing practices and traditions. As such, they are likely to be anchored within preexisting beliefs about technology and relationships in the modern world and should thus allow for more gradual – and less disruptive – adaptations in personal lives.

Mediating and Moderating Variables

One important caveat to the above is that, when dealing with both direct and more indirect changes, we cannot adopt a simple one-size-fits-all model. Several mediating variables are likely to influence the extent to which social change leads to transformations in either general beliefs and values or specific relationship behaviours. These include individual differences, group variations, and cultural influences. I describe these in more detail below.

Individual Differences and Change

The effects of social change on different individuals vary greatly (Elder, 1998; Silbereisen & Wiesner, 2002). Not everyone is equally influenced by change in a society, largely because not everyone's daily life conditions change following a social transition. Instead, individuals have to believe that a change has personal relevance before it significantly influences their relationships with others – any change must have "goal relevance" (Lazarus, 1991). Furthermore, although individuals may have only limited opportunities to resist a large-scale societal change, individual differences will influence how a member of a society appraises these direct changes, even if they can do little about them. And, of course, some may have benefited from a regime and system of living that would make them very unwilling to change their everyday lives. Thus, while radical social change might create challenges for most citizens in a society, some may perceive this as a threat, whereas for others it is a more positive challenge (Silbereisen & Wiesner, 2002).

At the individual level, Weber (1958, pp. 26ff) notes the importance not just of the rational but also the "disposition of men to adopt certain types of practical rational conduct" when dealing with social change. One important feature may be the seeking of meaning when faced with the stresses of rapid change and stress. In *Man's Search for Meaning*, Frankl ([1946], 1984), when describing his experiences in a Nazi concentration camp, claims "Man *can* preserve a vestige of spiritual freedom, of independence of mind, even in such terrible conditions of psychic and physical stress" (p. 74; original emphasis). "[A]ny man can, even under such circumstances, decide what shall become of him – mentally and spiritually" (p. 75). This suggests the significance of individual coping strategies, with different personalities allowing for different coping styles (Schmitz, 1994) and abilities to cope with change (for example, Berry, 1980). A sense of control over events is likely to be important (for example, Ho & Chau, 1995). Perceived mastery over a particular situation may buffer the relationship between the stressors and distress (Pearlin & Schooler, 1978), with individuals more likely to actively cope with a situation when they feel more in control (Carver, Scheier, & Weintraub, 1989). When an individual sees a situation as unchangeable or uncontrollable, he/she is more likely to use emotion-focused coping strategies (Roth & Cohen, 1986) or may try to deny or avoid the threat (Amirkhan, 1990; Lazarus, 1991). Avoidant strategies can be useful in reducing stress and preventing anxiety from becoming crippling (Roth & Cohen, 1986), but whilst this may be functional over a short time, approaching the issue is more likely to be useful over a longer period, especially when the situation is at least partially controllable. Often having a sense of control takes very material forms. During the Hong Kong transition to China, for example, such control included the possession of an overseas passport or the presence of family abroad (Goodwin & Tang, 1998). At the same time, personal identification with a group in transition can be important (Ho & Chau, 1995). In the years leading up to this handover to China, those who identified themselves solely as Hong Kong citizens rather than as Chinese were far more uneasy about the handover (Lam et al., 1995; Lau et al., 1995). Other beliefs are also likely to be significant. Individuals with a strong belief in marriage permanence, for example, are more likely to invest in resolving the problems that arise during a time of anxiety than those who hold less negative attitudes towards divorce (Amato, 2004).

Finally, educational level and age are likely to be significant in predicting individual adaptation to societal change. Higher education and youth are usually seen as a significant aid in adopting to individualisation processes within society, although this may be specific to the change under consideration (Reykowski, 1994). High youth unemployment, for example, can lead to considerable mobility that may challenge established relationships. The age structure of a total population is also likely to influence sexual behaviour across that population, with societies with large numbers of young people exhibiting significantly different baseline figures for sexual activity (Wellings, Nancharhal, et al., 2006). Generational differences may be particularly important in societies with higher life expectancies, particularly where there have been substantial changes in levels of security experienced during childhood (Inglehart & Baker, 2000). In societies that have experienced rapid economic growth over the last half-century, younger people are far more secular in their values, but there is no such pattern in low-income societies (Inglehart & Baker, 2000).

Groups and Change

When studying change in societies, race, ethnicity, social class, regional factors, and immigration status are all likely to impact on the experiences of those involved (Edin, Kefalas, & Reed, 2004). Different cultures and subgroups hold different values and express them in varying ways (Bardi & Schwartz, 2003). Following a major political transformation, compare the life changes required of a forester living in a remote location with those facing a manager of a large industry in the capital city. The former may have had little contact with events occurring in the larger cities; the latter may be used to job security and a whole set of patronages strongly bound up with the "old regime." Or consider the situation of a young, educated, linguistically and technologically talented student, able to seize the opportunities provided by a new social order, compared to that of a retired pensioner, dependent on state benefits and without the resources to deal with rapid inflation. We can see the impact of group differences in the (relatively successful) adaptation of the communist nomenclature following privatisation at the end of the communist era – although, as we see in Chapter 6, such privatisation may have been at the cost of the development of family relationships and broader social networks.

Kohn and his colleagues argue that the complexity of life activities carried out may have an impact on personality independent of education or previous employment, even when that person is unemployed or retired (Kohn, Zaborowski et al., 2000). According to Kohn et al., this is because activity helps define us: "I do, therefore I am" (p. 188). Work that is routine, heavily supervised, and low in complexity (generally characteristic of lower social class jobs) tends to produce a sense of hopelessness and alienation that undermines beliefs about the possibility of control in other aspects of life and causes psychological distress (Basic Behavioral Science Task Force of the National Advisory Mental Health Council, 1996). Kohn et al. conducted a large-scale interview study in Poland and the Ukraine during a period of rapid social change and uncertainty (the early 1990s). Their data suggest that, for both those employed and unemployed, complexity of activities was significantly related to their personality, and the centrality of those activities to people's lives was correlated with the size of the relationship between complexity and personality. Thus, those who were engaged in complex activities – at work or even when not working – had a self-directed orientation, a sense of well-being, and a higher level of intellectual flexibility. Although their data in this particular study did not allow for a full test of this, the authors argue that such a relationship is reciprocal, with personality affecting activity and vice versa. Changes in social organisations (and in particular in the division of labour) are also predicted to lead to subsequent alterations in child-rearing practices, a transmission pattern I discuss further in Chapter 6 (Cole, 1990; Kağitçibaşi, 1996). In Britain, changes have also occurred in activity patterns and social class over the last few decades (Gershuny, 2005). Here, patterns of activity formerly associated with lower social classes – such as long working hours – are now increasingly indicative of higher social status; low social status is now associated with the inability to find any paid work.

The different sexes may also respond differently to a particular social change. Men and women may react differently to a new regulation that prohibits women from working or that limits male–female interaction in public. Gender norms reflect the value placed on men and women and can continue to prescribe labour divisions and responsibilities even during times of transition. Increases in decision-making equality may improve marital quality among wives more than husbands, whilst an increase in housework done by husbands may improve the marital quality of wives but erode that of the husbands (Amato et al., 2003). The family, too, can be seen as a small group with varying levels of resources (Silbereisen & Wiesner, 2002). R. Hill (1949) describes an ABCX model to deal with social change and the challenges to the family. An event (A) interacts with the family's resources for meeting crises (B) and the family's definition of the event (C) to produce a crisis (X). Typical family level resources include the health and the well-being of its members, as well as the financial situation of the family (Rice, 1992). The family only suffers stress if it has appraised the event as threatening (McCubbin & Patterson, 1983). Although the family does not exist as a unit on its own (it is likely to comprise quite different individuals), some families are better able to offer help than others. Small stressors can also add up at times of social change (Rice, 1992) – a fractured family undergoing a divorce may offer little support for its members during a time of broader societal transition.

All of this suggests that particular group norms can be an important influence on individual behaviour. However, it is important not to overstate the importance of any simple social groupings for the impact of change on an individual's daily life (Beck & Beck-Gernsheim, 2002). These authors suggest instead that it is better to talk of "collective life situations" rather than simple class classifications. Edin et al. (2004) follow Weber in arguing that social scientists need to understand the meanings that individuals give to actions and to identify what occurs "inside the black box" of class. Social class is not just education or income but a "historically specific pattern of interaction with other socio-economic and political groups or institutions" (Coontz, 2000, p. 292). It also means the creation of "historically and regionally specific 'social locations' where families and individuals fashion their strategies and mean-ings" (ibid.). This emphasis on situating change in particular life circumstances can allow for us for a more tuned understanding of how broad social change may impact on a particular family or individual (Beck & Beck-Gernsheim, 2002).

Culture
In coping with an event, we are informed by our culture's history of struggles (Lazarus, 1991). Culture is generally slow-changing, helping demark and restrain the kind of coping mechanisms that are appropriate or indeed permitted when faced with change (Lazarus, 1991). For example, regulations and cultural expectations concerning age at marriage are likely to partly dictate age at first sexual intercourse (Wellings et al., 2006), whilst the wealth of a nation is also strongly correlated with women's control over their sexual lives, the number of children they may have, and whether or not to use contraception (Murphy, 2003). Cultures can instil in us important beliefs and values about the world as a whole, as well as the "rules of the game" that underlie the conventions and rules of everyday social life (Rohner, 1984) – what Giddens calls the "practical consciousness" of everyday life (Giddens & Pierson, 1998). Compare, for example, how a culture with an established high level of fatalism (such as Taiwan) might deal with change, compared to a country of greater optimism (for example, Norway; Leung & Bond, 2004), and how this might impact on a willingness to develop social networks and trust others. In more collectivistic cultures, where interdependence with similar in-group others is

valued, changes in internal attributes and feelings may also have a less direct impact on performed actions (Markus & Kitayama, 1994), mediating the relationship between social change, value acquisition, and behaviour. Inglehart claims that there may be a "baseline" reflecting long-established historical patterns upon which change takes place (Inglehart & Klingemann, 2000). In an analysis of the value change that has accompanied the move from preindustrial to postindustrial societies, he argues for "distinctive cultural zones" based primarily on shared histories (such as communist rule or colonialism) and religion (Inglehart & Baker, 2000, p. 30). Trust, he argues, is higher in interpersonal relationships in Protestant rather than Catholic societies, even when economic development level is controlled. These religious traditions are seen as an inherent part of culture, and, as such, they are likely to be transmitted over generations (Inglehart & Baker, 2000). On a shorter time scale, most communist societies were low on subjective well-being (a combination of happiness and life satisfaction) during the communist era – especially those exposed to a longer history of communist rule (Inglehart & Klingemann, 2000). These low levels of well-being persisted after the end of the regime and appear to have a persisting influence on interpersonal transactions across the region (Goodwin, 2006).

Research in the United States also shows that different ethnic groups use different coping strategies in times of stress (Basic Behavioral Science Task Force of the National Advisory Mental Health Council, 1996) and respond differently to the challenges of a changing environment. In the United States, nonmarital child rearing, cohabitation, and divorce have increased in all sectors of society, but they are most frequent amongst low-income groups and particular disadvantaged minorities (Edin et al., 2004). Culture also influences the extent to which migrating individuals are able to deal with the changes in their lifestyles (Liebkind, 1996). Different migrant groups utilise family ties in differing ways, with some able to use these ties to a greater extent than they had done so "back home" (Coontz, 2000). Lalonde et al. (2004), in their study of migrants from South Asia in Canada, report that those with a strong identification with their heritage had a greater sense of family connectedness and a higher preference for traditional attributes in their partners.

Shared cultural experiences are also likely to be important for the social challenges faced when cultures merge. Elder (1998) and Silbereisen and Wiesner (2002) examined the "quasi-experimental" situation of German Unification in 1990. They hypothesised that this will lead to a rapid diminishment of the differences between those living in East and West Germany. Whilst they found that the timing of the child first leaving the parental home varied between East and West, a sharing of West German media on both sides of the divide meant more commonalities in relationship attitudes than they had predicted. As a consequence, they argued, the unification of Germany had only a minimal impact on the private romantic relationships of individuals in these countries. Furthermore, although some aspirations did change in their samples (a desire for relatively "unrealistic" jobs – such as fashion models and flight attendants – in 1991 had changed to more realistic labour expectations by 1996), intimate expressions of behaviour (such as timing of first sexual experience) were best predicted in both East and West by association with groups of "deviant" peers.

How different cultural groups and individuals appraise a change is likely to be partly determined by how the message of change is transmitted. We can learn about social change from a variety of sources, with transmission of information from "vertical transmission" agents (such as parents) and "horizontal agents" (such as peers), as well as the more "oblique agents" (including the media and others around the individual) (Phalet & Schönpflug, 2001). Whilst friends and family may be significant for evaluating events and appraising change, these other media are very important for the wider interpretation of occurrences in a society. The media can also lead debates on crucially sensitive areas of relationship change, such as fertility rates, divorce, or sexual behaviour amongst the young. At the same time, of course, public trust in the media will also vary across cultures, subgroups, and individuals with the topic under discussion and the nature of the regime discussing these issues.

DIRECTIONALITY AND SOCIAL CHANGE

The preceding suggests that social change can have important impacts on a range of relationships, but that these changes are moderated and mediated by individual, group, and cultural factors. I also suggest that changes in core relationship *values* are usually slower than changes in more overt behavioural change (Horenczyk & Bekerman, 1993), which may result from behavioural changes imposed or necessitated sometimes literally overnight.

Nevertheless, although I divide direct and indirect effects in my model, not all such societal changes can be so simply categorised, and it is often hard to distinguish the interplay between direct enforcement of regulation, value adaptation, and relationship change (Boudon, 1986). Most variables can act as antecedents, mediators, and consequences (Lazarus, 1991), and – as the idealists reviewed above note – values and beliefs can drive change as well as emerge from it. Furthermore, as previously suggested, some social change may be resisted – particularly when it touches on well-established beliefs and traditions – or it may lead to excluding groups who become marginalized by the particular turbulences of change. An example is the case of war. A war can have the direct effect of breaking up families and reducing the number of available partners (usually males). It can also have the effect of creating greater anxiety in a society (perhaps leading to a greater valuing of close relationships) and can challenge earlier social divides. Remarque ([1929]; 1996) describes this clearly in the novel *All Quiet on the Western Front*:

... earlier values don't count any longer, and nobody really knows how things used to be. The differences brought out by education and upbringing have been almost completely blurred and are now barely recognizable (p. 191).

Later he notes:

No one will understand us – because in front of us there is a generation of men who did, it is true, share the years out here with us, but who already had a bed and a job and who are going back to their old positions, where they will forget all about the war – and behind us, a new generation is growing up, one like we used to be, and that generation will be strangers to us and will push us aside (p. 206).

Family life can be directly influenced by new societal regulations concerning, for example, female employment or family size, but it can also change over time as a result of shifting values and changing demographics (for example, Kağitçibaşi, 1996; Sinha, 1991). Similarly, certain sexual behaviours may be challenged by new restrictions, but more incremental changes in values may challenge these restrictions (as I discuss in Chapter 5), whilst the move from arranged to free-choice marriages may follow the end of a religious regime or a general shift in Westernised values (Hatfield & Rapson, 1996). The Catholic Church in Central Europe, for example, played a central role in promoting particular (and for many, "traditional") values following the end of communism in this region. It promoted general changes in beliefs and values that had indirect impacts on relationship beliefs and behaviours (for example, in discussions of "the woman question" and the role of women in these new societies (Einhorn, 1993)). At the same time, through its influence with the Solidarity movement, it was able to help introduce legislation with a direct impact on relationship practices (for example, through new regulations concerning abortion). This example suggests that whilst the framework above provides an organising heuristic for much work on relationships and change, it must be seen as an organising guide, with considerable potential for reciprocity and interactions between the pathways.

SUMMARY

Although work on social change dates back several millennia, there is considerable disagreement about how to define such change and the best ways in which historical changes can be modeled. In the first part of the chapter, I described theories of change that portray change as developmental and evolutionary, accounts that stress cyclical change and functionalism, and approaches that stress the role of ideas in driving change, before considering how individuals and groups might be resistant to change. In the second half of the chapter, I developed a broad framework for organising my subsequent review in this book, dividing social change into two: direct and rapid transitions, such as that which typically occurs following a revolution, and more indirect and gradual transitions, such as the industrialisation and modernisation process in Britain. I argue that whilst the former may have direct impacts on relationship behaviours – perhaps through the introduction of particular strictures on interpersonal behaviour or social networks – the latter is likely to lead to more gradual value changes, which will then impact on personal relationships. All such changes, however, are likely to be mediated by individual, group, and cultural influences that may diminish or accentuate their impacts on the personal relationships of members of these changing societies.

CHAPTER 2

The Myth of Modernisation?

In the first chapter, I suggested a framework that divided social change into two forms. The first, rather dramatic change is often the outcome of unexpected, sudden events, such as wars and large-scale natural disasters, or results from the direct imposition of new legal frameworks. More gradual change occurs primarily through shifts in societal values and beliefs and is often linked to industrial development or to other changes in mass economics. One of the most discussed – and controversial – of these latter shifts is the process of modernisation, a concept often linked to "Westernisation," "globalisation," and "individualisation" (Goodwin, 1999; Segall et al., 1990).

Ideas about modernisation – and its impact on personal relationships – date back at least a century. Tönnies ([1887]; 1957) described the societal shift from *Gesellschaft* (small-scale neighbourhood communities) to larger and more competitive *Gemeinschaft*. According to Giddens, sociology itself can be defined as "the reflexive analysis of modernity" (Giddens & Pierson, 1998, p. 69). Giddens and Pierson (1998) characterise modernity as a set of attitudes that views the world as open to human intervention, as well as a group of economic institutions and other practices (such as mass democracy). A number of definitions cite the influence of a dominant culture on another as key to modernisation, with the traditional society often forced to borrow customs and behaviours from the other (Divale & Seda, 2001). From this perspective, modernised societies are more complex than their more traditional counterparts. Frequently, modernisation is associated with economic change: Modernisation theory is "a broad term that applies to any theory that describes the cultural values that are associated with economic development" (Allen, Ng, & Leiser, 2004, p. 160). The "associated with" in the above definition underlines the idea that modernisation theorists do not necessarily insist that the economic forces come first, reminiscent of the chicken-and-egg materialism vs. idealist debate I discussed in Chapter 1. In revised modernisation theory, Inglehart and Norris (2003) see the ideational and material as working together, with "economic, political, and cultural changes as evolving in coherent trajectories, without claiming ... that the changes in the processes of economic production drive the superstructure of value change, or that, conversely, cultural processes such as the rise of Protestantism cause the socioeconomic developments" (p. 15). Nevertheless, there is clearly a strong bias towards the view that it is industrialisation that leads to a range of largely predictable social and cultural consequences (Inglehart & Baker, 2000).

The World Values Survey (http://www.worldvaluessurvey.com), initiated by Inglehart and his colleagues, has studied more than 160,000 respondents in some 80 societies that cover 80 percent of the world's population. Data were collected in a series of waves; first in 1981 (as part of the European values survey) and subsequently in 1990, 1995, and 2001. Analysing these data, Inglehart (1997, 2003) identifies two major trends in value changes: from traditional to secular/rational values (reflecting a move away from traditional religion) and from survival to self-expression values (a shift in priorities to well-being, rather than concerns for simple survival). These changes follow the movement from preindustrial societies, where life was strongly conditioned by natural forces, to the greater taming of nature evident in industrialisation. Such value changes were also accompanied by alterations in those values relevant to close relationships. Preindustrial societies were largely intolerant of abortion, divorce, and homosexuality, and they tended to emphasise social conformity, traditional family life with male dominance, and deference to parents (Inglehart & Baker, 2000, pp. 23ff). An emphasis on survival meant an atmosphere of distrust and little tolerance of out-groups, with a strong emphasis placed on traditional gender roles and sexual norms. Industrialisation has been accompanied by changes in these gender roles, as well as sexual norms and a decrease in fertility (Inglehart & Baker, 2000, p. 21). In postindustrial societies, neither machinery nor nature dominates everyday lives. Instead, personal encounters and services become more prominent. Self-expression is particularly important, and this often means challenging traditional views about relationships and family life. Individuals also value trust and tolerate those who are different, whilst cultural and sexual diversity become valued.

Inglehart argues that whilst human development may lead to changes in cultural attitudes, values also reflect a society's religious and historical experience. Thus, modernisation may lead to systematic changes in gender roles, but it is economic industrialisation that led women into the workforce, reduced fertility rates, and encouraged education and democratic participation. In a nine-culture study of Eastern and Pacific nations conducted in 1982 and then some 20 years later, Allen and his colleagues found that economic development and value change seemed to go hand in hand, although some values seem to complement certain stages of development better than others (Allen, Ng, Ikeda, et al., 2004). Similar to Inglehart, they held that once a society reached a certain level of economic development, there was likely to be a substantial shift in values.

Modernisation has been associated with a wide range of consequences, both good and ill. Modernisation tends to mean increased mobility and the expansion of the middle classes, an increased importance of white-collar workers, greater exposure to the mass media, and the development of "change-orientated" personalities (Inkeles & Smith, 1974; Lauer, 1977). In many poorer countries, it can mean promises of better water supplies, health improvements, and the development of a cash economy (Super & Harkness, 1997). Modern behaviour is "rational" rather than "traditional" (Boudon, 1986). However, since the Middle Ages modernisation has been associated with corruption and vice (LaPiere, 1965). Modernisation is certainly often stressful, although sometimes one particular group may benefit at another's cost. In a postindustrial age (Bell, 1973), blue-collar work becomes less significant, as does the traditional work ethic. New values are seen as emerging, among them pleasure seeking and hedonism. Modernisation is also correlated with an increase in obesity (Townsend, 2003), self-centeredness, and a strongly competitive orientation (Yang, 1996).

What are the consequences of this modernisation for personal relationships? Many traditional theories of privatisation emphasise how traditional family allegiances and common solidarities have been disrupted by this new modern world order (Allan, 2001). Personal lives have become restructured and social networks renegotiated or diminished. For Parsons (1959) and Goode (1963), the modernisation of established social structures has damaged the traditional family. Marriage as an institution has become a shell of its former self, with family breakups threatening a broad range of extended relations (Almond, 2006). Modernisation thus represents a precursor for societal alienation and anomie (Yang, 1996) and is responsible for the decline in sincere and meaningful exchanges characteristic of our "McDonaldized" world (Ritzer, 1993). Beck and Beck-Gernsheim (2002) describe a "categorical break" between the "modern situation" and earlier times. They claim that demands for individual freedom have undermined the integration associated with shared-value communities. Reykowski (1994), in Poland, argued that the decline of the socialist state arose as a result of the incompatibility between modern working conditions and older notions of obligatory group commitments. For some, gender roles have also been threatened. During the modernisation process in Colombia, collective living arrangements were disrupted and replaced by a patriarchal nuclear family, where women became dependent on men's wages (Sered, 1990). Women's roles were then changed and largely diminished, as they moved to less productive service employment (Divale & Seda, 2001).

Some of the dilemmas that modernisation can produce are evident in Liu's (2006) analysis of lay (social) representations of important concerns in Chinese life. Liu noted that since the rapid economic changes of the 1980s – which marked a movement towards a market economy – new public discourses have emerged concerning the quality of life. These have been reflected in two themes that echo the materialistic versus the postmaterialistic worlds described by Inglehart. The first concerns the achievement of profit (*guanxi*), whilst the second considers the development of intimate personal relationships as an antidote to loneliness. The two produce a tension between a positive embracing of the new opportunities and new freedoms, accompanied by worries over social alienation, insecurity, and the new risks of the market economy.

Whilst primarily associated with within-society economic developments, modernisation can also arise as a consequence of other external factors. Cha (1994), for example, describes the historical changes that have occurred in Korean society since the 1950s as initially originating in the materialistic values that emerged as a result of civil war. During the 1960s, the military regime encouraged self-reliance, and industrialisation began to grow in the country. This significantly challenged many traditional family values in society, with the extended family and clan being replaced by governmental institutions – such as the school – for the focus of collective activities. Such actions can at times lead to potentially "subversive" challenges within a society, with rippling effects higher up in the societal hierarchy (Turiel, 2002).

INDIVIDUALISATION

Frequently allied to modernisation is a process of individualisation. Turiel (2002) defines "the individualistic cultural orientation" as one that is "highlighted by detachment from others, nonconformity, self-reliance, a lack of respect for authority, indulgence of the young by parents, and the pursuits of personal needs, desires, interests, and pleasures" (p. 49). Many of the changes described in the thesis of individualism date back as far as the Renaissance and courtly society of the Middle Ages, as well as the more rapid changes during the second half of the twentieth century. However, most commentators see these changes as resulting chiefly from the social and economic changes of late modernity (Allan, 2001). Marriage in the eighteenth century was rooted in established social orders and persisted in its moral and legal form, despite social movement. Although the husband may have been away during a time of industrialisation, a strong moral and legal code to marriage was emphasised by the Church in many countries (Beck & Beck-Gernsheim, 2002). In contrast, modern society is seen as leaving moral responsibility to the individual. Whilst this individualisation has been associated with some positives – including higher levels of autonomy and independence in personal lives, a liberation from traditional roles and constraints, and a greater open-mindedness and cognitive flexibility (Inkeles & Smith, 1974) – high levels of individualism are seen as distinctly double-edged. Birthrates have fallen against a backdrop of individualised career paths, which prioritise the fulfilment of individual needs. Individualisation involves a new responsibility for identity and livelihood, with more requirements to negotiate formerly "taken-for-granted" social roles and relationships. Beck-Gernsheim (2002) argues that the very lack of fixed obligations or values poses important challenges, with personal freedoms undermining traditional relationships. She talks of a "dramatic plunge into modernity," with social risk now individualised and very personal. Bauman (2001), Bellah et al. (1985), and Etzioni (1996) all warn of the destruction of both private lives and the community through individualisation. From their perspective, it is the *I* rather than the *We* that now dominates, with interpersonal connections – as well as broader civic involvement – threatened by an isolated individual faced with bewildering choices but little support from the family, social institutions, or the wider community. From a communitarian perspective, both individuals and the State have failed in their responsibilities. Bauman summarises this sense of uncertainty well: "Ours is an experience akin to that of passengers in a plane who discover, high in the sky, that the cockpit is empty" (2001, p. 111).

In an individualised world, a narcissistic form of love based on gratification is seen as having made marriage more fragile, with few willing to show persistence in loyalty when things are difficult (Elliott & Lemert, 2006; Huston & Metz, 2004). A freedom for individuals to make their own decisions and rules can result in considerable confusion and vulnerability: In this individualised world, citizens are free to fail in their own personal relationships. In a newly individualistic world, there are numerous questions and tensions that arise from changes in society, with new "possibilities to choose" (Beck & Beck-Gernsheim, 2002). Individuals are "condemned" to individualisation, constantly having to assert themselves even, in reality, when the market serves to restrain their opportunities. Old traditions are less assured (Giddens & Pierson, 1998); self-expression and individual risk taking come accompanied with new apprehensions and anguish that arise from the risks associated with a globalised world (Elliott & Lemert, 2006). An increased opportunity for education and work may have different meanings and lead to new tensions for both sexes. Men may compare their experiences with those of their fathers, women with the more traditional background of their mothers, women who may have lived mainly "for others" (Beck & Beck-Gernsheim, 2002). As I will describe in Chapter 5, sexual relationships have become more open, although women still bear the greater risks to their reputation, the health problems associated with some contraceptives, and the danger of unwanted pregnancies.

With individualisation, rights are also now located with the individual rather than the family and can sometimes be seen as acting against family cohesion. New relationship partners from different regions, classes, and countries marry and are then confronted with significant new issues: Which country shall we live in? What is our legal status? Which language do we use? Who does what work at home? (Beck & Beck-Gernsheim, 2002). In societies facing increasingly high levels of divorce, there are new negotiations to be conducted over everyday life, with the potential complexities of where the children will live and their relations to their parents and other relatives. Family life is lived at a "new rhythm," with different social institutions, organisations, and working hours of partners creating new complexities. In this individualised and compartmentalised reality, children may have to deal with the new partners of their parents and with new concerns over pocket money, discipline, location, and even family membership. Fears over behaviour towards stepchildren also come to the fore: What is the appropriate expression of intimacy from a new partner on the scene towards a teenage child of the opposite sex? Hence, in this free-floating world new arguments and challenges become routine within the "normal chaos of love" (ibid.).

A further challenge provided by individualisation is that traditional social groupings may be less available for reliable support if failure occurs. Old communities are now more mixed, with the formerly reliable boundaries less certain. Previously established, secure social networks (strong neighbourhoods or friendship networks, long-term partnerships) now seem to be less secure. The emergence of the welfare state provides some (minimal) security beyond the family, allowing individual members to separate if they choose. In Eastern Europe at the end of communism, for example, citizens of this region appeared to be some of the most individualistic peoples in the world (for example, Smith, Dugan, & Trompenaars, 1995). As I will describe in subsequent chapters, this appears to have had a number of serious consequences for the development of positive social networks in these countries.

GLOBALISATION

A further allied concept to modernisation and individualisation is that of globalisation. Arnett notes that "in recent years, *globalization* has become one of the most widely used terms to describe the current state of the world" (Arnett, 2002, p. 774, italics in original). It has been argued that the Roman Empire was the first globalised culture, with the springing up of new amphitheatres and other signs of Roman rule echoing the more recent emergence of streets of identical coffee shops across the world (Hingley, 2005; Hitchner, forthcoming). Such globalisation is now associated with free markets, consumerism, and individualism, as well as shifts in the movement from rural to urban and an increased "mixing" of peoples. This is seen as having important interpersonal ramifications. In rural Africa, for example, household size shrinks as youth move to the cities. Schools open up new educational opportunities for women and with this, new expectations about gender relations. In Southeastern Asia, there is an increased seeking of opportunities overseas, opening up the possibility of new interpersonal liaisons. However, Arnett (2002) notes that this has not led to a simple one-way process: Instead, many young people have a bicultural identity – part local, part global. So whilst the "internet generation" can communicate internationally with ease, a continuing sense of local obligation and an identity located at least partly in the immediate community can lead to a hybrid identity. Furthermore, whilst outcomes may be easy for some, for others there is a sense of marginalisation and confusion that can then lead to depression, suicide, and drug use. Breaking away from traditional kin networks and relationships may lead to considerable personal sacrifices. This notion of rapid change as leading to new potential stresses emphasises my earlier discussions about the continuing personal challenges posed by rapid social change. Resistance to modernisation has received little attention by relationships researchers, even though more violent protests propagated through terrorist activities – often ironically facilitated by the use of modern technology such as the internet – have inevitably captured greater attention.

CRITIQUES OF MODERNISATION AND RELATED THEORIES

The theories cited above largely assume that there will be considerable convergences across the world, that "the peoples of the world are on the march towards industrialization" (Kerr et al., 1964, p. 3). They also assume that this will have definitive psychological and sociological effects (Giddens, 1989). Several theorists have challenged these assumptions, however, and have drawn attention to the weaknesses in such accounts. They have also alerted us to the positive impacts of any modernisation processes, often neglected by the rather gloomy prognoses of commentators in this area. As this is likely to be important for an understanding of the study of relationship and modernisation, I list some of the most common objections here.

One concern is the easy conflation of terminology in this field. Industrialisation, for example, does not necessarily coexist with modernisation: It is possible for a society to industrialise but not to modernise, with modernisation concerning social and political changes rather than simple economic transition (Allen et al., 2004; Lauer, 1977). A number of commentators have pointed out, for example, that the nucleation of the British family occurred well before industrialisation (for example, Kağitçibaşi, 1996, 2006; Wagels & Roemhild, 1998). Furthermore, as I will discuss in Chapter 6, the idealised joint family in both Western and non-Western societies – such as India – were in fact reality for a minority (Laslett & Wall, 1972), as only the wealthier families could avoid this structure (Kağitçibaşi, 2006). In addition, the young and better educated may espouse particular "modern views," but there may be few changes in population movement or industrialisation (Micklin, 1969). Instead, in some cases industrialisation may reinforce traditional practices (Lauer, 1977). Kinship networks, for example, can be highly important when individuals seek to build businesses (ibid.; Kağitçibaşi, 1996), as can the religious ties often associated with reduced modernisation (Lauer, 1977).

A related issue concerns the measurement of many of the central terms and concepts used by modernisation theorists. As noted above, modernisation can incorporate many concepts, and it is sometimes unclear exactly *what* has to occur in a society before it can be deemed to be "modern." Thus, Rothenbacher (1998) argues that the movement from premodern times into modernity has not yet finished (he talks of "unfinished modernity"). Additionally, some countries (particularly in the Mediterranean) moved directly from an agrarian to a service society, omitting the industrial stage. Quite "normal" and everyday conflicts and struggles with social norms during both childhood and adulthood can easily be overinterpreted as evidence of movement along over-simplified cultural divides (Abu-Loghod, 1991; Turiel, 2002). Some commentators have questioned the measures used in the World Values Survey to measure modern and postmodern states, suggesting that the manner in which the items are used reflect relatively temporary social and economic conditions (Davis, Dowley, & Silver, 1999). Here, the forced categories used to measure modernity values in this survey are seen as leading participants into only a limited range of responses (Davis & Davenport, 1999). Others have questioned Inglehart's hypothesis that security leads to postmaterialistic values, using Canadian and German data to show that rising unemployment is also related positively to such values (Clarke et al., 1999). Whilst Inglehart and others do recognise the significance of period effects and local conditions, such challenges underline the difficulties in asserting modernity or postmaterialism in any one particular time or location.

A second set of critiques has questioned the very existence of a modernising world, with some arguing that there has in fact been relatively little evidence of change in global values, at least during the last few decades (Hofstede, 2001; Schwartz, 2006). This is particularly the case for the majority of the world's population living in less economically developed countries (Kağitçibaşi, 1990, 1996). Huntingdon (1996) rejects any convergence hypothesis, drawing attention to the "clashes" in civilisations. In his analysis, he contrasts the values evident in seven great systems: Confucian/Chinese, Japanese, Hindu, Islamic, Western, Latin American, and African. Inglehart suggests that religion in particular moderates any changes in values, claiming that cultural change is "path-dependent" (Inglehart & Baker, 2000, p. 49). As with any analysis of social change, there are considerable variations within cultural groups as to the extent to which any modernisation in values is occurring (Allen et al., 2004; Diez-Nicolas, 2003; Lauer, 1977). Modernisation is also likely to be differentiated by age, with arguments for greater modernisation amongst both the young (Mishra, 1994) and the old (Turiel, 2002), depending on setting and resources.

Certainly, modernisation processes are unlikely to be fast – indeed, the speed of these changes is often exaggerated (Schwartz, 2004, 2006). Many analyses of modernisation concentrate on ideal preferences when in fact such preferences or choices may not exist. Thus, strong family pressures as well as legal practices may constrain the actuality of becoming divorced even when the individuals concerned may desire this (Allan, 2001). Moghaddam and Crystal (2000) have argued that in twentieth-century Japan and Iran the same norms for relations with authority and the treatment of women have persisted for centuries, despite marked economic changes in these societies. In examining the postindustrial hypothesis proposed by Bell (1973), Giddens (1989) argues that growth of the service sector at the cost of the manufacturing sector has been largely exaggerated. Instead, he claims, there is a wide heterogeneity in the service sector, with many "service jobs" actually part of a continuing manufacturing industry. Some of the fragility of the modernisation process can be seen in Tannous's (1941) study of a Lebanese Arab village. In this village, the introduction of silk factories led to a cash-based economy that challenged the traditional symbols of prestige, such as old age and kinship networks. Cash and individual profits then became an important determinant in choosing a mate, whilst female employment in the factory allowed for previously unknown unsupervised contact between the sexes. However, the introduction of rayon led to the collapse of the silk industry. This led the community to return to a reliance on traditional farmlands – much of which had been neglected during the rise of the silk industry – and a consequent return to traditional activities in work, as well as in family relations.

Modernisation theories are therefore often seen as providing an unacceptable gloss on a plethora of complex changes within a society. Any social change within a particular society is likely to be influenced by diverse factors, including religion, population movement, societal heterogeneity, and the influence of foreign rulers (Allen et al., 2004; Giddens, 1989; Schwartz, 2004, 2006). Particular structural circumstances, such as location and the broader culture, are still likely to remain significant (Allan, 2001). All of these factors may have differential impacts on the development of particular values or the maintenance or rejection of specific relationship behaviours. Rapid economic changes can lead to a series of other changes that introduce both modernising and traditionalising pressures into a society. For example, the collapse of the former Soviet Union was accompanied by a decrease in self-expression values in many of these countries, accompanied by an increased preference for postmodern values (Smith, Bond, & Kağıtçıbaşi, 2006). As I will demonstrate in Chapter 6, the rapid economic modernisation in China in the last three decades led to a demand for greater self-expression but, with the process of decollectivisation of farmland, a return to more traditional power relationships in the family. Continued military threat may also mitigate against the development of modernisation. For example, respondents in the World Values Surveys from Israel and South Africa emphasised survival values rather than self-expression values, despite considerable political and economic developments in these countries (Kotzé & Lombard, 2003; Yuchtman-Ya'ar, 2003).

A third common criticism suggests that a simple opposition between modernity and traditional ways of life is problematic. This assumed dichotomy rests heavily on the evolutionary assumptions of progress discussed in Chapter 1 and simplistic stereotypes of traditional societies (Lauer, 1977). Instead, many societies seem to combine "the old and the new" in a highly adaptive fashion (Allik & Realo 2004; Lauer, 1977). Inkeles (1977), one of the founders of theories of modernity, notes that "individual modernity is found, and apparently lives compatibly, alongside many orientations and behaviours which some analysts consider to be part of traditionalism" (p. 162). Many at least moderately collectivistic societies, such as Japan, are also highly modern cultures, whilst many traditional, collectivistic patterns of values persist in the most modern of cultures (evident, for example, in the relatively high values of hierarchy and social embeddedness in the modern United States; Schwartz, 2004). Similarly, the modern United

States appears to exhibit very strong evidence of persisting family ties (Kağitçibaşi, 1990, 1996). Thus, despite Bellah et al.'s (1985) assertion that "American individualism has difficulty ... justifying why men and women should be giving to one another at all" (p. 111), individuals maintain significant social relationships, even though these relationships are not necessarily based on traditional household and neighbourhood structures (Allan, 2001).

Others have argued that independence and personal agency coexist in many non-Western cultures, with much depending on the social roles held and situational constraints (Turiel, 2002). Thus, only certain aspects of life may have changed (Yang, 1988). One example is when someone from a traditional society behaves in a very modern way at work, but in a far more traditional manner at home. Kağitçibaşi (2006) argues that too often a false dichotomy has been posed between autonomy and relatedness; instead, these can be seen as underlying dimensions on which there is cultural variation, and in many sociocultural contexts one does not imply a lack of the other. In particular, migrant families, such as recently migrated Hispanic families in the United States, may maintain many of their collective, family-orientated values, which can be vital for economic survival and psychological adjustment when moving to another society (Kağitçibaşi, 2006). Furthermore, rather than modernisation reducing the role of families in our lives, individuals in modernising societies often appear to embrace traditional family structures as a sense of security in an insecure world (for example, Lasch, 1977; Vergin, 1985). Thus, over time, migrants may mix the "old" and "new" rather than simply assimilating the host country's values, combining material independence with a retained and emotional and psychological interdependence (Kağitçibaşi, 2006). Sometimes this can take form in apparently banal behaviours. Thus, in South Korea friends in a McDonalds will act in a "traditionally collective" manner by pouring the contents of their packets of chips onto a tray and eating together from the pile (Watson, 1998).

For many, such adaptations put the lie to the more pessimistic conclusions of the doomsayer analysis of modernisation. They argue that the equalisation of gender roles that has arisen from the reduction of traditional sex-based boundaries has opened the door for greater intimacy in personal relationships, particularly for women who can now play a more equal role (Hatfield & Rapson, 1996; Huston & Metz, 2004). Data from two of the largest social survey data collections to date – the World Values Survey (for example, Inglehart, 1990) and Hofstede (2001) – demonstrate a positive correlation between individualism and interpersonal trust. Examining social networks and trust, Allik and Realo (2004) compared the relationship between individualism and collectivism and social networks ("social capital") within the United States and across 42 countries, reporting that "in societies where individuals are more autonomous and seemingly liberated from social bonds, the same individuals are also more inclined to form voluntary associations and to trust each other" (pp. 44ff). Even Beck and Beck-Gernsheim speak of an "ethic of 'altruistic individualism'" that requires a social sensibility to others. It is also clear that new alliances are forming across international boundaries, partly meeting persisting demands for traditional family orientation – for example, in the seeking of Eastern brides by Western men.

Throughout this book, I will argue that there are undoubtedly structural and economic changes occurring continually in the world that will impact on personal relationships. Thus, Inglehart (1997) is probably correct in noting that certain cultural and political changes do seem to be linked with modernisation, if not to all aspects of a society. Whether we see these changes as reflecting "late modernity" (Giddens, 1991) or if societies are still evolving an embryonic modernity, social relationships are undoubtedly changing as the physical and geographic structures of everyday life are transformed (Allen, 2001). Thus, it is probably wrong to throw out the modernisation baby completely; instead, particular characteristics that meet the demands of the local ecology are more likely to be accepted (Diez-Nicolas, 2003). Both values and behaviours emerge from particular issues or problems in the environment or are a result of particular experiences (such as the low levels of mastery exhibited in Eastern Europe following the end of communism), with these often emerging as an attempt to avoid potential troubles and immediate threats (Schwartz, 2004). The largely adaptational nature of these changes means that there is no *inevitability* in the direction in which further relationship patterns will develop; indeed, as seen in examples above, "retraditionalisation" does occur under some circumstances. Furthermore, as I argued in Chapter 1, patterns of behaviour are moderated by important individual and group influences, as well as persisting cultural dynamics. A comprehension of these is thus central to any understanding of any modernisation or individualisation processes and their implications for personal relations.

SUMMARY

In this chapter, I discuss some of the key features of theories of modernisation and related concepts of individualisation and globalisation. I then consider some of the critiques of these notions. In particular, I question the extent to which there really is evidence of simple convergences in values and relationship behaviours across the world and whether some of the ambiguities in the meanings and operationalisation of such terms as "modernisation" really allow us to assess this. I also contend that an easy contrasting of modern and traditional ways of life is too simplistic and misses the mixing of the two that occurs for large parts of the world's population in their everyday lives. I conclude by suggesting that whilst there is evidence of certain trends in both value and behavioural change across the world, these changes are often more fragile than assumed, and, as adaptations to environmental conditions, they can be influenced again and in different directions by subsequent societal changes.

CHAPTER 3

More Beautiful than a Monkey: The Achievement of Intimacy

A Russian saying that gained particular vogue after the massive decline in the male population following World War II proposes that to be an eligible partner, "A man only has to be slightly more beautiful than a monkey." This saying, of course, reflected the real issue of restricted partner opportunities following a conflict in which more than twenty million Soviet men died. Such a "direct" impact on the formation of close relationships may seem extreme, but, as we will see, a range of factors external to an individual may have an important impact on their relationship formation. In addition, one of the defining aspects of debates around modern society concerns the extent to which individuals are able successfully to form and maintain intimate relationships with others when faced with other, competing desires and priorities. In this chapter, I discuss the way in which both direct and indirect factors may influence the achievement of intimacy in contemporary societies.

THE FORMATION OF INTIMACY IN A MODERN WORLD

Romantic love is likely to exist across all cultures (Goodwin, 1999). However, some have argued that the role of passion in marriage is both culture- and period-dependent, with many of these changes reflecting the modernisation and industrialisation processes described in the previous chapter (Giddens, 1992; Shumway, 2003). Discussions of love and romance are seen here as portraying patterns that have evolved over several centuries and reflect developing economic trends within particular societies.

Most cultures have recounted stories about the dangers of love and the impact of a "bad match" on both the individual and the wider family. Historically in Britain, marital relationships have rarely been based purely on romantic or passionate love (Giddens, 1992). Despite evidence of some literature that described passionate love as early as the twelfth century, Shumway (2003) argues that marriages in the Middle Ages were based on monogamy and commitment, rather than a more passionate or romantic love. These relationships could best be envisaged as property relationships that reflected wider societal institutions. Passion, when it occurred, was often portrayed as unfortunate, as love was potentially disruptive to a social group. Despite Shakespeare's romantic comedies, marriage was still a largely arranged affair.

There was some evidence of change in this in the late seventeenth century, as various political, economic, and cultural changes challenged the role of the family in marital choice (Coontz, 2004). In the eighteenth century, the revolutionary fever of the times was echoed by a new idealised love in Western Europe and North America (Coontz, 2004). However, it was the emergence of capitalism in the nineteenth century, and the loosening of traditional social bonds that accompanied this, that really allowed for a more individualised and romantic conceptualisation of love (Giddens, 1992; Ingoldsby, 2003; Shumway, 2003). This new romantic love meant a committed relationship, where the other's (largely psychological and personal) qualities took precedence over past expectations and traditions (Giddens & Pierson, 1998).

This discourse of love was propagated initially through the pulp novels of the eighteenth and nineteenth centuries, where the idea of everyone having a "right match" became an accepted part of discussions on marriage (Shumway, 2003). In *The Sorrows of Young Werther* (Goethe, 1774), Goethe's hero, Werther, falls in instant – and painful – love with Lotte, despite the fact that she is already engaged to another man. Because Lotte is unable to requite his love, Werther commits suicide. In this new discourse of love, the couple became of prime significance, even more so than their children. This love had no obvious sense of duty, but revolved around emotional communication between partners, as well as the individual's self-reflections on his/her ideal partner (Giddens & Pierson, 1998). Such love was more than simple conquest but was about new freedoms and self-realisation. The state of "sublime love" became more important than sexual passion, with the other chosen as a special character rather than simply a sexual other. For some, this sense of intimacy served as a new "functional social glue," holding together couples from very different backgrounds (Goode, 1963). Intimacy and love were seen as a treasured refuge from an increasingly harsh and disconnected world (Shumway, 2003; Ting-Toomey, 1991; Waterman, 1981), providing meaning for an otherwise "empty" future (Giddens & Pierson, 1998). This new romantic love created a "shared history" separable from other aspects of family, and it was endowed with "a special primacy," a "meeting of souls," in which the "flawed individual is made whole" (Giddens, 1992, p. 45).

A particular feature of this new love relationship was a new balance between autonomy and attachment. In this romantic era, verbal openness in particular became valued, so that by the 1960s "the relationship" became a topic of much debate amongst intellectuals and the wider public. Intimacy was seen as the defining characteristic of marriage, an ideal towards which the couple had to work (Shumway, 2003). Love allowed for opportunities to express the "real self" and was particularly significant in more individualistic societies (K. K. Dion & K. L. Dion, 1993). Good relationships were characterised by open communication and a lack of violence, with both parties equal and autonomous. These democratic relationships allowed for the possibility of divorce, giving women in particular new opportunities through modified divorce laws. Modernity has been seen as creating a whole new way of intimacy, with emotional communication at its core. Such communication is now viewed as essential for the maintenance of the relationship (Giddens & Pierson, 1998). With economic prosperity and a decline in family size, sexuality became increasingly separated from pregnancy and childbirth to become "a potential 'property' of the individual" (Shumway, 2003, p. 27). Women began to see their roles in life beyond those of simply a wife and mother, no longer accepting "as fate" their primary role in looking after children and the home.

Not everyone is convinced that the achievement of intimacy is possible when faced with the pressures of "modern life" on personal relationships. Instead, close relationships are viewed as suffering as a result of both economic transitions and broader changes in personal values. For some, the selfishness of modern individualism is incompatible with love (Bellah et al., 1985) – or at least it presents individuals with a "double-edged sword" as they struggle to reconcile personal control with shared relationship needs (Dion & Dion, 1993). In particular, extreme "self-contained" individualism has been viewed as dangerous for a partnership, liable to lead to distrust and little caring for the partner (ibid., 1991). For Bauman (2001), the formation of a love relationship is an action cloaked in risk: Love involves subordination of the self, "signing a blank cheque" to the other. Whilst Giddens is largely positive about the democracy and openness of relationships in what he terms "late modernity," he also notes that those marriages that form as a simple escape from a hostile world may contain relatively little emotional involvement (Giddens, 1992). Indeed, there is considerable potential for conflict between short-lived sexual excitement and a more durable and caring love. Trust relationships built on kinship networks now have to be negotiated, with high ideals to be satisfied if the relationship is to "work." Close relationships are burdened by implicitly high expectations, and there is the constant risk of love as obsession as traditional strictures lose their potency (ibid.). Coontz (2004) illustrates the irony of this:

No sooner was the ideal of the love match and lifelong intimacy invented than people who took it seriously began to demand the right to divorce. ... In other words, the very values that we have come to think of as traditional, the very values that invested marriage with such emotional weight in people's lives, had an inherent tendency to undermine the stability of marriage as an institution even as they increased the satisfaction of marriage as a relationship ..." (p. 978).

In a time of female sexual emancipation and greater autonomy, ideals of the "one and only" may also be challenged by a desire for multiple sexual experiences (Giddens, 1992). The development of "plastic sexuality" and the emergence of a "pure," idealised relationship have considerably strained some marriages, although some of the problems here may result from men's determination to hold on to some aspects of power in a changing world (Giddens & Pierson, 1998). We see the emergence of a new form of love – "confluent love" – an active and contingent love that stresses reciprocal sexual satisfaction (Giddens, 1992; Giddens & Pierson, 1998). At the same time, individuals carry with them significant "red flags": remnants from previous relationships that might encourage cynicism about longer-lasting relationships and that can seriously inhibit the development of trust. These red flags, internal memos that an individual accumulates with negative experiences, remind individuals of patterns of personal failure and can often lead them to discriminate unfairly against a new partner when behaviours "remind" the partner of a previous liaison ("My ex appeared to be a real gentleman at first – and look how that turned out!"). In the words of the Sarnoffs:

Today ... a heavy cloud of existential uncertainty is afflicting spouses with anguished doubts about where to place love in their scale of values. At the same time spouses are extremely susceptible to the divisive pressures of separate careers and individualistic pursuits. In fact, given the destructively self-centered thrust of the contemporary world, it is a great accomplishment for *any* couple to create and develop a loving relationship (Sarnoff & Sarnoff, 1989, p. 5, emphasis in original).

CHOOSING A PARTNER: EVIDENCE FROM ACROSS THE GLOBE

Evidence from many societies does indeed seem to support the loosening of family influences on mate selection. Across the globe, greater freedom to choose a mate has led to an increased idealisation and affection towards the partner (Medora et al., 2002) and the growing importance of love in mate selection (Goode, 1959; Goodwin, 1999; Rosenblatt & Anderson, 1981). Often this change reflects the influence of national political decisions, alongside the more gradual shift in values associated with modernisation and related value change. In Vietnam, for example, the 1959 Marriage and Family Law abolished arranged marriage, giving men and women freedom to choose their own partners (Wisendale, 2000). Polygamy was made illegal, and equality between men and women was expected both at home and in the wider society. This led to a rapid decline in arranged marriages. Subsequent legislation allowed also for interethnic and cross-religious marriages. In Turkey, traditional patterns of arranged marriages were challenged, and conjugal affection and sexual equality were actively encouraged by the regime in the legislation that followed the war of independence, as part of a concerted campaign to promote secularisation and Westernisation (Hortacsu, 2003).

Studies in Africa also suggest a trend for the declining influence of the family and the social group on partner choice. Takyi (2003) argues that a combination of increased contacts by Ghana with the Western world – particularly through the experience of colonial rule, urbanisation, and the development of cash-based economies – has severely undermined the traditionally strong influence of family in mate selection. This has resulted in individualistic partner preferences taking predominance in this society, particularly amongst the younger generation, although a substantial proportion of women (around 20 percent) do still seek family consent, blending together their individualistic choices with recognition of the importance of the family. In Kenya, too, individuals are increasingly seeking their own partners, with individuals meeting their partners in a number of locations, including schools, colleges, and religious settings, as well as through more established social networks (Wilson, Ngige, & Trollinger, 2003). Once again, parental consent and advice are valued, with individuals attempting to mesh traditional practices and views with newer mores and values. However, factors outside of the family have been influential here in disrupting established family allegiances: These include wars and other conflicts, economic difficulties, migration, and, of course, the presence of AIDS.

One country to have witnessed particularly dramatic social change in the last 50 years is China. Here, the role of State regulation alongside modernising forces provide an important insight into the impact of macro factors on partner choice. These changes have served to challenge many traditional beliefs and marriage customs, with the choice of partner closely following the social and economic changes that have occurred (Xia & Zhou, 2003).

During feudal times, the economic background of the Chinese family was of primary significance in mate selection. Before 1949, arranged marriages, organised through parents but often with the help of a professional matchmaker, were seen as the key to maintaining family heritage (Xia & Zhou, 2003; Xiaohe & Whyte, 1990). Women were chosen for their ability to produce and care for children; men were seen as providing valuable resources to the family (Xia & Zhou, 2003). Much of this was abolished following the 1949 revolution. The right to choose one's own spouse was guaranteed by the 1950 Marriage Law, alongside equal rights for the sexes and the protection of women and children (ibid.). This led to an increase in free-choice marriages (Whyte & Parish, 1984). Marital decision power was now with the individual, with women encouraged to join the labour force, although traditional patriarchal family dominance died slowly, especially in the countryside. During the Cultural Revolution, the State actively discouraged traditional weddings and marriage, with those married during this period having less expensive weddings and encouraged to choose their own partners freely. The State also actively encouraged later marriages: Spouses' marriage ages were required to sum up to atleast 50 (Pimentel & Liu, 2004). Political ideology may be an important factor in mate selection in a society where there has been recent instability (Medora et al., 2002). In China, the political background of the individual and family became important for partner selection, especially from 1949 to 1987, following nationwide political campaigns, with some groups favoured and others considered "antirevolutionaries." Once again, these preferences could be seen as reflecting a desire for economic stability and security. During the 1950s, cadres of the Chinese Community Party were most desirable for young women. In the 1960s, technicians and workers, especially those in such industries as railroads, were the most desired. Military officers were particularly popular during the 1970s, because they could allow families to move to the better living conditions found in urban areas and provide particular privileges (Xia & Zhou, 2003). Parental influence and wider group participation in the process nevertheless continued, and during the Cultural Revolution the political background of the couple's family became an important consideration. Even in the 1980s, informal matchmaking between party members was actively promoted by the State, with couples often matched on the basis of their "moral character" (Honig & Hershatter, 1988). It was only in 2003 that the State stopped demanding that couples gain permission from their workplace before marriage and allowed them to divorce without workplace approval.

The economic and social changes of the 1980s in China meant that being rich was no longer viewed as being dangerously antirevolutionary. In the years of economic decollectivisation, parental and family pressures reasserted themselves, as wealth again became a criterion for marriage. This marked something of a return to prerevolutionary patterns, despite the 1980 Marriage Law, which emphasised that marriage should be based on mutual affection (Honig & Hershatter, 1988). "Retraditionalisation" meant a return to bride price and dowry payments, largely missing during earlier times, which now had a considerable impact on family budgeting (Harrell, 1992; Whyte, 1992). There was also evidence of the return of marital exchanges between relatives and other prerevolutionary marriage patterns, with some girls sent to live with a boy's family as early as four or five years of age, with the intention of early marriage (Honig & Hershatter, 1988). Correlates of wealth, such as high levels of qualification for men in particular, were also now valued, alongside the traditional expectation of a beautiful, gentle woman and a taller male mate (ibid.). Nevertheless, social change is occurring rapidly in China, and mass migration to the cities serves once again to threaten the influence of parents and other family members in the mate selection process. Arranged marriages are decreasing particularly rapidly in the cities. In a study of 3,000 married men and women, Xu (2000) reported that health and honesty are the main factors sought in mate selection.

Within the United States, Simpson et al. (1986) found a marked increase in the significance of love as a prerequisite for marriage in the decade between 1967 and 1976. Buss and Barnes (1986) suggested a structural powerlessness hypothesis, whereby the importance women place on men's economic resources should decrease as women get more resources. Buss and his colleagues (2001) examined changes in the characteristics that North Americans sought in a mate over six decades, analysing student partner preferences in 1939, 1956, 1967, 1977, 1985, and 1996. Over time, the importance of physical attractiveness increased for both sexes, with men in particular increasingly valuing good financial prospects in a partner. Education, intelligence, and sociability were also characteristics that increased in importance across the decades, whilst mutual attraction and love became more important for both sexes after 1967, suggesting to Buss and his colleagues that marriage might be moving from an institutional to a more companionate form after the "sexual revolution" of that decade. Over time, chastity decreased in importance for both sexes. For men, the traditional seeking of a woman who was a good cook and housekeeper decreased over time, whilst the woman's education and financial prospects became increasingly important. However, a "dependable character," emotional stability, maturity, and a pleasing disposition were highly valued for both sexes across all decades, whilst politics was viewed as unimportant across the decades. Overall, the data provided some evidence of convergence in the sexes' ordering in the importance of mate qualities, with, in particular, sex differences in the stress on economic resources decreasing over time.

For all this, there are also some signs of stability in attitudes towards partner choice in many countries. Furthermore, most societies maintain clear expectations about who is suitable as a partner. Men tend to marry into their own or a lower social class, women into a higher class. Social class is often more important than other traditionally significant factors, such as religion and age, in mate choice (Ingoldsby et al., 2003). The desire for a good job and education for both sexes may be particularly high in societies where there is strong competition for work (Medora et al., 2002). In Korea, Brown (1994) reported very little change in attitudes towards the parental role in arranging marriage between 1965 and 1989, with most believing that the parents should have at least "equal say" in selecting a mate. Despite the rapid social changes that have been so evident in India over the last five decades, traditional Hindu marriage is still a social and cultural duty rather than simply an expression of affection between the partners. As such, marriage within religion and caste remains important, and most young Indians feel that they are unable to choose their own suitable mate wisely without substantial input from their parents (Medora, 2003). Parents or other kin screen selected partners with similar social, cultural, economic, and family backgrounds, often suggested by friends or the extended family, with the clear expectation that this is a nonsexual process aimed at providing a marriage partner, although a newly emerging, self-arranged marriage does allow for prescreened couples to partake in a short courtship process prior to marriage. Amongst the wealthy and educated elite, families may also place advertisements in publications such as the *Times of India* and screen potential candidates using photos before they allow for a telephone conversation or a chaperoned meeting. Thus, even amongst this highly modernised and mobile group, parental approval is still highly significant (ibid.).

Most researchers would argue that greater education, participation in paid labour, urban living, increased geographical mobility, and dispersal of the family have played important roles in increasing an individual's choice of a partner (Corwin, 1977; Fox, 1975; Rosenblatt & Anderson, 1981). Yet in some instances, we see evidence that just such changes may have only limited impact or indeed may operate in a different direction than expected. Oppong (1980) reported that love-based marriage in Ghana was the traditional basis for marriage. However, the development of a cash-crop economy not only led to greater migration and social mobility, but also produced economic challenges that have led to an increasingly materialistic emphasis in marital partner choice. Preferences may also persist for partners from a familiar setting: Feldman (1994) found in a study of Peruvian and Mexican rural peasants that there was still a strong preference to marry someone from the home town, even following migration to a city. Religion – and in particular Islam – may have an influential impact on willingness to allow the family to choose a mate (Al-Thakeb, 1985; Fox, 1975), whilst the introduction of Christianity to a culture is often associated with a decline in polygamy (McKinney, 1992). One fascinating set of studies conducted by Tashakori and Thompson (1988, 1991) analysed the impact of the Islamic revolution of 1979 in Iran on close relationships in that country. They showed how respondents questioned in 1982 were more traditional than a sample collected some eight years earlier, before the revolution. This was

evident in the respondents' desire for earlier marriage and greater
parental involvement in partner selection. This pattern was moderated
by education, however, with "traditionalisation" greater in those from
less educated backgrounds. In addition, amongst high school children
there was evidence of an increasing desire for women to seek
further education and paid work, suggesting that many attempts to
"retraditionalise" may not have been completely successful.

Located at the southeastern edge of Europe, Turkey is a secular
society with a predominantly Muslim population. As such, it provides
an interesting example of many current debates about partner choice,
religion, politics, and modernisation. Modern-day Turkey combines
the traditional and the new, with approximately half of new marriages
arranged, but with evidence of an increase in "Western style" partner
selection, particularly among the young and educated, where women
are far more active as initiators of a match than in previous years
(Hortacsu, 1997; Medora et al., 2002). Modern arranged marriages
provide prospective families with an introduction, using their social
networks to seek a suitable mate. In the case of a groom, this would be
someone with higher social status and education and good character.
For the bride, this would include a good (unscandalous) family reputation and similar education, money, religion, and values. Other
traditional exchanges (such as the provision of bride wealth to the
family and the marriage of a woman to her dead husband's brother) are
increasingly uncommon. Yet even amongst the young and educated
urban elite, where an individual is most likely to choose his/her own
spouse, family approval is likely to be sought, with the groom asking for
the hand of the young woman from her father. Furthermore, whilst the
search for the "one and only" is of course primarily an individualistic
pursuit, this does not mean that in those situations where partnerships
are arranged by the family, mate choice selection has not changed over
time, too. Thus, even in the more traditional arranged marriage, strong
interpersonal attraction and the development of spousal love is strongly
encouraged by the family, even when the family had a major role in
attempting to restrict the choice of partners available and in overseeing
the courtship process (Medora et al., 2002).

BECOMING ATTACHED OR STAYING SINGLE

In a "post-materialistic," modern world, where the intense, private,
and "internal" emotions are of primacy (Suh et al., 1998), loneliness

may be a key predictor of life satisfaction. Indeed, some have argued that such loneliness may be of greater everyday concern to citizens of contemporary affluent societies than the material worries that occupied the lives of previous generations during less materially affluent times (Inglehart, 1997; Tornstam, 1992). Some of this is likely to result from an increasingly large number of single people living alone. This is partly associated with a lesser willingness to marry in general, as well as cohabitation after divorce for social benefit reasons and the lesser availability of men due to their higher mortality rate. Concerns about marital rates have been a frequent topic of discussion in various Asian countries. Jones (2005) considers the "flight from marriage" in Southeast and Eastern Asia, with nonmarriage for women more commonplace in some big cities than in the West. A rising urban and educated population has meant parents may be less keen for their daughters to marry until their economic capacity can be appreciated. New models of independent young women who are earning money and remaining single have allowed for the development of new norms of "nontraditional" lives. In Thailand between 1980 and 2000, the proportion of Thai males who were still single in their forties doubled. In Singapore, marriage rates are lower amongst poorly educated men and highly educated women. This is because educated men may be happy to marry women younger and less educated than themselves, but highly educated women are rejecting less educated men, leading to a shortage of mates. In Malaysia, the large number of educated women has led to a lack of local spouses and the emergence of Islamic marriage agencies to help find partners.

The timing of marriage is also likely to be influenced by economic participation and the related variable of education, as well as mate availability. Sheela and Audinarayana (2003), in Tamil Nadu, India, note how higher levels of education for girls and greater economic participation for women makes the postponement of marriage more likely, with women more likely to marry a man of a similar age. However, this was moderated by caste, with lower-caste members more likely to enter matrimony at an early age in comparison to those of a higher caste. Furthermore, despite laws forbidding the marriage of women under the age of 18, many of these regulations are ignored amongst the rural poor. Thus, some 30 percent of rural female adolescents are married by the time they reach age 15 (Adler, Ozer, & Tschann, 2003). Sumbadze (2006) describes the influence of the difficult economic circumstances of the last decade on marriages in the

Republic of Georgia. Here registered marriages dropped from 37,000 in 1990 to 14,000 in 1999. One factor in this reluctance to marry may be the particularly grandiose expectations for the wedding feast, which would impose financial burdens on families already going through a period of severe economic challenges.

Wong (2003) discusses Becker's (1963) economic independence hypothesis, which argues that as women gain greater economic independence the rationale for the traditional division of labour in the household will be weakened. As a result, there will be less for women to gain from marriage overall. Hong Kong has gone through very rapid socioeconomic development in a short time, and women's gains in educational attainment have been marked. Sustained and rapid economic growth drew many women into formal employment. Wong argues that rising educational and employment opportunities for women have led to the postponement, but not abandonment, of marriage. However, the relationship between education and marital formation is complex. Indeed, better-educated women could often find a more attractive partner, as they can contribute more to the household. This can lead to a positive relationship amongst education, earnings, and marriage. Wong's data suggest that women with the highest levels of education are the most strongly inclined to marry and to expect more from marriage, especially in the area of personal fulfillment. At the same time, these women wish to marry later than those who are less educated.

In Britain, rates of living alone have increased markedly in the last three decades. Barber (2004) used time series data for England, Wales, Scotland, and the United States to examine the role of female marriage opportunities and their relationship to single parenthood. He notes that women are spending increasingly more of their reproductive age unmarried as a result of diminished marriage market opportunities. Over the last three decades, the British population has grown 5 percent, but single-person households have increased more than six times (*Social Trends*, 2003, p. 42). These patterns are likely to persist within individuals across time. Using linked census data records from 1971, 1981, and 1991, Williams et al. (2005) found that living alone in an earlier census predisposed one to living alone again and that this pattern was increasingly marked. The numbers of singletons may also reflect an understandable unwillingness of those who have experienced divorce to remarry, with several data sets from the United States and the United Kingdom showing that the higher the divorce rate, the lower the remarriage rate. In the United States, there has been an increase in single men aged 20 to 29 from 1961 to 1981 and rising numbers of separated men. There was also some increase in the numbers of nonresidential biological fathers during the late 1970s and 1980s, although this leveled off during the 1990s (Gupta, Smock, & Manning, 2004).

A key debate for those concerned about the impacts of modernisation concerns its implications for the formation of close attachment relationships. We can envisage several different kinds of relationship between culture, social change, attachment, and the consequences of attachment for intimate relationships (Goodwin & Kunowska, 2006). These make different assumptions about the universality of particular parenting experiences, the impact of those parenting experiences on attachment, and the relationship between attachment and other psychological variables, such as personality, relationship schemata, and love styles.

Stemming from Freud's (1914) work on attachment and love and Bowlby's (1969) work on attachment styles, a universalist approach to attachment suggests that particular parenting behaviours lead to specific attachment styles, with consequences for later adult relationships. Early attachment experiences are seen as influencing general relationship schemata, and these then affect adult love schemata (Collins & Feeney, 2000; Hazan & Shaver, 1987, 1994). Indeed, Doherty et al. (1994) argued that attachment styles are more important than culture in shaping love styles. Others see culture as a significant moderator of childhood attachment, with later consequences for adult relationships. From this perspective, there may be cross-cultural differences in the proportions of both childhood and adult attachment styles. These may then reflect cultural differences in child-rearing practices (Keller, 2002). There is some evidence of cultural differences in the association between attachment and marital relationships (for example, Onishi & Gjerde, 2002, in Japan). Most of this work assumes that the parenting experience/attachment link works in the same way across cultures, although some (for example, Rothbaum et al., 2000) question the Western bias of measures used here.

Of particular interest here is whether adult attachment styles and the "internal working models" they reflect may be subject to subsequent changes independent of parenting experiences. Certainly, as we see in this book, there is evidence of some rapid changes in core aspects of adult interpersonal relationships, such as in trust levels in

Eastern Europe following the fall of communism. Indeed, one of the very definitions of an "avoidant attachment" style (Hazan & Shaver, 1987) is: "I am somewhat uncomfortable being close to others; I find it difficult to trust them completely." Work on affiliation and anxiety demonstrates that when people are more scared, unexpected new attachments form (Schachter, 1959). Furthermore, attachment style represents an important personal resource, and therefore it may be critical in appraising societal change. This opens up new, largely unexplored possibilities about how an individual's sense of relationship security might be influenced in a time of social change. I return to this when I consider the implications of terrorism threat on social network maintenance in the next chapter.

SOCIAL NETWORKS, DATING, AND THE INTERNET "REVOLUTION"

Many reports from Asia have suggested that both the Chinese and Japanese prefer to socialise in groups and feel shy and awkward when with members of the opposite sex (Reischauer, 1988; Xiaohe & Whyte, 1990). However, it is clear that informal networks are playing an increasingly important role in bringing couples together in urban areas, with residence patterns playing a significant moderating role in the development of relationships. Xu (1997, cited in Xia & Zhou, 2003) interviewed 3,200 married couples from four Chinese regions. Although parental opinion is still important in final marriage matches, Xu found that whilst some 80 percent of Shanghai couples met at school or work or through mutual friends, only 37 percent of those from the underdeveloped rural province of Gansu met this way, with almost half introduced by relatives or neighbours. Between 1987 and 1996, the dating of classmates and friends/colleagues had more than doubled (from 27 percent to 56 percent), with the dating of individuals met through relatives showing a similarly proportional decline.

One topic that has attracted considerable media attention in recent years is the growth of dating agencies, in particular the impact of the internet on the development and maintenance of close relationships. In an early North American study of dating agency interaction, Green, Buchanan, and Heuer (1984) found that, in common with the partner preferences discussed above, females chose men who had high status and were attractive, whilst women were chosen primarily on the basis of their physical appearance. A more recent study of more than 2,000 users of a commercial dating service found that dating preferences were based almost completely on physically observed attributes (attractiveness, weight, height, and age) (Kurzban & Weeden, 2005). I examined the social background and communication competencies of members of the largest UK dating agency (Goodwin, 1990). Although the use of dating agencies was less well spread than is currently the case, I argued that dating members were typically more educated than the general population but were weaker on communication skills than nonagency members.

The internet increasingly allows for the meeting of individuals who would have had little opportunity previously to interact. Websites such as *MySpace* and *Facebook* attract tens of millions of users who may become "friends" purely on the basis of being logged on to a service at the same time. Boase and Wellman (2006) contrast the two dominant views on internet relationships. The utopian perspective sees the internet as a great democratising agent for personal relationships, allowing for a revolutionary expansion of social networks across the world. In contrast, a dystopian views the internet as one further agent of modernisation, eroding family life and "real" relationship interaction. Boase and Wellman's review shows that the internet allows for the development of more spatially and socially dispersed networks and a higher velocity of exchanges. It may also allow for a greater amount of interaction with friends without affecting less voluntary and routine relationships, such as those shared with family members. In some special circumstances, a neighbourhood-based internet service can also help develop neighbourhood relationships. Their evidence suggests few differences in offline interactions or social engagements between those who do and those who do not regularly use the internet, although the internet may limit the time spent on some other media (such as television). Instead, for them internet use must be seen in the context of an array of other individual personality and social network factors that determine how the internet is actually used. It should also be seen as another functional means of communication in a society where there are already physically distant relationships, dispersed social networks, and relatively easy to form (and end) relationships. Thus, the internet allows for the achievement of particular relationship goals (for example, through the emailing of a large and loosely bound network or the maintenance of an already long-established closer relationship over distance), rather than representing a transforming agent in itself. Overall, they claim that this technological intervention has much the same impact as other technological inventions discussed in Chapter 1: It neither destroys existing relationships nor revolutionises social interactions.

In a considered analysis of the distinction between "typing, doing, and being," Ross (2005) considers the internet as both "a new form of expression of the self (or selves) and a non-traditional social and sexual setting" (p. 342). Ross considers the old technology and social-change debate, contrasting views that see the internet as just a mirror of the noninternet world but with different technology and those that see the possibilities offered by internet interactions as providing a distinct new space for intimate interactions. He sees the internet as a "gap between thinking, doing and being – and especially, an oppor-tunity to do and not be, or to type and not do" (p. 344). For Ross, online can be a romantic place, with a new script being created by the playwrights at their typewriters. It can accelerate the development of intimacy due to the absence of normal social cues and conventions. At the same time, of course, the internet allows interactants to remain at a distance and to engage in particular behaviours without censure, allowing for the free rein of fantasies. Thus, the internet can allow for a number of more "removed" and nonintimate sexual relationships, where normal disclosures can be avoided and relationship interactions can be primarily functional in form (Ross, 2005). Sexual encounters in particular may be anticipated from the first logging on to the site and may encourage a strong exchange of feelings, desires, and preferred behaviours that may allow participants to feel they already know much about their partner. Certainly, a number of websites now exist that aim to establish anonymous sexual contacts between strangers with minimal commitment (Gabrenya, 2004) – very much the plastic sexuality described by Giddens. The psychological profile of those using these services has not been extensively studied, although Gabrenya did examine the use of "cybersex" (online sexual interac-tions) in the United States, using items from the World Values Survey. As might have been expected, the use of cybersex was negatively related to religiosity or conservative views (Gabrenya et al., 2006).

Yurchisin, Watchravesringkan, and McCabe (2005) focus on the ways in which individuals manage their identities through internet dating. They suggest that the internet allows individuals to create and re-create identities and to present aspects of themselves they may refrain from exhibiting in public. Their informants claimed they began to use the internet as a result of a particular trigger event or a desire for achieving personal growth, often seen as a "moving on" in life – for example, after a divorce. For some, honesty was important; for others, "hoped-for" aspects of their selves were stressed and explored in an anonymous space. Internet dating was particularly important for allowing marginalized groups – for example, homosexuals – to "come out" in a safer and possibly less judgemental environment. Such dating also allowed others to receive positive feedback that bolstered their self-image and positively influenced their offline identities, helping overcome interpersonal awkwardness. As such, internet dating allowed individuals to learn about themselves and whom they could become, thereby aiding them in overcoming the stresses of difficult life transitions.

As with many areas of modernity and personal relationships, the existence and ease of cybersex has aroused some controversy. For some, cybersex reflects today's individualistic and materialistic society (Waskul, 2004). In this analysis, cybersex is seen as having a generally negative impact, not only on a healthy relationship with the immediate relationship partner, but also on children and siblings (Delmonico, 2003). Bauman (2003) sees cybersex as signaling a death in moral relationships, where individuals are objectified and seen as simple consumption objects and where interactions are shallower and less intense. Philaretou, Mahfouz, and Allen (2005) examined internet pornography and men's well-being. Whilst they recognise that cybersex can help some marginalised groups and help those in a healthy relationship expand their sexual repertoire, they use survey data to claim that around 7 percent of the male adult internet population in the United States spend more than six hours a week involved in "excessive" cybersex. They claim that this compulsive behaviour is of increasing importance to professionals and is associated with delusional and faulty thoughts. They suggest that cybersex obsession is likely to lead to a neglect of interpersonal relationships with partners, friends, and family, as well as leading to a feeling of distress when offline. Such an obsession can also lead to lying to cover up otherwise unacceptable activities and is related to physical symptoms such as disturbed sleep patterns. They see obsessed men struggling with their obsessions and experiencing guilt, depression, anxiety, and problems with the formation of "real-life" relationships.

For others, there are several positive aspects to cybersex. Ross (2005) argues that cybersex provides extra sexual possibilities that add to human sexual interactions and gives the opportunity for new connections – "a new social niche for sexual expression" (p. 351). As in the case of dating relationships, Ross notes that the internet allows for the development of new surrogate and transformed individuals, able to meet a wide variety of sexual needs that are not satisfied locally or within their off-line relationships. For Ross, cybersex can undermine existing (and repressive) power relationships and, in being the ultimate "malleable" relationship, offers possible empowerment to women in particular. It also allows for others to "come out," providing a first opportunity for many to experience behaviours and language they may not otherwise feel confident in accessing. This may be particularly important for some communities who feel under threat or who feel the need for important relationship disclosures. McKenna, Green, and Smith (2001) argue that those unable to express their individual sexuality through their offline relationships are more likely to go online to express them. This is seen as "demarginalising" sexual selves, acclaiming a positive sexual identity when before there was isolation and shame. Indeed, there is evidence that specific groups – such as women, older adults, and gay men – seem to be using cybersex in particular ways (Delmonico, 2003). Carballo-Diéguez et al. (2006), for example, studied internet-using Latino men who had sex with men and found that the internet provided an important opportunity for disclosure of their serostatus. Thus, the internet can serve those with stigmatized sexual choices and help them develop a new community that would otherwise be impractical by creating new "communities of identity and interest" (Ross, 2005, p. 349). The internet may allow for the socially and physically disadvantaged, allowing poor communicators to reflect on their interactions, those who are less attractive to compensate, and those who are less mobile to still enjoy romantic and sexual experiences. Thus, it becomes "not unlike a sexual version of ebay or online catalogues, providing a globalised marketplace in place of a local sexual economy" (p. 347). At the same time, not all cybersex users are necessarily socially marginalized or relationship losers. Indeed, there is evidence to suggest that those who engage in cybersex are more likely to have offline partners than those who do not (Daneback, Cooper, & Manson, 2005).

One notable development in recent years has been the emergence of the "mail-order" partner; usually, but of course not exclusively, the bride. Constable (2003) considers pen pals and mail-order marriages, often seen as a situation of exploitation by rich Western men out to find cheap, young, subservient women or by manipulative women desiring glamorous shopping expeditions. Constable argues that Third World women in particular are often seen as subjugated in their marriages to Westerners, but she suggests that this image arises partly from sexist and racist stereotypes of these women. Instead, she sees possible advantages for both men and women in these situations, with women presenting themselves in not too dissimilar a way to American teenagers "preparing" for a Western date and often having far more power than is portrayed (indeed, more than they may have "at home"). Whilst, of course, some exploitation does occur, the development of a truly international pattern of partner exchanges, conducted through a wide range of media, is likely to be an increasing feature of a more globalised society, although the extent to which this will substantially change established patterns of relationship interaction remains to be assessed.

Finally, other forms of electronic communication are also beginning to gain attention for their impact on close relationships. A report by the think tank Demos (2003) suggests that "by their nature, electronic networks like the internet or mobile [telephone] are 'technologies of connection.' They allow individuals to communicate ... and build relationships" (p. 59). The mobile phone has become a major part of everyday communications, allowing for the development of new methods for initiating, organising, and terminating both intimate and nonintimate social connections. Texting, like other forms of electronic communication, allows the shy an opportunity to control their interactions without the embarrassment of a face-to-face interaction, whilst the strong relationships between teenagers and their phones may even be seen as public expression of their identities (compare, for example, the range of phone ring tones that can be heard on a typical London underground [subway] journey). As yet, we know little about how this new form of communication is impacting the quality or diversity of the relationships formed. It does seem, however, that such means of communication are, like their computer-based counterparts, largely about the maintenance of new relationships, rather than acting purely for the formation of new liaisons.

SUMMARY

Throughout history, many societies have worried about the dangers of love between "unapproved" parties. The increase in freedom to select your own partner of choice has signaled a greater egalitarianism in relationships, but the self-centred nature of modernity has made some question the stability of these relationships. Across the globe, mate choice has been influenced by local environmental, political, and religious factors, whilst education, for women in particular, has delayed marriage in many societies. New technology, most noticeably the advent of the internet, has offered new opportunities for establishing partnerships, particularly between previously marginalized groups. However, the development of such technology is likely to mean the extension of social networks rather than a diminution in the significance of face-to-face interactions for the development of longer-term relationships.

CHAPTER 4

Friends and Social Networks

Whilst it may be relatively easy to see the impact of dramatic social changes on regulations about contact between the sexes or on divorce, less immediately obvious are the impacts of these changes on friendships and social networks. Yet the manner in which social solidarities have emerged in response to the pressures of "modern life," as well as the apparent decline of social relationships in an era of individualism, have also been the subject of speculation by many social scientists – even when there have been few data to support their views. Consequently, we find ourselves faced with the familiar debate between those who argue that the modern world pulls apart loyalties and intimacies and those who posit that it is the very challenges of a harsh and unforgiving outside world that reinforces those loyalties.

PATTERNS OF FRIENDSHIP OVER TIME

"Friendship" is a difficult word to define and is likely to cover a whole range of informal relationships. In addition, the meaning of friendship has changed over time (Adams, 2004; Pahl, 2000). Pahl (2000) has traced the development of friendship since antiquity. The Aristotelian notion of friendship, which divided friendships of pleasure and utility from the more "whole-person" friendship of virtue, was primarily framed in terms of male friendship. Pahl notes that despite claims that modernity has destroyed old patterns of virtuous friendships, writings dating back at least eight centuries have demonstrated the instrumental notion of friendship and, in particular, the utility of friends for finding work and performing other practical tasks. However, sociological literature suggests that friends were not a prominent feature in the nineteenth and early twentieth centuries in the Western world, a time marked by economic depression as well as increasing social and geographical mobility (Adams, 2004; Pahl, 2000). Living arrangements were important in what friends did together; the nineteenth-century home was ill suited for visitors, so friends were rarely invited inside. Giddens (1992) argues that during Victorian times male friendships were particularly marginalized, although they were significant in helping to cope with unfulfilling marriages.

Modernity may have changed this. For Pahl (2000), there is evidence of something akin to Aristotelian intimacy in modern-day friendships. He argues: "Friendship may be seen as an increasingly important form of social glue in contemporary society ..." (p. 1). "[T]here is something about friendship that appears to be quintessentially post-modern, ... [with] connotations of freedom, choice, individuality and, crucially, subversion" (p. 166). Our everyday culture is increasingly "mediated" through our friendships (Pahl, 2000, p. 3); the weakening of traditional family bonds has meant that "[f] riendship is the archetypal social relationship of choice, and ours is a period of choice" (p. 171). Friends may play a particularly important part during the most significant periods of our life, especially when there is no romantic partner to provide this support (Adams, 2004). Social diversity has allowed for the growth of new ties, forming new "informal solidarities" that help frame the wider social network (Allan, 2001). This new and very personal friendship incorporates a lack of obligation and the possibility to express opinions and feelings freely (Pahl, 2000). Such friendship is also potentially burdensome, expecting a great deal as other marital relationships or class unions become challenged (Vernon, 2007). Friendship networks may be particularly significant in allowing us to make sense of the world around us, enabling us to resolve personal issues and helping us create our sense of self (Allan, 2001). In an ever more mobile world, close friends can help replace kin in psychological value. Even when performing "individualistic" tasks such as gardening, friends provide an audience, with shared activities creating valuable sentiment. Furthermore, new relationships with former lovers or partners and the increased sharing of social activities with other couples (such as when traveling together on holiday overseas) represent a move away from the compartmentalised couple relationships characteristic of the 1970s (Pahl, 2000).

Allan (2001) notes that many key friendship relationships will be emergent rather than long established, reflecting the changed circumstances associated with increased social and geographical mobility. Social diversity has also allowed for the development of new ties that go beyond the local area. Friendship patterns may also become increasingly undifferentiated by gender, despite some persistence in the tendency for friendships to be primarily single-sex (Baumgarte, 2002). An expanded higher education system in particular has given women new opportunities to make friends. For many, friendship has moved beyond simple face-to-face interactions, with the potential to become far more diverse with the advent of the internet and other mobile forms of communication (Adams, 2004). Often new ties are established with people with whom we have less in common than in traditional friendships. Such ties tend to be geographically diffuse, with low network density – we only know a few of our friend's networks. This allows for a range of individuals to be included and for friends to portray themselves differently when in different groups (Allan, 2001). Giddens describes how networking becomes increasingly important amongst otherwise disconnected people, who may rely less on established roles and traditional associations (Giddens & Pierson, 1998). This requires the development of an "active trust" (p. 121). As a result, relationships can be more egalitarian, but also require new types of negotiation that were less necessary in earlier times.

As with previous critiques of some aspects of modernity, Giddens and others are aware of other limitations of these new forms of relationships. Pahl (2000) notes that urban living and increasingly longer commuting times in many cities may also serve to undermine some traditional patterns of friendship interaction, curtailing friendship as the "pure relationship." New friendships may represent a form of "stripped-down" intimacy, which is often essentially relatively superficial and utilitarian (Giddens & Pierson, 1998, p. 121). In the workplace, perceived insecurities and rivalries may undermine the development of stable relationships, with many workplaces providing relatively low-trust environments (Adams, 2004; Pahl, 2000). Allan also recognises that "different individuals ... have different capacities and freedoms to modify and change their lifestyles and identities" (Allan, 2001, p. 337). Social groups still moderate the way in which individuals' friendships have evolved alongside changes in daily circumstances: Social ties and the practices they perpetuate can be seen as one part of the response of occupational groups to the constraints and realities of external circumstances (Pahl, 2000; Williams, 1990). Friendships are still likely to be constrained within one social class group and are more likely to develop in a particular geographical area. Contrary to popular myth, people from low socioeconomic status usually have only limited access to support from friends (Liem & Liem, 1978). However, as we saw in the previous chapter, new forms of communication, such as the internet, do allow for the rapid and easy maintenance of social networks, with many such networks maintained from the office desk during working hours. In particular, those who may feel their identities are marginalized in wider society may particularly welcome the opportunities presented through association with like-minded friends. Hence, for many gay people friends represent "families of choice," who can be trusted to provide support not provided by others in their family or community (Allan, 2001).

Some of the enduring power of friendship is demonstrated in a study by Sugawara and Akiyama (2004) in Japan, where the family plays a central role. Cabinet Office data showed that one-third of older adults live with married children in Japan, compared to only 42 percent in the United States and 2.4 percent in Sweden. Previous research in Japan has tended to indicate that friends provide a main source of companionship and emotional support in young adulthood, but after marriage the spouse and family become the major support source (for example, Carbery & Burhmester, 1998). Couples are then seen as separate units rarely socializing together. Sugawara and Akiyama, however, provide evidence of a different pattern of friendship, one that emphasises the role of friends across the life course. In their analysis of more than 500 respondents aged 20 to 75 in a middle-sized Japanese city, they found that friends were the primary source of companionship across all life stages. These friends functioned as important confidants in all life stages, sharing this role with the family for those who were married. Indeed, spouses functioned as companions less than friends, reflecting the separate social lives lived by many Japanese couples.

FRIENDSHIP DURING TIMES OF RAPID CHANGE

In totalitarian countries, friendships may have a very different, even life-threatening, meaning (Mamali, 1996; Markova, 1997; Shlapentokh, 1984). Friendships can challenge social orders (Adams, 2004), and totalitarian societies often discourage friendships, seeing them as a challenge to State authority and as a breeding ground for conspiracy. Friendships can also provide a route for bypassing State regulation and control (Pahl, 2000). They may challenge social inequalities sanctioned by the State and can help encourage wider social engagement, civic engagement, and democracy, all of which may not be widely welcomed (ibid.). In addition, by providing power to those with the right social connections, they may also be viewed as a source of corruption and inequality.

During the communist era in some Eastern European countries, up to one in three adults had at some time acted as informants for the State. Corruption was widespread, and the State ideology emphasized collectivistic and depersonalized relationships (Mamali, 1996; Markova, 1997); indeed, the most intimate of interpersonal liaisons and conflicts could provide a source of blackmail and control for the Communist Party. As a result, an atomisation of relationships and a reluctance to trust others was perhaps unsurprising, alongside a widespread belief that "commitment to [other's] welfare [was] foolhardy at best and self destructive at worst" (Schwartz & Bardi, 1997, p. 392). At the same time, despite the risks involved, friendships were also often viewed as vital resources in a political system seemingly run in an often arbitrary manner (Shlapentokh, 1989). Popular was the Russian phrase "a hundred friends are worth more than a hundred roubles" (Rose, 1995).

The end of communist rule in Eastern Europe signaled a major change in the societal structure of these countries. For many, the new competitive lifestyle propagated new social tensions between former colleagues and friends. The absence of a common, often somewhat absurd State apparatus against which to unite appeared to weaken former alliances. The author and Nizharadze, Nguyen Luu, Kosa, and Emelyanova (1999) examined intimate disclosures on a number of topics during the period of *glasnost* in Russia, Hungary, and the Republic of Georgia. We compared the disclosures of three groups: entrepreneurs, who lived in a highly competitive environment and operated in an atmosphere of distrust and conflict; manual workers, whose traditional workforce loyalty was becoming increasingly threatened by high levels of unemployment; and university students. Like Wellman (1994), we found that in Eastern Europe, friends did provide some of the material assets vital for economic survival and gave valuable informational support at a time of uncertainty. Yet, we also found that disclosure to friends was moderated by the target of the disclosure and the culture of the respondent. Age was also a significant independent moderator of disclosure, as was a fatalistic worldview. Hungarians were the most likely to disclose, Russians the least, reflecting a broader cultural theme of distrust in the latter country, also revealed in an analysis of the newsprint media of that time. Students were more likely to disclose to close friends than manual workers or entrepreneurs were. Indeed, younger respondents in general were also more likely to disclose intimately to others across a range of topics. This reflected our older respondents' experience of the "years of stagnation" that followed Khrushchev, an era characterised by particular distrust and disillusionment (Lane, 1992). At the individual level, psychological fatalism also predicted poor disclosure to others, reflecting other findings that highlight the importance of beliefs for adjustment to changing societies (Jerusalem & Mittag, 1995).

SOCIAL CAPITAL

According to Furstenberg (2005), "[I]t is hard to find a recent concept in the social sciences that has been greeted with more enthusiasm than the notion of social capital" (p. 809). The presence (or indeed, absence) of social capital has become central to the discussion of social cohesion in modern societies (Edwards, 2004) and thus relates to many of the essential ideas discussed so far in this book. Although ideas on social norms and networks date back to Durkheim (1951), the concept is usually attributed to the work of Coleman (1988). Furstenberg defines social capital as "the stock of social goodwill created through shared social norms and a sense of common membership" (2005, p. 810). Bourdieu et al. (1983) distinguish amongst three types of capital, each of which can function as a form of symbolic capital. The first, economic capital, includes assets such as income and material possessions. The second, cultural capital, involves such resources as educational qualifications and language. Finally, he identifies social capital – the social network and contacts an individual has and may use in his/her everyday life. Thus, social capital is "the sum of resources, actual or virtual, that accrue to an individual or group by virtue of possessing a durable network" (Bourdieu & Wacquant, 1992, p. 119). This would also include the friendships discussed above. Putnam defines "social capital" as "connections among individuals – social networks and the norms of reciprocity and trustworthiness that arise from them" (2000, p. 19). Most of these definitions focus on networks, norms, trust, and resources. Social capital is deposited largely in the family, providing a key resource that allows for linkages between individuals and outside groups and these resources (Coleman, 1990). As such, this analysis forms part of a functionalist perspective on families and communities.

The notion of social capital has often been tied to ideas of community cohesion and responsibility. Social capital is frequently seen as a major part of the "social glue" that cements societies. For the political right, social capital offers an important replacement for State support. For the left, voluntary associations and the like can act as a corrective to excessive individualism within capitalist societies (Edwards, Franklin, & Holland, 2003). Strong and connected community networks appear to be important in mobilising political activity, particularly amongst relatively politically uninvolved groups, such as ethnic minorities and migrant communities (Fieldhouse & Cutts, 2006). The British Labour Party leadership has recently embraced the notion of social capital, echoing Durkheim in seeing it as a major (and relatively cheap) panacea to social disharmony in British society (Baron, 2004). Former Prime Minister Tony Blair directly cited social capital work when describing how "inter-connected communities" are healthier (Roberts & Devine, 2004). In remarks on the March 2003 white paper *Respect and Responsibility: Taking a Stand Against Antisocial Behaviour*, former British Home Secretary David Blunkett claimed, "We need a fundamental cultural change in our society, where we take pride in our communities and challenge those who try to damage them" (cited in Edwards, 2004, p. 4).

A loss of social capital is seen as having wide implications for the broader functioning of society and is associated by many with a broader moral decline (Edwards, 2004; Edwards, Franklin, & Holland, 2003). In one of the most important texts investigating social capital, Putnam (2000) provides an exhaustive account of the decline in social capital in the United States during the second half of the twentieth century. Putnam has a particular concern with economic well-being and democratic participation, although for him social capital can take many forms, including extended families, civic organisations, professional affiliations, and civic organisations (p. 21). Using a variety of sources, but drawing most heavily on organisational records and national survey data, Putnam argues that societies high in social capital are more trusting and that social capital influences economic involvement, democratic participation, and individual health and happiness. According to Putnam, social capital has both individual and collective components. Thus, whilst individual networking can help an individual get jobs or favours from others, social capital is also a "public good," positively influencing the wider community. Such capital allows for the protection of a local neighbourhood and the raising of money for charitable ends. Putnam distinguishes between the "bonding" and "bridging" functions of social capital. Bonding capital is inward and reinforces exclusive identities, such as membership in a fashionable country club. This form of social capital does not necessarily just furnish the more privileged, but can help less fortunate community members – for example, in the way that minority ethnic communities may help new members of a host society. Other forms of social capital serve to include a wider diversity of members (such as in civil rights movements). This bridging social capital can help members "get ahead," allowing members to expand their activities. This capital also links members to external resources. These capital ties can be both weak and strong. In Putnam's words, "[S]trong ties with intimate friends may ensure chicken soup when you're sick, but weak ties with distant acquaintances are more likely to produce leads for a new job" (p. 363).

Central to Putnam's arguments are the ways in which social capital has changed over the past century. He does not argue that this has been a constant, steady decline. Instead, he argues that this has been a story of change over recent history. Simply put, he maintains:

For the first two-thirds of the twentieth century a powerful tide bore Americans into ever deeper engagement in the life of their communities, but a few decades ago ... that tide reversed and we were overtaken by a treacherous rip current. Without at first noticing, we have been pulled apart from one another and from our communities over the last third of the century (p. 27).

Putnam provides evidence of these trends under a number of subheadings, and here I discuss those most relevant to interpersonal relationships. First, consider social networks. Putnam argues that whilst American voluntary organisations have proliferated in number, these groups tend to be much smaller since the 1960s. Groups now tend to be part of wider political debates, rather than debating local affairs, and encourage remote involvement rather than attendance at regular meetings. While nearly half of Americans in the 1960s spent some time each week in clubs and local associations, this number had dropped to less than a quarter in the 1990s. Putnam gives the example of membership in parent–teacher associations, which actually rose until around about 1960 then declined sharply over the next three decades. Turning to workplace connections, Putnam notes how, despite the rhetoric of "team building," workplace connections tend to be casual and not deeply supportive, reflecting the concerns of many students of friendships at work cited above. In particular, Putnam claims that structural features in the nature of work, such as the proliferation of temporary jobs and shorter job tenure, tend to limit work ties. Similar decline is evident when it comes to more informal social contacts. Putnam argues that we send fewer greeting cards, spend less time with neighbours, participate less in sports, and visit friends less frequently (p. 115). Putnam also sees altruism as part of social capital. He provides evidence to suggest that involvement in community life and relationship ties with family, friends, and neighbours are powerful predictors of giving money, blood, or favours to others. Despite greater prosperity in the last decades of the twentieth century, he claims, Americans became less generous, with the caveat that an increasing number of retired people performed more voluntary activities, such as youth mentoring.

Putnam considers a number of possible reasons for this decline. He examines the decline in family structure (more divorce, fewer children, more living alone) but argues that neither marital nor parental status predicts wider social capital. Indeed, modern families do not necessarily lead to the spread of social capital, with these unions forming with relatively little outside pressure and with personal attributes favoured over those that may strengthen common communities (Furstenberg, 2005). Putnam also considers the possibility that we are just too busy trying to get by financially, so that we have little time for social connectedness. Whilst he recognises that the growth of two-career families has had the effect of reducing women's community involvement (in that they traditionally played a larger part in these communities), he concludes that neither time nor financial pressures play a major part, as social connectedness has decreased for both sexes, working or not. Putnam also examines the growth of urban sprawl, including the development of the "impersonal mall" and increases in commuting – but he argues that this again only contributes a relatively small amount to the decline in social capital. Furthermore, contrary to many modernisation theorists, he notes that market capitalism has been around for several centuries, but the decline in social capital in the United States is much more recent. More important, he suggests, has been the increase of television viewing, which he characterises as the single most consistent predictor of civic disengagement and to which he attributes some 25 percent of the decline in social connectedness. Television, he argues, not only "privatizes our leisure time, it also privatizes our civic activity, dampening our interactions with one another" (p. 229). "TV watching," he claims, "comes at the expense of nearly every social activity outside the home, especially social gatherings and informal conversations" (p. 237). Such television viewing is also related to loneliness and emotional difficulties. Finally, he posits generational effects; a very "civic" generation, partly shaped by the experiences of World War II, was replaced by generations who were less engaged. This, he argues, may account for half of the decline in social capital.

The implications of this decline, Putnam says, are multiple. Social capital allows people to collectively solve joint problems and smoothes business and social transactions. People with good social capital do better in the economic marketplace. Weak ties are particularly important here in helping those at the margins prosper. Social capital provides an important physical safety net: Those with good social capital are noticeable when they are absent, and cohesive communities care enough to get involved and help out. Members of collective movements are less cynical and more tolerant of others. Social capital allows individuals to cope better with trauma and to fight physical and psychological disorders more effectively; and at the collective level, social capital also encourages safer, more democratic societies. Putnam argues that nations in U.S. with high social capital have flourishing children and low crime rates. Where social capital is lacking, the negative effects of employment and family breakdown are magnified, particularly in poorer areas, where there are greater educational and financial challenges. Immune resistance may be triggered by social capital, helping people fight distress and cope with stress. People who are disconnected are more likely to die from all causes, compared with similar others with close family, friendship, and community ties. Indeed, Putnam asserts, "[I]f you belong to no groups but decide to join one, you cut your risk of dying over the next year *in half* [original italics]. If you smoke and belong to no groups, it's a toss-up statistically whether you should stop smoking or start joining" (p. 331).

Putnam does consider some counter-evidence to his thesis of social decline. He acknowledges that small self-help groups have formed that may substitute for other intimate ties (for example, Alcoholics Anonymous). Evangelical (mainly Christian) movements have also shown a rapid increase. Environmental movements and the like have rapidly increased their memberships over the last few decades, largely through direct mailings, but these tend not to encourage local involvement. Technological changes have played their part, too. The telephone has allowed for greater social contacts with friends and has not necessarily led to disconnection. The internet may help facilitate some forms of social ties, both weak and strong, although Putnam claims this cannot be seen as a substitute for these relationships. Putnam also recognises "the dark side of social capital" – in particular, the notion that social capital may reduce freedom and encourage intolerance. Nevertheless, overall, he concludes, those who are engaged in communities are more tolerant of others and that, at both the individual and the group level, social capital is "good for you."

Finally, Putnam considers the question: "What is to be done?" He points out that if we look at historical precedent we see that at the end of the nineteenth century the United States faced a similar problem of social decline, when industrialisation, urbanisation, and massive immigration also changed American life. New market pressures greatly transformed the social landscape of British and American societies, with new modes of communication, economic changes, and restructuring of the workplace echoing more contemporary changes. But the end of the nineteenth century also witnessed a huge boom in association building in the form of voluntary organisations. This investment seemed to be a requisite of the building of broader social capital. Whilst some of these new groups (for example, the Ku Klux Klan) seem to emphasise exclusion, Putnam argues that "civic inventiveness" is urgently needed to help invigorate civic societies through the establishment of collective initiatives. These can take the form of a range of extracurricular events and learning programmes. It should be accompanied by other forms of "social-capital formation on the job" (p. 407) and a decrease in time spent commuting.

Changing Social Capital in Communist Societies

"Active citizenship" was often seen as a mechanism for dissent in communist Eastern and Central Europe during the 1980s (Einhorn, 1993). The "second economies" in Hungary and Poland offered important spiritual and intimacy fulfillment, as well as providing much needed material needs. In our work in the Republic of Georgia, we found strong social networks to persist amongst entrepreneurs

well into the mid-1990s, primarily in order to help them deal with the
challenges of the new market economy in that country (Goodwin,
Allen et al., 2002). An interesting example of changes in women's
nongovernmental organisations and women's groups after the end of
communism is provided by Haskova and Krizkova (2003). As is
common in totalitarian societies, the Communist Party that took
power in Czechoslovakia in 1948 saw civil society as a potential threat
through its promotion of individual and group sovereignty. With the
Communist Party in control, nongovernmental organisations fell away
dramatically or were unified into new national bodies. The Church
was monitored through official organisations such as the Czechoslovak
Association of Catholic Clergy, which supported the regime. Leisure
activities for both the young and adults became State controlled.
Opposition or dissident groups faced persecution, although some
quasilegal mutual-benefit networks did persist and were important in
challenging official sources of information. By the end of the communist rule in 1989, there were approximately 2,000 organisations
within Czechoslovakia. However, this number increased rapidly,
reaching 37,000 in 1996. Yet despite this, civic participation fell significantly, especially amongst women. Financial restrictions limited
the opportunities to participate in social groupings that involved
travel or other financial costs. In addition, workers were too busily
engaged in two or three jobs to have time for a social life. Broad
social participation across Central and Eastern Europe was further
hindered by the concentration of wealth into the hands of a few
dominant "oligarchs" and an associated cynicism and lack of "public
spiritedness" (Fukuyama, 1995). Indeed, there is evidence now of a far
greater social and economic polarity, with these countries exhibiting a
marked unevenness in their distribution of wealth and opportunities
(Kennedy & Kirwil, 2004).

One characteristic of many communist societies in Eastern Europe
was the bridging capital provided by the school and accommodation
in these countries. With the majority of the urban population living in
large blocks and with schools organised around geographical rather
than explicit social class principles, groups of children who might
never have met under previous economic arrangements were brought
together. This created social relationships that initially continued to be
of value in the uncertainties that followed the collapse of these systems
in the late 1980s. However, a growth of private schools and fee-paying
universities in the 1990s and an increased dispersal of the middle class

into separated (and often gated) communities led to a homogenisation of networks within social classes. This has been coupled with large-scale migration from countries such as Poland to Britain and other Western European nations. Although the long-term consequences of this on the home population have yet to be assessed, early data suggest that severe strains are being placed on established social networks "back home" through such migration. Furthermore, as yet there is little evidence of compensatory support from within the ethnic groups for these migrant populations in their new countries (Goodwin, 2007).

Vietnam became the Socialist Republic of Vietnam in 1976 under Communist Party rule. In 1986, a policy of renovation known as *doi moi* liberalised trade and decollectivised farms. This was accompanied by a substantial increase in industrialisation and a decrease in agriculture, with mass migration to the cities. Dalton notes that along with an improvement in general living standards and a reduction in poverty, social networks became increasingly significant, with the development of new community groups such as sports clubs (Dalton & Ong, 2004). At the same time, the family remained extremely important in helping structure social activities. Comparing data from the 2001 World Values Survey, Dalton noted a specific culture effect, in that Vietnamese spent less time with their friends – and more with their family – than other Asian cultures, such as in China and Japan. There was also a moderating effect for social class: Those with higher income and greater affluence increased their participation in all social networks, whilst those who were better educated enjoyed greater family activity and participated more in friendships, work, and social group networks. The younger Vietnamese participated most actively in social networks. Dalton contends that economic development has not led to a movement away from the family, but has increased the density of social networks, leading to greater participation in such networks.

Trust

Central to most conceptualisations of social capital is the notion of trust. According to Fukuyama (1995, p. 26) "Social capital is a capability that arises from the prevalence of trust in a society." Defining "trust" as "the expectation that arises from a community of regular, honest, and cooperative behaviour" (ibid.), Fukuyama (1995) argues that if people in a business trust one another, they operate according to shared ethical norms, reducing the costs of business. If people do not trust each other, business requires formal rules and regulations, involving further transaction costs. Thus, trust also contributes to "a nation's well-being, as well as its ability to compete" (ibid., p. 7). Low-trust societies, such as China and Italy, are "taxed" by a necessity to "fence in" their peoples. State intervention becomes necessary because of a lack of trust. The family may act as a strong bond but may provide little opportunity for the development of trusting bonds beyond family networks. Low levels of trust are also related to a general permissiveness towards corruption (Moreno, 2003). Putnam (2000) argues that trust acts as a lubricant against the frictions of social life (p. 135) and is an important indicator of charitable giving, political and community participation, greater tolerance towards minorities, and other indices of civic virtue. Thus, "people who trust others are all-round good citizens, and those more engaged in community life are both more trusting and more trustworthy" (p. 137). Putnam distinguishes between "thick" trust – characterised by the exchanges of dense social networks – and a more "generalised," "thinner" trust, which is arguably even more valuable for the wider society in general. Those who "have" in a society are generally more trusting than the "have-nots," and city dwellers trust less than those in rural areas, probably as a result of both the local normative environment and actual experiences.

Reflecting a common theme, Fukuyama believes that high levels of individualism in a society may also restrict the capacity for genuine association between people. Highly individualistic societies are characterised by a weak voluntary sector, as in contemporary Russia or inner-city USA. This suggests that too much family-orientated collectivism as well as too much individualism is inhibitive of strong and broad social bonds. In contrast, higher-trust societies, such as Japan and Germany, as well as more rural parts of the United States, can allow for the development of large organisations without State help. Such societies can provide more responsibility lower down in the organisation, and camaraderie may develop even within a competitive workplace environment. This then reduces costs for both business and the wider society.

Like social capital, trust levels can change markedly over time. Putnam suggests that social trust in the United States rose from the mid-1940s to the mid-1960s and then, like social capital, declined. As a result, people turned to litigation and other formal institutions to solve issues that formerly would have been dealt with through informal social networks. There is some evidence to suggest that trust may be very fragile: Specific events are likely to lead to a decline in trust, such as the Watergate scandal in the United States, particularly when these events are seen as compromising moral goals (Turiel, 2002). Religion and long-established ethical habits can be important predispositions to trust within a society, alongside particular local histories. According to Fukuyama (1995), France in the Middle Ages was a relatively high-trust society. This trust was lost in the sixteenth and seventeenth centuries by a centralising monarchy. In Italy and China, a lack of spontaneous sociability and citizenship arose from the dominance of centralised but rather arbitrary state controls, which limited associations between individuals and groups. This resulted in an "immoral familism," particularly in regions such as Southern Italy, where blood oaths helped build new "trust" relationships on the basis of a fear of violence (Fukuyama, 1995). Elsewhere, such as in Korea, large kinship groups, regionalised identities, shared university class, compulsory army service, and shared hobby groups have helped Koreans go beyond narrow families and build wider communal solidarities (ibid.). In the Chinese family, urbanisation and geographical mobility have weakened lineages and replaced larger extended families with con-jugal ones. However, as I argued above, since the economic reforms of the late 1970s the Chinese family has reconstituted itself along more patrilineal forms, reinforcing older bonds that survived the most radical changes of early communist rule (ibid.). Emerging from a history of overpopulation and strong competition, as well as consid-erable periods of poverty and starvation, the Chinese family and associated businesses act as a vital defence against a traditionally hostile and volatile environment.

Fukuyama's analysis echoes Putnam's in his views on the con-sequences of a decline in trust. Such a decline in U.S. society he sees as leading to a rise in violent crime, civil disintegration, and the break-down of family. Because communities are seen as depending on mutual trust, a lack of trust has also led to the decline of intermediate social structures such as neighbourhoods and churches. In atomised communities, such as can be found in many modern African cities, delinquency is common. Contrary to many stereotypes of cogent African communities, levels of benevolence and universalistic gener-osity to others are particularly low in many African societies (Schwartz & Bardi, 2001). In contrast, Giddens (Giddens & Pierson, 1998) is more optimistic about modern societies. He argues that while trust is traditionally associated with commitment and moral principles, a modern society requires new risks and the new trusts associated with this. Consistent with Giddens's model of modern friendships, such trust is not passive but active and is built on new partnerships and networks, rather than established institutions.

The relationship between trust and democracy is likely to be complex, particularly during times of rapid social change. The collapse of the economic, social, and political systems of Eastern Europe in the late 1980s and early 1990s led to a desperate search for material security for many citizens of these countries. Materialist societies are low on interpersonal trust, and the difficult postcommunist experience has led many to continue to hold low levels of trust towards others (Inglehart, Norris, & Welzel, 2002). Inglehart and Baker (2000) argue that this emphasis on survival values led to greater misery and distrust, particularly towards out-groups. In East Germany, secret files were kept on an estimated six million people by the feared *Stasi* (the East German secret police) (Rainer & Siedler, 2006). Rainer and Siedler analysed longitudinal data from the German General Social Survey data between 1994 (shortly after German reunification) and 2002. They found that levels of *institutional* distrust (such as distrust in parliament or the legal system) fell between 1994 and 2002. However, *social* distrust continued to be high. This may reflect the ambiguity many East Germans felt over the benefits of unification, particularly given the new, fierce levels of competition for work and resources that they now faced. East German women – and in particular East Germans who had experienced unemployment since reunification – were the most distrusting. In contrast, greater personal economic success was associated with higher levels of social trust.

CHANGING SOCIAL CAPITAL? A CRITIQUE

Social capital has rapidly been widely accepted as an "analytical, empirical, and policy panacea" (Fine, 2001, p. 189). For the World Bank and other such organisations, social capital is seen as a means to alleviating poverty and removing corruption, allowing individuals to take part in local decisions and to develop "community feeling" (Roberts, 2004). Conceptually, social capital is seen as providing a "missing link" between the social and economic structure and individual relationships. Yet, common to similar debates over individualism and modernisation, there have been a number of questioning voices and critiques of the very notion of social capital, as well as the suggestion that it is on the decline. Given the growing influence of the concept of social capital and its part in the analysis of social change, I consider a number of these in detail.

First, a number of writers have questioned the definition of "social capital," seeing it as a slippery notion that is hard to operationalise (for example, Edwards, Franklin, & Holland, 2003; Fine, 2001; Roberts, 2004). Fine points to the confusion between defining what social capital *is* and what it *does*, describing the notion as "a sack of analytical potatoes" (p. 190). Furstenberg notes that social capital is notoriously difficult to measure, providing "a plethora of items and scales based more on convenience than conceptual rigor" (Furstenberg, 2005, p. 817). Roberts argues that many commentators make broad empirical judgements based on a rather arbitrary choice of social indicators, with the same voluntary activity seen as social capital in one context but not in another (Roberts, 2004). For Fine, new indices of social capital are absorbed into the concept far too easily, making it difficult to objectively test or evaluate. Social capital "has a gargantuan appetite. . . . [I]t can explain everything from individuals to societies, . . . whether the topic be the sick, the poor, the criminal, the corrupt, the (dys)functional family, schooling, community life, work and organisation, democracy and governance, collective action, transitional societies, intangible assets or, indeed, any aspect of social, cultural, and economic performance" (Fine, 2001, p. 190). The concept seems to be surrounded by a "protective belt" of associated ideas reminiscent of Lakatos's critique of falsifiability in the philosophy of science (1970). For Fevre (2000), social capital represents yet another example of the colonising attempts of economics to make itself the main science of human behaviour. He argues that the inclusion of so wide a variety of social components (including "undergraduate degrees, church coffee mornings, business networks, and rain forests" (p. 96)) is essential in order to fit the concept into models of economic rationality. Tonkiss is particularly critical of the introduction of the family into considerations of social capital. For Tonkiss, the family cannot simply be reduced to formal contracts and rational self-interest (2004, p. 19). While family relations may indeed involve trust, the relationship is often far more complicated: Families are not simple voluntary organisations, and trust in families is often ambivalent given the levels of dependency inherent and the more repressive sides of traditional gender roles

(Edwards, 2004). Unfortunately, the relationship between families and their surrounding communities is rarely systematically explored, despite the extensive literature on social capital (Furstenberg, 2005).

A second critique has pointed to the narrow and selective historical perspective used when analysing data in this field (Fevre, 2000). The cosy notion of an old-fashioned supportive society – where interpersonal trust and community ties merged to protect and nurture otherwise vulnerable individuals – is a popular one when discussing social capital (Turiel, 2002). Also popular, Turiel notes, is the notion that the end of the twentieth century has been a time of moral failure, with the good of society sacrificed for the sake of personal desires, a theme promoted by the late Pope John Paul II and many other religious and political leaders. Regional movement and family breakdown are seen as challenging social capital, with serious deleterious effects (Edwards et al., 2003). For some, too, women's increasing labour participation is seen as a threat to genuine community bonds and social cohesion in a time of change. These are hardly new themes, echoing earlier notions of social decline. In the 1920s, changes in young people's lifestyles (including their peer relationships, sexual patterns, and sex roles) led to reactions similar to the current communitarian worries over the decline in society (Turiel, 2002). Jazz and modern dancing were seen as contributing to this moral decline, both in Britain and the United States, as well as at various times in the Soviet Union and its satellites. In this earlier critique of social change, working women were seen as part of the problem, contributing towards the decline of the family unit and a subsequent increase in crime, prostitution, and other social ills.

There are, however, serious questions to be raised about the data being used to support such arguments of social decline (Allen, Ng, & Leiser, 2004). During the 1990s in the United States, for example, crime rates and teenage pregnancies fell, although there seems to be little evidence of a return there to traditional or community values (Turiel, 2002). Putnam's evidence, in particular, has been seen as selective: Turiel argues that his data presents a depreciation of the significance those activities that have increased (Turiel contrasts soccer, which has increased, with bowling, the decline of which provided the title for Putnam's book). Evidence elsewhere also suggests that certain particular local conditions can either inflate or deflate levels of social capital and trust. Ladd (1999) argues that it was only a marked increase in common purpose following the Second World War that led to unusually high levels of civic engagement and social participation.

Mehmet and Mehmet (2004), analysing war-torn Cyprus, found that the shared traumas of the war led to the cementing of family ties, with the family providing labour when the official labour dried up, as well as shelter, food, and other basics. In this situation, a lack of intercommunal police bodies led to households banding together to become defenders of their homes and villages, with formal channels of support supplemented by nonformal family ties. Maloney in Britain charts a growth in local voluntary organisations since the 1990s (Maloney, Smith, & Stoker, 2000). Analysing Britain's second city, Birmingham, he finds an increase of at least one-third in the number of voluntary organisations over the last three decades, with a notable increase in ethnic minority representation in these organisations. These new organisations encompass a wide range of activities, including housing, education and training, and civic advocacy. Maloney also charts evidence of high levels of trust between these voluntary organisations and the City Council. Furthermore, whilst parents' opportunities to perform voluntary work or to maintain their wider family networks have been affected by paid work, child care networks for working mothers have become increasingly prevalent. Such networks complement more-formal care provision, allowing informal carers to help with family emergencies and provide important flexibility during the school day (Dex, 2003). Overall, Turiel argues, more attention should be paid to why people join organisations and the goals of their membership. He speculates that whilst some people refrain from joining mainstream groups, they do look for other ways to address their problems. This may involve the inclusion of trusted communities and groups outside of a simple analysis of established community organisations. Hence, while traditional social groups, such as student fraternities, may be spurned, more-informal networks may develop. As we see with many trends in personal relationships over time, there are likely to be "good" or "bad" network changes and growing and declining liaison, depending on the particular social grouping, location, or time.

Fukuyama's data can also be critiqued on a number of counts. Contrary to his comparisons between "high-trust societies," such as Germany, and "low-trust societies," such as Italy, large-scale representative data from the World Value Survey data (1999–2001) show that there are similar levels of agreement across the United States, Germany, and Italy with the statement that "most people can be trusted" (around one-third of participants answer "yes" to this). Representative European Social Survey data collected in 2002 for

Germany and Italy gave almost identical scores for a similar item on a ten-point trust scale (4.54 for Italy, 4.61 for Germany). In contrast, in China, a supposedly low-trust culture in Putnam's analysis, more than 50 percent agreed with the statement that "most people can be trusted." This clearly suggests the need for further data to support the claims of Fukuyama and others on trust levels across cultures.

A third critique has focused on the underemphasis on the negative aspects of social capital. Because social capital is so generally seen as a "good thing," there is some tension between the positive impacts and the less enhancing aspects of such capital. In rule-based societies, such as modern Russia, the uncertainties of social change may lead to a reliance on personal social capital that can become essential for the development of business. Such a process may encourage the selective application of rules and the production of "perverse norms" (Fernandez-Dols, 2002), where a cynical attitude towards the social system leads to a series of legal violations and corrupt practices. An example can be found again by turning to Mehmet and Mehmet's analysis of ethnic conflict and the ways in which families and family communities act as a supplemental form of social capital. They note how perverse social capital develops in such circumstances, as when communities work at cross-purposes within gangs or drug cartels. Allen et al. (2004) note that whilst horizontal social ties at the micro level may seem to foster economic development, successful economies may move away from such civil ties as they are seen as restrictive of economic growth. Societies with high civil social capital may exhibit a lower growth level, and it is indeed rarely clear how particular trust interactions generate broader social trust. Indeed, in an eight-nation study, Allen et al. found that civil and governmental level social capital were negatively correlated. In particular, there is real ambivalence about whether strong social links within families are positive or negative for the wider society (Zontini, 2004). Social capital can of course mean corruption and nepotism, the mafia, and religious sects, as well as "healthy" social networks favouring friends and relatives (Furstenberg, 2005). Social capital exchanges are likely to enable some, but may restrict or oppress others, with exclusivity a major consequence of enhanced social capital amongst friends (Pahl, 2000). Economic inequality can also be reinforced through the perpetuation of "old-boys' networks" (Bourdieu, 1983).

Finally, social capital research has been criticised for focusing on individual relationships, rather than on the properties of individuals or institutions (Furstenberg, 2005; Maloney et al., 2000). Fine (2001) notes how economy, formal politics, nation states, power, and the divisions in a society are largely ignored in social capital accounts. Self-help notions for the poor typically ignore wider causes of their poverty, and there are significant issues involved in how individuals actually become involved and socially connected in "everyday life" (Maloney et al., 2000; Roberts & Devine, 2004). Certainly, there may be deeper structural factors behind why people may or may not be involved in groups (Roberts, 2004; Roberts & Devine, 2004). For Roberts (2004), workplace policies that have isolated and historically margin-alized groups are responsible for much of the apparent "capital decline." Social capital may operate quite differently across social classes (Furstenberg, 2005), with the middle classes able to provide a greater reach in terms of connections than working class families, which are more dependent on local resources. Some thus see in social capital a "soft" but powerful defence of capitalist societies (Fevre, 2000). As such, it represents part of a wider conservative agenda on social change (Edwards, Franklin, & Holland, 2003; Franklin, 2004), with responsi-bility for social ills removed from the government, and the social dis-ruptions that might follow broad governmental or economic transitions left to individuals or local communities to pick up the pieces. From this perspective, social capital can also provide cheap social policing, help-ing maintain order, however unjust that order is (Edwards et al., 2004). An emphasis on "good citizenship" values often misses structural inhibitors of behaviour and the contextual factors that limit engagement in the shared social activities (Maloney et al., 2000).

SOCIAL SUPPORT AND SOCIAL CHANGE

Above, I discussed the notion of social capital and social change in some detail, as these concepts have played an important role in broader debates about the nature of social change in societies. Closely related to the concept of social capital is a wider notion of social support, broadly defined as "the resources provided by other persons" (Cohen & Syme, 1985, p. 4). Social support, like social capital, has generally been viewed as a good thing and a key resource during times of social transition: Amirkhan claims that seeking social support reflects a "primal need for human contact in times of duress" (1990, p. 1073). Those with strong support networks exhibit better psychological and physiological well-being (Pahl, 2000; Sarason, Sarason, & Gurung, 1997), with social support promoting a sense of self-worth (George, 1989) and helping individuals positively appraise undesirable events (Sarason et al., 1997; Schwarzer & Leppin, 1991). Schwarzer, Hahn, and Schröder (1994) examined levels of social integration and social support amongst East Germans at the opening of the border to West Germany. In a three-wave longitudinal study, conducted between 1989 and 1991, 428 East Germans completed a range of measures assessing both their perceived levels of support and the actual support they had received. In this study, receiving social support was a significant buffer against the negative impacts of long-term unemployment.

Yet for all this, social support, like social capital, is likely to be multiply determined along the lines of the key factors I identified in Chapter 1. Hence, the ability to garner support in challenging or threatening situations is dependent on both the individual's personal characteristics and his/her wider group memberships and environment. Not all individuals possess the capabilities to utilise support effectively (Cummins, 1989, 1990), and those seeking support require personal skills that allow them to obtain aid from others. Expectations about one's self-efficacy are likely to influence to whom individuals turn for support, the appropriateness of that choice, the level at which they embrace the help given, and the trust they demonstrate towards the supportive person. A fatalistic outlook on life, for example, acts as an inhibitor to the development of active coping strategies, including the seeking of social support (Kobasa & Puccetti, 1983; Markova et al., 1998). In our studies in the former Soviet Union (Goodwin et al., 2002), fatalism was a significant predictor of social support and had a small, but significant, mediating effect on the beneficial impact of social support on mental health. In addition, those we approach for support must have the personal characteristics that enable them to understand the request for help, and the individuals giving support must also have sufficient resources of their own to do this. The support offered needs to fit the particular needs required: It should be the "appropriate" person who does the "right things" (Hobfoll, 1998; Sarason et al., 1997). Different sources of support may also be more appropriate in particular circumstances (Sarason, Sarason, & Pierce 1994; Wan, Jaccard, & Ramey, 1996). We can also distinguish between global evaluations of support ("helping behaviour that might happen"; Norris & Kaniasty, 1996, p. 498) and reports of the support received after a stressful event (Barrera, 1986; Dunkel-Schetter & Bennett, 1990; Sarason et al., 1994). Although both inevitably reflect an individual's perceptions of support (Barrera, 1986), the former may be better seen as reflecting a stable personality characteristic in its own right (Lakey & Cassady, 1990), reflecting individual self-esteem in particular (Goodwin & Hernandez-Plaza, 2003), whilst the second is more functional and attuned to a particular event or domain (Sarason et al., 1997). These two types of perceived support might be only weakly correlated (Barrera, 1986; Martínez & García, 1995). Finally, a particular transition or event may tire all the available supporters so that few have the energy to help. According to the conservation of resources theory (Hobfoll, 1989), a commonly shared threat to a vital condition resource (such as employment) can undermine supportive networks. Norris and Kaniasty (1996) observe that a general deterioration of emotional support often follows stressful events. Indeed, seeking social support can be associated with increased symptomology in certain situations (Amirkhan, 1990). This is most likely to occur in situations of uncertainty, where support allows an individual to focus on his/her emotional distress for a prolonged period of time (Carver et al., 1989).

Culture is also likely to be a key factor in determining support provision. In collectivist cultures, the basic unit of survival is the group (Hui, 1988). Hence, support from others is very important in these societies (Triandis, 1989, 1994), providing a strong buffer against life stresses (Triandis, Bontempo, & Villareal, 1988). Those in collectivist cultures have been found to enjoy close, supportive networks and to actively share in the lives of others in their in-group (Gudykunst, Nishida, & Schmidt, 1989; Triandis et al., 1988). In contrast, those living in individualist cultures exhibit fewer skills for interacting intimately with others and are more emotionally detached from their in-groups (Goodwin & Hernandez-Plaza, 2000; Triandis et al., 1988). In addition, local, "emic" traditions, such as the social norm of *tolong-menolong* (helping one another) have been well established within Indonesian village society (Higgins & Higgins, 1963) and may explain a willingness to aid strangers (Goodwin & Giles, 2003).

Further macro and ecological factors, such as differences in financial resources and educational opportunities, may be of great significance for support provision, with such factors influencing both the ability to provide support (Hobfoll, 1999) and the location, size, and homogeneity of the social network (Triandis, 2001). Employment situations influence both the opportunities for supportive interaction (Jerusalem & Mittag, 1995; Wellman, 1985) and provide normative frameworks for how these relationships should develop (Allan, 1993). As such, employment can be a major factor in determining reactions to social change. Groups with low economic status often report lesser support availability, even from family and friends (Liem & Liem, 1978; Norris & Kaniasty, 1996). In one study conducted in the mid-1990s (Goodwin, Nizharadze et al., 2002), we examined the support networks of students, manual workers, and business people in Russia, Georgia, and Hungary during a time of rapid change. As was the case with trust and friendship, the role of broader social support in these formerly communist countries was paradoxical. On the one hand, members of these societies relied on the support of kin and other informal networks simply to survive (Schwarzer et al., 1994; Sik & Wellman, 1999). This had a number of consequences on the structure of living arrangements, with, for example, members of Eastern European countries often living together in a single (often cramped) residence (Scharf, 1995). At the same time, considerable social movement and stressful life events following the break-up of the communist system contributed to a breakup of established social networks (Kraus, Liang, & Gu, 1998; Schwarzer et al., 1994). Because of the shared nature of these strains, turning to others for support led to an extra burden on those already under considerable duress (Coyne, Wortman, & Lehman, 1988; Hobfoll & London, 1986). Manual workers in Central and Eastern Europe had certainly suffered greatly from the economic uncertainties that followed the transition to a market economy (Kryshtanovskaya, 1992; Teague, 1992), with their support networks likely to have been particularly undermined by long working hours, economic uncertainty, and a climate of distrust that have arisen from the growing threat of unemployment (Barner-Barry & Hody, 1995). In contrast, the new entrepreneurs of Central and Eastern Europe were far wealthier, with greater access to material support; but, as I noted above, they also inhabited a highly competitive and distrustful world, where resources were strongly contested (Kryshtanovskaya, 1992). As a result, they were often characterised as "people who learned to rely on themselves" (Smith, 1990). Furthermore, their work involved a great deal of travel away from family and friends, restricting their opportunity to interact with friends and family and providing them with only a moderate degree of emotional support from others. In our studies, we found that both perceived and actually received support was highest for students and lowest amongst manual workers (Goodwin, Nizharadze et al., 2002, study one). Support levels were highest in Georgia and lowest in Russia. In qualitative interviews (ibid.), Georgian business people reported far greater support levels than their counterparts in the other countries, with the full development of social networks amongst Georgian entrepreneurs not only providing individuals with a major economic resource, but also allowing for the extension of "grey economy" relationships established under the former Soviet system. Furthermore, although the Georgian entrepreneurs recognised that they spent only limited time with their spouses and family, respondents here noted how the enhanced social standing that arose from their economic activities reflected positively on their social networks and the status of their family group. In this way, their work activities helped bolster their close family relations. This finding is consistent with other work on Georgian communities that emphasises the high levels of mutual support that characterise this society and that were critical for survival for many people during the turmoil of the last decades (Sumbadze, 2006).

One further moderating effect on social support in a time of social change is generation or age. Taiwanese life expectancy, for example, increased 20 years between 1952 and 2000, whilst total fertility dropped by almost five births (Lin et al., 2003). This led to a near quadrupling in the percentage of those aged over 65, from 2.5 to 9 percent, but also a lack of sufficient institutional support for assistance for the elderly. This has led to an increasing likelihood that today's parents will live alone or have just one child when they are in their older years, reducing the support available for their kin. Rapid social changes can leave little opportunity for adjustment amongst the elderly in a society. Iecovich et al. (2004) suggested that the major socioeconomic and political changes at the end of the former Soviet Union profoundly affected the social network of the elderly in these countries. They examined social support networks and loneliness amongst elderly Jews in Russia and the Ukraine. During the Soviet era, the State took on the responsibility of meeting all the (basic) needs of its peoples, but the rapid collapse of the communist system in the early 1990s led to the withdrawal of much of the previous safety net provided for the most vulnerable parts of the population. In the words of one of their respondents: "For us elderly people, the former regime provided everything and we felt secure, but now we feel abandoned and neglected" (Iecovich et al., p. 313). This meant that responsibility now lay on the existing informal networks, such as family members. At the same time, of course, the ability of those in the family network to provide such support was stretched by their own financial troubles. Amongst the Jewish population, large-scale emigration, primarily to Israel, further weakened their established community, particularly in the Ukraine.

Iecovich et al. examined two models of how individuals compensated for their loss of social support: a model of substitution, where support providers from one source of support replaced another, and a complementary/task-specific model, which stressed the importance of particular support providers for meeting particular needs. They found evidence for both models: Both kin and non-kin were necessary providers of support, but during this transitional time there was some evidence of compensation – for example, when an individual who lacked kin or close friendships locally maintained good relations with neighbours. Wellman, working in the generally more stable community environment of Toronto, Canada, reported similar findings, suggesting that although spouses provide the widest range of support, individuals maintain different portfolios of ties that enable them to access different resources (Wellman, 1994). Thus, for example, strong (voluntary and socially close) ties, such as the family, provide high levels of support, whilst the ties provided by others living nearby can provide other services. Most of his Toronto sample had changing relations; shifting networks, which – contrary to the fears expressed by many social capital theorists – were constantly re-forming and evolving. Thus, Wellman claims, although individuals may feel they live in a "community of strangers," this apparently privatised community still provides a great deal of support, although interactions may be more home-based than in the past. Social change within Canadian society has not, therefore, destroyed social communities but re-formed them from neighbourhood and other location-based networks to networks of personal choice.

We also examined the relationship between age, social support perception, and mental health consequences during a period of social transition in the former Soviet Union with data from four countries: Russia, Belarus, the Ukraine, and the Republic of Georgia (Goodwin, 2006). My colleagues and I questioned more than 2,500 manual workers, students, civil servants, managers, and retired respondents across these countries. Our analyses showed that older respondents reported lower levels of perceived support. Consistent with previous work, gender was also a significant predictor of support perception, with women reporting greater support. Social support was, in itself, a small positive correlate of mental health, although such support had only a limited and partial mediating impact on the relationship between age and mental health. This may reflect the potential costs of seeking or providing support during periods of psychological uncertainty and transition (Hobfoll & London, 1986). Notably, it was the more tangible forms of practical support, rather than emotional support, that was the most highly related with positive psychological outcomes. This might well reflect the high importance of security and material needs in countries undergoing significant economic hardships. Again, the exact efficacy of social support was partly mediated by culture. As in our previous studies, support levels were highest in Georgia, the most collectivist of the societies under examination.

MIGRANTS, SOCIAL CAPITAL, AND SOCIAL SUPPORT

Some of the further complexities in the operationalisation of social support networks can be demonstrated in studies of immigration. The personal relationships of migrants are subject to complex challenges, with the evolution of new relationships with friends, family, and acquaintances varying between groups and as a consequence of community size (Maya Jariego, 2006). Immigrant communities may be heavy users of family-based social capital, often also utilizing other bodies such as churches and community organisations to help link families (Furstenberg, 2005). Migration "is typically a family project, for which information is gathered collectively and resources are pooled" (Nauck & Settles, 2001, p. 462). Strong ties are likely to be important in any migration process, with family members in a society often needed to obtain legal permission to enter a country (Nauck & Settles, 2001). Once started, the migration process can become a pattern of chain migration, with the migrant group preparing for their wider kin to move to the new country after them. As such, migration is not simply a response to a labour market, but typically involves the thoughts of the wider family and their own additional investments in this (ibid.). For all this, the local trust and capital networks so praised by Coleman are often less evident in transnational or migrant communities (Zontini, 2004). Instead, social support is usually based in the family rather than the network, with "ethnic group solidarity" or "ethnic communities" often something of an outsider's myth (Nauck & Settles, 2001).

The availability of confidants and emotional support will depend in part on whether a migrating individual is moving to a community where there are several fellow country members or whether he or she will be part of only a small community. Most migrants have support networks that consist primarily of family members (Maya Jariego, 2006), but length of residence, degree of family restructuring following migration, and the generation and size of the compatriot community are all factors that influence the availability and strength of the kinship community. Generally, the personal support environment is small at first and consists largely of compatriots and kin (ibid.). This can be stressful for both the new migrant and his or her ethnic community in the new country, as the new migrant may not only be demanding of his/her ethnic networks, but may be able to offer relatively little in terms of support him-/herself. Over time, the migrant's network expands, becoming more diverse, although this will, of course, depend on the availability of supporters from the receiving country and their willingness to welcome members of the incoming community (ibid.). At the same time, there is likely to be a limit to the number of active bonds a new migrant can make in addition to the demands from "back home." These often lead to requests for material assistance or the provision of opportunities for migration for other family members. Perhaps unsurprisingly, therefore, international migrants tend to live within relatively weakly integrated communities in their receiving country, whilst at the same time facing considerable challenges balancing the demands of their new society with their duties to those they left behind.

Zontini (2004) provides an example of social support and capital formation amongst Italians migrating to the United Kingdom and then returning to Italy some years later. In Italy, despite the existence of new role models for women and greater female independence, families continue to live close by and maintain important economic and emotional links. Following migration to the United Kingdom, the family proved itself to be a flexible social unit, reformulating to meet new challenges. Thus, migrating groups drew on specific family values and norms for their advantage (such as when grandparents were used to look after grandchildren) and on important family-based economic resources (particularly significant when starting up a new enterprise, such as a restaurant). However, more problems were faced by those returning to Italy to rejoin their families. Here, there were often unexpected difficulties in finding sufficient support, particularly for the elderly and those who could not find suitable employment on return. In this situation, expectations about social capital provision often ignored significant changes within Italian culture, making the "back transition" process far from easy.

Nauck and Settles (2001) note the moderating effect of ethnicity on the acculturation process. Turkish families in Germany tend to use a collectivist strategy, utilizing high levels of intergroup support. In contrast, Russian Jews in Israel have less intergenerational support available and use more individualist approaches when dealing with migration issues. In both cases, this leads to highly segregationist tendencies, partly because of the actual number of minority members. For Turks, priority is given to accumulation of transferable economic capital and the maintenance of strong, interrelated, and reliable social relationships. This is most likely within strong kinship systems, as alternative ties in the receiving society are seen as insecure and unreliable. This contrasts with the strong investment in language skills and the acquisition of cultural capital (such as professional qualifications) sought by their Russian counterparts in Israel.

Edwards (2004) claims that particular ethnic minority subgroups are often ignored in the study of social capital, despite the complex family and relationship choices often faced by such communities. People of South Asian origin represent one of the largest ethnic minority populations in Britain. When their families migrated to Britain, significant differences in cultural values and traditional cultural practices and beliefs were often transported across several continents – in the case of British Indians, from India to East Africa and then to the United Kingdom. These heritages had an important impact on relationship beliefs and practices in the United Kingdom (Goodwin & Cramer, 2000). The maintenance of extensive support networks, in Britain and also transnationally, served both to bolster and test these relationships, with the marital relationship in particular forming a symbolic figurehead for both the couple and their wider families. Individuals and couples in this community are likely to live within an extended-family household or nearby (Owen, 1994), and both Asian parents and children are more likely to turn to their family members for both practical and personal help than a comparable British sample. They are also less likely to use either friends or professionals as confidants when dealing with personal problems (Stopes-Roe & Cochrane, 1990).

In our analysis of 70 Gujarati couples from the British Midlands, we found support from the family playing a valuable role in married life (Goodwin & Cramer, 2000). The family was a major promoter of relationship commitment, with financial aid from the family helping reduce the strain on the couple, whilst practical help with parenting helped provide an important bridge between the couple and their wider family. Informational support was supplied in the handing down of language and cultural traditions, with many of our older respondents stressing the importance of a transmission of a moral code between the generations. This transmission helped to reinforce cultural and social identity of the community. At the same time, the family provided a formidable barrier to relationship breakdown in a community where sanctions against relationship dissolution were manifested in a number of ways and where even the siblings of divorcé(e)s were likely to be treated with suspicion by a prospective partner. Given that nearly all our respondents had lived with the extended family at some time during their married life, the public viewing of their marriage provided a lesson for the younger unmarried members as to how problems could be surmounted, as well as allowing the elder generation to aid the newly married couple when problems arose.

SUPPORT FOLLOWING TERRORIST ATTACKS

New threats to a society can provide important challenges to existing patterns of social relations. The terrorist attacks on the United States on September 11, 2001 in particular left an indelible mark on perceptions of security and threat across the world. Individuals developed new fears about their own personal safety and that of their loved ones, with potentially important implications for where they located themselves and moved between locations. Witness the uneasy dilemma faced by the long-distance couple that no longer feels secure when flying between cities to meet. In addition, interaction with particular groups now seemed more dangerous, with a sense of one's own mortality reducing the likelihood of particular out-group interactions (Pyszczynski, Solomon, & Greenberg, 2003). Although most research on this topic is relatively recent, there is mounting evidence of the significance of the fear of terrorist attack on everyday personal relationships.

During a time of stress, close relationships can act as a fundamental anxiety buffer, providing a "symbolic shield against the awareness of one's finitude" (Mikulincer, Florian, & Hirschberger, 2003, p. 37). Attachment theorists note that an important way of coping with personal threats to one's safety and mortality is to seek support from others (Bowlby, 1969), with primary support likely to be derived from romantic partners, friends, and family (Lazarus & Folkman, 1984). Terror management theorists have emphasized the importance of the support provided by romantic partners during times of mortality salience (fear of death) (Pyszczynski et al., 2003). For example, Florian, Mikulincer, and Hirschberger (2002) have argued that romantic relationships provide a sense of security that allows people to function with relative equanimity during times of personal existential concern. In particular, death awareness leads to a desire for long-term, committed, and emotionally driven relationships with significant others and the avoidance of conflict with these others during times of anxiety. Thus, Nakoney, Reddick, and Rodgers (2004) examined divorce rates from 1985 to 2000, following the Oklahoma City (Murrah Federal Building) bombing in April 1995. Using terror management and attachment theories, they predicted and found a significant decline in divorce rates in the state of Oklahoma one to two years following the bombing, with this effect decreasing over time. This they see as suggesting that those who might otherwise have divorced sought comfort from their spouse at this time. In addition, individuals may also seek to socially share with others their anxieties in an attempt to reduce such anxiety or may feel reassured by significant members of their social networks about the risks posed (Dumont et al., 2003). Hatfield and Rapson (2004) describe a process of "emotional contagion" in which people "catch" emotions, mimicking those of others around them.

We examined this in two studies conducted in London, England. In the first, conducted in London in 2003 following the 9/11 attacks on New York City, we found that normative fears of an attack (that is, those fears shared with family and friends) predicted an individual's greater expected probability of future attack (Goodwin, Willson, & Gaines, 2005). A sense of personal threat to family and friends was positively correlated with greater contact with friends and family following the 9/11 attacks. In a subsequent study, conducted in four monthly waves immediately following the London bombings in July 2005 (Goodwin & Gaines, 2006), we again found those who had fearful friends and family were more anxious about the threat of further attack and more likely to perceive such an attack as probable. Those who were anxious were also more likely to report greater contact with friends and family following the attacks. As of yet, work on terrorism threat and its implications for personal relationships is in its infancy.

However, with the apparently continuing threat of attacks (particularly against those in countries where social scientists are actively researching this topic), we expect the emergence of future work and theorizing that should further explain the processes underlying relational changes that might occur following terrorism threat.

SUMMARY

Friends from increasingly diverse backgrounds may be replacing kin networks as central supporters in our lives. During times of rapid change, these friendships may be of particularly significance, but persisting cultural beliefs may limit the development of such relations. Social capital can have a wide range of benefits for both individuals and societies, and its potential decline can have serious impacts on societal well-being. Trust is a core element of this capital, and it can be undermined by high levels of individualism in a society. However, the much-hyped evidence for a decline in social capital and trust has been marred by a lack of clear definition of these terms and the selective nature of the data discussed.

Migrants in particular are likely to benefit in multiple ways from strong supportive networks, although the expectations of those back home may often place additional stressors on an already stressful migration. Finally, social networks may be disrupted by fears of terrorist attacks, but the desire for association that accompanies these fears may, in the short term, help cement our relations with those we hold closest.

CHAPTER 5

Sex and the Modern City

While sexual relationships are, of course, a feature of all societies, the appropriateness of sexual behaviours varies a great deal over time and place (Goodwin & Cramer, 2002). Societal prohibitions can influence the performance of State-controlled actions, such as the abolition of abortion in State hospitals in Romania under Ceauşescu, whilst other proscribed behaviours, such as homosexual practices, will persist despite being officially forbidden. Particular societal conditions, such as extreme economic deprivation, may change behaviours in previously unimagined ways, with, for example, "respectable" individuals turning to prostitution to provide for themselves and their families. Other environmental factors, such as cramped living conditions, can greatly reduce the opportunities for privacy and can severely stress a couple's intimate relationships (Einhorn, 1993; Honig & Hershatter, 1998). One important aspect of the way in which people think about their families and sexual relationships has been the impact of mobility. Migrants are often exposed to the possibilities of high-risk sexual behaviours (Wellings et al., 2006). In Eastern Europe, Hillhouse (1993) argues that migration reduced traditional social controls and allowed premarital sexual behaviour to be more openly acknowledged. American children change residences more frequently than children in other industrialised countries (South, Haynie, & Bose, 2005). South et al. discuss residential mobility in the United States as a moderator of adolescent sexual activity. Drawing on the National Longitudinal Study of Adolescent Health, which questioned more than 90,000 adolescents in grades 7 to 12, they found that recently mobile adolescents were more likely to initiate sexual activity than nonmobile ones. This they attribute to their greater tendency to affiliate with low-performing, relatively delinquent peers, with higher-status, more academic networks less willing to accept the newcomers. Smit (2001) discusses the plight of migrant workers, who may rarely have a chance to live together with their families; if they do so, they are likely to live in very limited living space and probably in shared rooms. As a result, any sexual intimacy has to be conducted in rooms full of people, sometimes even in beds shared with the children. In the far more affluent West, high house prices can still mean that children increasingly stay at home with their parents into their late twenties (for example, Cicchelli & Martin, 2004, in France). This leads to a new group of *jeunes adultes* (adult youth), autonomous in some areas of their personal lives but at least materially dependent on their parents.

In discussing patterns in sexual behaviour, we also see a number of speculations concerning the nature of more gradual social change and the part played by more general value change. Here we see the familiar themes of societal decline, often expressed in media headlines in terms of "loose behaviour," sexual permissiveness, and the increasing acceptance of the unacceptable and immoral standards. Frequently, this decline is postulated as stemming from the influence of "corrupting" forces, such as American television, which has been seen as leading to the uncritical acceptance of modernisation values, particularly by the young. Also at risk have been those vulnerable populations markedly affected by societal changes, such as the growth of prostitution associated with the fall of communism in Eastern Europe and as a result of extreme poverty in parts of sub-Saharan Africa. Beyond some of the more sensational bylines, Wellings and her colleagues list a number of factors that influence trends in sexual behaviour around the world (Wellings et al., 2006). These include changes in poverty, education, and employment, as well as migration patterns and changes in public health policies and strategies.

There is certainly evidence of some changes in premarital sexual behaviour in many economically developed societies. Along with beliefs about greater freedom and control over life, modernisation has been closely related to notions of sexual liberation, a greater tolerance of sexual relations between unmarried people, and a greater acceptance of homosexuality (Inglehart, 2003). For more than a hundred years, men and women in the United States were expected to live within tightly defined standards of action. Although in colonial America the sharing of beds meant that children were exposed to adult sexual activity at a relatively early age (Coontz, 2000), there were carefully drawn normative boundaries about overt sexual activity. Sex before marriage was generally frowned upon in Britain during the Victorian era, at least amongst the middle classes. Indeed, marriage in Victorian times and the early twentieth century was seen as posing rational restraints on irrational sexual urges. Women were divided into two parts: virtuous and nonvirtuous women, with only those women at the top or bottom of a society free to escape from this classification (Giddens & Pierson, 1998). In general, public interest was seen as being served through an institutionalisation of sexual relations and the tight regulation of marriage and divorce.

Giddens contrast this situation with postmodern society. In this society, the role of nature in sex has been diminished as sexuality becomes separated from reproduction. The introduction of the birth control pill and other contraception has greatly increased the opportunities for potentially lower-cost sexual intercourse. In this society of "plastic sex," sexuality has to be actively invented, with the emphasis now on sensation and pleasure giving (ibid.). The age of sexual maturity is falling, with children in many societies more integrated into a highly sexualised consumer culture (Coontz, 2000). Many societies report evidence of a greater tolerance towards sexual freedoms, including sex between unmarried partners. Thus, the Japanese Association for Sex Education reported higher levels of intercourse amongst students in the 1980s (Hatano, 1990), indicating a greater acceptance of premarital sexual activity.

Giddens suggests that the sexual emancipation he associates with postmodernity can be a positive thing. In his words, sexual emancipation: "can be the medium of a wide-ranging emotional reorganisation of social life ... as the *radical democratisation* of the personal. Who says sexual emancipation ... says sexual democracy" (1992, p. 182, italics in original). Such a democratisation rejects violence, including emotional abuse, and requires openness with the partner. There is a strong notion of trust and accountability, with pure relationship partners complementing each other and holding equal resources. Sexual emancipation has led to the rejection of repressive male sexuality, which includes male domination over the public sphere, and a questioning of the sexual division of labour, sexual double standards, and the division of women into marriageable versus the "impure." There is now increased tolerance of previously proscribed behaviours, growing individual freedom over personal behaviours, and less emphasis on obedience to previous standards. This has been coupled with greater egalitarianism, increased challenging of responsibilities of the genders, greater relationship diversity, and more "thinking for oneself" within the relationship (Thornton & Young-Demarco, 2001). Giddens thus provides an optimistic prognosis: "The transformation of intimacy, together with plastic sexuality, provides for conditions which could bring about a reconciliation of the sexes" (1992, p. 156).

Bauman, however, is more critical of the development of this new "freedom to seek sexual delights for their own sakes" (2001, p. 223). He sees eroticism as having been "culturally processed" and made into a commodity: We are now "socially and culturally trained and shaped as sensation seekers and gatherers" (p. 225). For him, postmodern sex is only about orgasm, with the ultimate sexual experience remaining an objective never truly reached. At the same time, sexualisation stands to diminish other forms of relationships: "All ... kinds of human relationships are ... purified of even the palest of sexual undertones that might stand the slightest chance of condensing those relations into permanence. Sexual undertones are suspected and sniffed out in every emotion ... in every offer of friendship" (Bauman, 2001, p. 236). For Bauman, casual remarks and interactions in the college or office are now open to suspicion, and nearly every sexual activity can be defined as rape. In this postmodern sexual environ-ment, Bauman claims, century-old fears about out-of-control children are replaced by new fears about the sexual exploitation of children *by adults*, with children now seen as sexual objects. Somewhat ironically, at a time of increased intimacy between consenting adults, children are dealt with warily, for fear of the adult being labeled abusive.

These changes in sexual behaviour are consistent with the findings of Wellings and her colleagues in Britain (Wellings, Fields et al., 1994; Wellings, Nancharhal et al., 2001). Wellings reports marked differences in sexual experiences over time in a series of large and representative cohort comparisons and longitudinal studies. She reports that first sexual experience in marriage is now almost unknown in Britain, a dramatic change from the previous half-century. For those women born in the 1930s and 1940s, more than 38 percent remained virgins until they were married, compared to less than 1 percent born in the late 1960s and early 1970s, with similar changes reported for men. For women born between 1931 and 1935, the median age for first sexual activity was 21; this dropped to 17 years for those born between 1966 and 1975. Similar trends were also evident for men. Older members of this sample, and women in particular, were likely to attribute their first sexual intercourse to resulting from being in love. In contrast, curiosity, surely a greater expression of sensation seeking, was a stronger reason for first sexual intercourse amongst the younger members of the sample. The National Survey of Sexual Attitudes and Lifestyles (NATSAL), conducted in 1990 and 2000 (Wellings et al., 2001), reported that the increase in the proportion of women reporting first intercourse before age 16 increased up to, but not after, the mid-1990s. This study also noted an increase in both homosexual and heterosexual intercourse between the times of the 1990 and 2000 study (ibid.) and a convergence of the sexual behaviour of young men and women and those living outside London. The increase in sexual partners, the authors suggest, may reflect the large number of those cohabiting, a trend associated with increased partner change. Encouragingly, this has been accompanied by an increase in condom use and a decrease in the number of those using no contraception at the time of first intercourse. Notably, only 2 percent of respondents in Welling et al.'s (1994) survey claimed extramarital sex was not at all wrong, and three-quarters of the respondents believed it was "always wrong" or "mostly wrong." Furthermore, two-thirds of the men and three-quarters of the women surveyed believed that cohabiting partners should be sexually exclusive, with young people supporting monogamy as strongly as elder respondents.

In the Netherlands since the 1960s, there is evidence of less restrictive sexual morals, particularly amongst women (Kraaykamp, 2002). Kraaykamp studied attitude change towards sexual permissiveness in the Netherlands (1965–1995), using items from eight waves of data from the Cultural Change in the Netherlands survey. Data were collected in face-to-face interviews in 1965, 1970, 1975, 1980, 1985, 1986, 1991, and 1995, with a sample size of more than 15,000. Kraaykamp found that in the Netherlands, as in the United Kingdom, respondents were more liberal towards extramarital sex between 1965 and 1975, but this was followed by a countertrend. In particular, women's greater workforce orientation and the experience of growing up in a time of increased divorce appears to have underlined the unique value of spousal bond and led to a more negative attitude towards extramarital sexuality. In similar work, Thornton and Young-Demarco (2001) collated data from five large-scale data sets, focusing particularly on changes between the 1960s and mid-1980s. Their work revealed that attitudes towards premarital sex changed dramatically in the 1960s and early 1970s, with attitudes becoming less restrictive. This trend continued into the 1980s and 1990s, but at a slower pace. Between the mid-1980s and the 1990s, there was also greater acceptance of unmarried cohabitation, which was no longer seen as a novel experiment. Sex and coresidence were increasingly separated from the institution of marriage, and there was an increased acceptance of unmarried childbearing, although unmarried parenthood was rarely seen as a goal. However, attitudes towards extramarital sex demonstrated a conservative backlash, with less permissiveness and a growing disapproval towards it in the late 1980s and early 1990s. Indeed, by the late 1990s, 90 percent of men claimed extramarital sex was always or almost always wrong, echoing a growing trend to emphasise the importance of the permanence of marriage. Thus, despite marriage becoming more voluntary, there is a recognition of the intimacy component in sexual fidelity: more freedom for the single, less for the married. This may lead to a postponed marriage until individuals feel they can be fully committed to a life-long match (Thornton & Young, 2001). I discuss this in more detail in the next chapter, where I consider changing attitudes towards family and marriage.

In some cases, this increased sexual freedom is part of a wider political discussion about the rights of the individual to express his or her needs and desires (Hatfield & Rapson, 1996). Thus, in China there has been continuing debate about the sexual morality of unmarried women, rooted in the political tides that followed the 1949 Revolution and the subsequent waves of political changes within that country (Honig & Hershatter, 1988). This was expressed in debates about the appropriate dress for women and the assertion of individual beauty, as well as concerns over the maintenance of "purity" until marriage. Given the relative confusion of political messages that were released over sexual behaviour, it was perhaps unsurprising that there is evidence of a great deal of ignorance about sexual matters in that country. As a result, the official Mainland Chinese press began to publish sex manuals for the newly married in the early 1980s, complete with attendant propaganda about the role of sex in "socialist reconstruction" (ibid.). This can be seen as a move away from both traditional and socialist concepts of morality, both of which were relatively puritanical in their attitudes towards sex (Tsui, 1989). In the last two decades, extramarital relations have become one of the major reasons for divorce (Honig & Hershatter, 1988). Some 80 percent of divorce cases in the Canton region mentioned extramarital affairs in their divorce proceedings, and 10 percent of couples reported having had extramarital relationships (Ruan & Matsumura, 1991). In Shenzhen, China, the new market economy has appeared to change perceptions of family and sexual relationships, with middle-aged men from rural, peasant backgrounds now keen to enjoy relationships with younger women along with their new wealth (Cheal, 2002). In response, some Chinese cities, worried about the apparent explosion in the numbers of such affairs, have made adultery a crime. Prostitution in China dates back to at least the seventh century BC, and it was prevalent throughout the country until the clampdown under communism in the 1950s (Ruan & Matsumura, 1991). In the mid-1980s, however, there was a strong revival of the practice, but a growing fear of sexually transmitted diseases, coupled with strong ideological opposition from the State, led to a second, harsher wave of suppression in the late 1980s (ibid.).

In Islamic cultures, too, sexual behaviour may be part of a wider debate about the evils of modernisation and the threats associated with Eros. Whilst Western younger generations may be more liberal on sex and gender issues, in Islamic societies both the young and the old are relatively conventional in their views and maintain traditional sexual mores (Norris & Inglehart, 2003). Many of these attitudes are reinforced in penal codes in Islamic cultures that have limited the apparent sexual displays of women, such as the wearing of lipstick. As a result, sexual activity has been politicised and is seen as part of a similar protest by those who reject these codes, along with the taking of drugs and the holding of private parties (Turiel, 2002).

It is easy, however, to overstate these changes in sexual behaviour when analysis is conducted on an international scale. Wellings provides an important analysis of sexual behaviour data from 59 countries, arguing that there is in fact no universal trend towards earlier sexual intercourse (Wellings et al., 2006). Instead, a movement towards later marriage, particularly in more developed countries, has meant that premarital sex is now more common. However, this later marriage has also meant a trend towards later sex in young women, particularly in Africa and South Asia. Wellings and her team also contend that monogamy is also "the dominant pattern in most regions of the world" (p. 1711), with most reporting just one sexual partner. In some societies, however, there may be clear differences between ideology and practice in sexual relationships (Goodwin, 1999). Thus, young women in Asia may see their activities as far more restrained than their Western "liberal" counterparts, but may both underestimate the degree of premarital sex in their own society and overestimate sexual behaviour in the West. In Western cultures, sexual activity is largely delayed by those in higher social classes. In Wellings's British data men and women in the upper social classes were two to three years older than those from the lowest class at the time of first sexual intercourse, and those with higher education were also more likely to have experienced first sexual intercourse at a later age. At the same time, sexual attitudes may actually be more liberal amongst the higher social classes in other societies. More modernised "liberal" attitudes towards sex were likely to be found amongst those with the highest social class in Zambia (Pillai & Roy, 1996) and the Netherlands (Kraaykamp, 2002), with the more educated having more permissive attitudes towards sexuality than those less educated. In many societies, ethnic group is likely to be important, at least in terms of actual sexual activity. In the United States, for example, the median age for first intercourse is 16.9, but it is 15.8 for African Americans compared to 18.1 for Asian Americans (Ingoldsby, 2003).

Patterns of child rearing and sexual activity have been greatly influenced by socioeconomic and legal changes in Africa. Calves (2000) examined premarital childbearing in urban Cameroon. Traditionally, across sub-Saharan Africa, girls married very early, as soon as they reached menarche, with a large emphasis on having children and extending the family. A child would be considered legitimate and belonging to the husband's lineage so long as bride-wealth payments began and the marriage process started, whether or not the husband was the biological father. However, marriage no longer marks the beginning of childbearing, with increased nonmarital sexual relationships outside patrilineal descent. In the 1980s, changes in Cameroonian laws dissociated the legal status of bride-wealth and marriage, and bride-wealth no longer determined paternity. Unmarried men may often have a "main" girlfriend whom they are expected to marry plus other girls they do not expect to marry. The postponement of marriage in most African countries led to men being selective about whom they acknowledged and supported as their children, with social ranking of those children born out of marriage. This new selective recognition of children then leads to further consequences, with an increased role for grandparents in raising children for their daughters, as the presence of a child restricts the young woman's ability to marry another man.

Age-of-consent limitations have only emerged in the last two to three hundred years, with individual biological maturity previously being more significant (Graupner, 2000). Currently, the minimum age limit for penetrative sex varies greatly across the world, even within large countries such as the United States, where there are different age limits for different sexual practices (Graupner, 2000; Waites, 2004). In most societies, there is evidence of major changes in age limits for sexual behaviour over recent decades. Age limits have been raised in most European states from 12 or 13 in the 1920s; in South Africa in 1988, the minimum age for sex between women and boys was raised from 7 to 16 (19 for lesbians) (Graupner, 2000). Age of consent currently stands at 12 in Malta (although this excludes "acts that deprave" until the age of 18), but it is 15 in most other European Union states and up to 18 in some states in the United States. Two countervailing arguments have acted either to increase or decrease this age. The first stresses protection and the risks of abuse by elders in particular; this is contrasted with a counterposition that emphasises the rights of the adolescent and the risk of criminalizing vulnerable teenagers (Waites, 2004). Many jurisdictions have a multistage approach, providing regulations on minimum age limits but also seduction provisions for acts of authority figures, with new regulations often leading to substantial changes in prosecution rates (Graupner, 2000). Thus, the 2003 Sexual Offences Act in the United Kingdom, which emphasised protection of the child, led to a marked increase in prosecutions for sexual activity with a child under 16.

HOMOSEXUALITY

Historically, same-sex relationships have been accepted in many cultures, but usually under specific conditions (Coontz, 2004). Giddens argues that male homosexuality has been tolerated or approved in more cultures than it has been disapproved. In particular, homosexuality has often been seen as part of a ritual designed to give boys sexual training prior to marriage (Giddens & Pierson, 1998). However, the notion of homosexuality outside any such ritual may only be a century or so old. Indeed, the freeing of homosexuality from perversion arose alongside the separation of sexuality from nature and tradition described above (ibid.). Cherlin (2004) sees same-sex marriages as an important part of "the de-institutionalisation of marriage," with same-sex marriages now legalised in several European countries and with gay couples as willing as their straight counterparts to value coupledom (Edin, Kefalas, & Reed, 2004). This recognition of a diversity of sexual proclivities has also meant the acceptance of different lifestyles. Indeed, part of the rebellion against many "traditional" aspects of marriage has been led by homosexuals.

Until 1967, male homosexuality was a criminal offence in Britain, and it was only removed from the list of psychiatric disorders by the American Psychiatric Association in 1974. This reflected an increasing trend towards equality for lesbians and gay men in the 1960s and 1970s (Graupner, 2000). The European Court of Human Rights ruled that a ban on homosexual behaviour violated the European Convention on Human Rights, whilst the European Commission on Human Rights rejected different age limits for heterosexual and homosexual relations (ibid.). However, whilst there has been some acceptance in the West of homosexuality, in some countries there has been far greater resistance. In Eastern Europe during communism, there was general repression of homosexuality and gay movements, although this varied by country. In the former Soviet Union, for example, homosexuality was seen as a crime until the end of communism. There was also little tolerance of homosexual practices in Poland until the mid-1980s (Goodwin, 1999). In Czechoslovakia, however, there was some tolerance towards homosexuality, and in the former German Democratic Republic there was a degree of protection for homosexuals. Somewhat ironically, this was often provided by the Church as part of its ongoing rivalry with the State (Hillhouse, 1993). Notably, this greater tolerance towards homosexuals, eventually accepted by the GDR parliament in the repeal of the 1967 Penal Code outlawing homosexual activities, was overturned following German unification.

In China, despite evidence of some increase in tolerance towards homosexuality, few Chinese admit to being homosexual. Although homosexuality was never specifically outlawed in the People's Republic, homosexuals on the Chinese mainland were politically suspect and under threat of being charged with "hooliganism" (Ruan & Matsumura, 1991). Strongly held public prejudices were reinforced by penal codes restricting contacts between gay individuals of either sex, although there is evidence of social class differences in that college men were more likely to admit being attracted to another man than peasants were (Liu, Ng, & Chu, 1992). However, there is some evidence of change, with the hooliganism laws repealed in 1997 and with homosexuality being taken off the list of mental illnesses.

CONTRACEPTION AND ABORTION

Chemical contraception techniques first appeared in France around 1850 (LaPiere, 1965), and the use of contraception and abortion has been a major topic of discussion for couples and governments alike ever since that time. The International Conferences on Population and Development, sponsored by the United Nations, have illuminated the considerable disagreements over the means couples should use to implement effective fertility decisions, the role of government in family planning, and the part played by abortion in this. Political leaders have often continued to promote either population control or growth, whilst religious and cultural contexts have been differently emphasised in different nations as justifications for fertility decisions (Townsend, 2003). Worldwide abortion laws have become generally more liberal, although even in the most developed countries there are exceptions, such as the United States, where 32 of the 50 states restrict an adolescent's access to abortion (Adler, Ozer, & Tschann, 2003). For many newly independent or developing states, a large population is associated with national strength (Moghadam, 2004), which often leads to direct State intervention in abortion practices at the State level.

In her review of sexual behaviour during and after the communist period in Eastern Europe, Einhorn (1993) claims, "[R]eproductive rights have always been on the borderline between the private and public domains, encompassing the dual, and sometimes seemingly incompatible, issues of 'a woman's right to choose' and the state's responsibility to intervene on behalf of the health and well-being of its members" (p. 74). Some of the highest abortion rates in world were in communist Europe, with abortion often performed in extremely unsanitary conditions. In these nations, abortion was frequently the most common form of birth control, with relatively few people having access to contraception outside the major cities. In republics such as Georgia, for example, only 3 percent of women used the contraceptive pill or intrauterine devices (Einhorn, 1993). Much of this was a result of labour requirements for the workforce and broader concerns about population numbers, which tended to override other ideological commitments to women's rights. In the German Democratic Republic, some young women had themselves sterilized to improve their chances in the job market (Einhorn, 1993). In the Soviet State between 1936 and 1955, legislation abolished abortion except in extreme medical situations, representing a complete turnaround from earlier commitments and reflecting the economic concerns of the time (Heer, 1965).

Other local contextual factors, such as religion, were also important in abortion legislation. Abortion was abolished, as was the importation of contraception, following the Islamic revolution in Iran in 1979. In

Islamic law, a foetus is generally seen as developing a soul once the mother can feel its movement. After this point, it is prohibited to abort the foetus, although different Islamic states vary on whether abortion is permitted at all. In Poland, pressure from the Polish Catholic Church after the fall of communism restricted the supply of condoms and oral contraception and the possibility of having an abortion except under particular circumstances (such as following rape). Indeed, the central role of the Catholic Church has meant that the very discussion of family planning and sex education has been severely curtailed (Danziger, 1996). The availability of contraception had an important influence on abortion rates. Abortion was liberalised in Czechoslovakia in 1957, with termination of pregnancy available during the first three months of gestation under some circumstances. This was revised in 1986, when termination became available on the woman's request within the first 12 weeks (David, Dytrych, & Matejcek, 2003). After the fall of communism in 1989, the greater availability of contraception led to a decline of more than 50 percent in abortions between 1990 and 1997.

Sex ratios are notably imbalanced in many societies, reflecting the widespread use of abortion of those seen as less valuable to the society (nearly always girls). Secondi (2002) considers the marked imbalance in sex ratios in many Asian countries, which have significantly more than 105 boys born for 100 girls. These have led to a debate about whether this indicates evidence of abortion of female foetuses or female infanticide. I return to this debate in more detail in the next chapter.

SEXUAL DISEASE

Sexual diseases, such as HIV/AIDS, have had both rapid and gradual impacts on individual behaviour and on governmental legislation. At the same time, politics and commercial concerns have acted either to reduce governmental interventions or attribute blame to particular groups in the face of the disease, with substantial differences in the ways in which cultural norms and codes have encouraged or inhibited open discussion about sexual epidemics and their wider social impacts. Thus, several governmental bodies have been reluctant to intervene against such morally charged diseases, leading to political obstacles that have blocked HIV and other prevention and care programs. In other cases, governments have sent unclear messages, concerned about the impact of the disease but worried about its economic implications and reputational impact on the country. One example was the initial reluctance by the Thai government to intervene in discussions about the HIV epidemic, in a country where sex tourism provides an important source of hard currency (Manderson, 1995). In China, too, the government was reluctant to intervene following a high incidence of HIV infection amongst paid blood donors: Approximately a quarter of a million donors contracted the virus due to selling their blood to illegal traders who mixed together the blood, removed the plasma, and re-injected the mixture into donors (Wang, 2004). Social stigma has continued to follow this infected group despite their particularly unfortunate method of contracting the disease. Compared with people with AIDS overseas, Chinese paid donors who contracted the disease had a lower quality of life and suffered greater emotional rejection (ibid.).

The HIV/AIDS epidemic is a relatively recent phenomenon in Eastern Europe, not beginning until the early 1990s. Although obtaining exact prevalence figures in this region is problematic, the World Health Organization's AIDS surveillance figures indicate a recent rapid growth in both HIV and AIDS in Eastern Europe. An estimated 1.6 million people in Eastern Europe and Central Asia were living with HIV in 2005, an increase of twenty-fold in less than a decade (UNAIDS, 2006). In most of these countries, transmission has been primarily through injecting and the sharing of needles and syringes (Donoghoe, 2003; Hamers & Downs, 2003), with an estimated 1 percent of the population of Eastern Europe and Central Asia injecting illicit drugs (UNAIDS, 2002a). Rhodes and his colleagues (Rhodes, Ball et al., 1999; Rhodes, Stimson et al., 1999) have identified a number of features of the "macro risk environment" that act as major factors in sustaining epidemic growth and mediate the efficacy of prevention responses. These include the deterioration of the health care system, an increased mixing of populations, community values that stress greater sexual freedom, and a widespread sense of hopelessness and fatalism that has helped promote risk-taking behaviours. The growth of prostitution as a means of obtaining hard-to-get Western currency was of particular concern in the early 1990s (Borisenko, Tichnova, & Renton, 1999; Headley, 1998; Kalichman, 1998). Prostitution also came to be seen as a way of expressing freedom in a time when sexual behaviour became an important expression of rebellion against the old Soviet ways. Einhorn (1993) quotes a humorous Russian "dilemma": "either getting married, which is not very attractive, or becoming a prostitute, which is much more attractive" (ibid., p. 136).

In much of the former Soviet Union, HIV/AIDS has remained a highly political subject. Frank discussion of sexual matters was largely taboo in communist Eastern and Central European countries (Goodwin, 1995): Perhaps unsurprisingly, therefore, Lunin, Hall, Mandel, Kay, and Hearst (1995) found that only 29 percent of Russian 16-year-olds thought condoms should only be used once. In Georgia, an article in *Akhali Taoba* (*New Generation*) (December 3, 1996) reporting official numbers of AIDS cases was contradicted a week later by the Department of Social and Economical Information, which reported that there were *no* AIDS cases in Georgia (*Kavkasioni*, December 11, 1996). Existing attitudes and prejudices have encouraged "folk" or "common sense" representations of HIV/AIDS that place the epidemic within fringe, "pariah" groups, allowing individuals to feel personally immune from infection, thus reinforcing existing prejudices against those thought to be infected.

We (Goodwin et al., 2003) examined variations in lay representations of HIV/AIDS across occupational and cultural groups to see the extent to which these informed actual sexual practices in these fast-changing societies. Data for this project were collected from five nations – Estonia, Georgia, Hungary, Poland, and Russia – during the late 1990s. These countries vary significantly, not only in the spread of the epidemic in each nation, but in political structure, the influence and nature of the religion(s) practised, and levels of economic investment and growth – all factors likely to have important implications for the spread of sexual infection. Estonia and Georgia were both parts of the former Soviet Union and had very low rates of HIV infection at the time of our study. In Hungary and Poland, infection rates were also relatively low and stable, and there was little evidence of a marked increase in the prevalence of HIV/AIDS. In contrast, the Russian Federation has seen a marked escalation in the HIV epidemic, with HIV infection now increasing at one of the fastest rates in the world. In our work, we studied two groups: health care professionals and business people. These groups lived in quite different social and economic conditions and faced a range of varying adaptational demands resulting from the economic and social changes of the past decade. Business people are a highly mobile group whose lifestyle and relatively high income permit them to engage in particular higher-risk activities (Barnett et al., 2000). Individuals in such a group are particularly likely to visit sex workers (Wellings, Fields, Johnson, & Wadsworth, 1994), an important risk group in this region for HIV infection (Towianska, Rozlucka, & Dabrowski, 1992). Given the inconsistent levels of screening and poor hospital conditions in some of these nations (Renton et al., 1999), health care professionals were also viewed as a relatively high-risk group. As social stereotypes influence health care professionals' commitment to treatment and prevention of infection, the representations of medical staff are likely to be highly influential in these transient societies.

Five hundred and eleven participants (104 each from Estonia and Georgia, 103 from Russia, and 100 each from Poland and Hungary) were recruited in the five countries in this study, consisting of half medics and half business people in each country. Our respondents participated in face-to-face interviews and gave free associations about HIV/AIDS. Our results demonstrated both similarities and differences in representations of HIV/AIDS across the five cultures studied. Thus, while both our interviews and free associations demonstrated an unsurprisingly negative set of associations around the AIDS epidemic, reflecting the results of other studies across the world (Sheeran, Abraham, & Orbell, 1999), it was also clear that beliefs about the origins and spread of HIV, prevailing conceptualisations of moral responsibility and blame, and attitudes towards the role of the government were unevenly represented across the sample. These variations at least partly reflect differences in testing regimes across these nations, disparities in media portrayals of HIV/AIDS across the cultures, and the varying influences of religious beliefs on the growth of the epidemic in different cultures. Conspiracy theories (for example, AIDS was developed as a weapon of warfare) were a prominent feature of the early Soviet reporting of HIV/AIDS (Headley, 1998; Sontag, 1989). It was perhaps unsurprising, therefore, to see such theories still playing a role in the representations of HIV of many of our respondents in the three former Soviet nations in our sample (Georgia, Russia, and Estonia). This latter finding may tap into continuing representations that see HIV/AIDS as a metaphor for a general loss of "moral standards" (Rosenbrock et al., 2000). Indeed, a widespread belief that HIV is an outsiders' problem associated with the "decadent West" contributed to a controversial AIDS regulation requiring the compulsory testing of foreigners visiting Russia for more than three months, reflecting calls for isolation common to epidemics across the ages (Sontag, 1989).

One intriguing group of respondents in our study was the relatively high number of Russians (some 30 percent) who believed that the problem of HIV was exaggerated or could be readily solved. At the same time, a similar proportion of Russian respondents emphasised the hopelessness of the situation in their free responses, reflecting an apocalyptic sense of doom frequently evoked in the early days of the Western epidemic and anchored in a wider range of fears about the future. In a parallel newspaper study across these five nations, conducted at the time of our interviews (Goodwin, 2000), Russian newspapers provided both the largest number of alarmist stories (with headlines such as "We Have No Hope," *Kommersant* [*Businessman*], October 27, 1999, p. 9) and the greatest coverage of "miracle cures," with one youth-orientated newspaper (*Komsomolskaya Pravda*) actively sponsoring an eventually unsuccessful AIDS "cure" (*Armenicum*). Whilst the relationship between media representations and individual-level behaviours is a complex one (Svenkerud, Rao, & Rogers, 1999; Wagner, 1995), such active newspaper "propagation" (Moscovici, 1961) can be argued to have had rather deleterious implications for the perceptions of HIV/AIDS and risky sexual behaviours amongst this newspaper's young, and increasingly at-risk, readership. This demonstrates that the media portrayals of a social relationship can act as a significant mediator in changes in behaviours and attitudes in this domain.

In our studies, particular groups were more likely to be identified as being particularly risky in each country. Respondents in Russia were particularly concerned about levels of morality and social breakdown in their country and its implications for sexual behaviour. At the same time, this was the country where respondents were most willing to see the epidemic as having "nothing to do with them." In a related questionnaire study conducted in the same five countries (Goodwin et al., in press), we found high rates of sexual partnerships amongst our Russian business respondents, with more than 20 percent of these participants reporting more than one sexual partner per week. Our interview and free-association findings suggest relatively conservative representations in Poland and, to a lesser extent, Georgia, where images of the "promiscuous" young condom carrier were accompanied by the strongest free associations between casual sexual activity and HIV/AIDS. Stigma and discrimination can act as important structural barriers to HIV prevention. The Polish and Georgian samples were the most likely to declare their religious affiliation, and our findings here are in line with other results amongst religious communities, which have also reported relatively conservative representations of sexual behaviour and HIV/AIDS, particularly in relation to condom use. It was in our "religious" nations – Poland and Georgia – that there was the greatest number of free associations between HIV/ AIDS and misfortune and intolerance, indicators of a more compassionate attitude towards those infected. Kachkachishvili (1999) in Georgia also found that older respondents in Georgia felt that public debate on sexual issues was unacceptable and immoral.

In a subsequent analysis of these data (Goodwin, Realo, & Kwiatkowska, 2004), we used multidimensional scaling to reveal two dimensions of associations of responses. One dimension groups together casual sexual activity, condoms, prostitution, and sexual activity in general and reflects the sexual component of the epidemic. A second dimension emphasizes the disease aspect of the epidemic and the fear associated with the epidemic. In the analysis of associations between specific stimulus words, Georgian respondents associated AIDS most closely with homosexuality and casual sexual activity. Such conservative representations may have significant implications for safer sexual behaviour (Paez et al., 1991). Older Georgians in particular have been described as holding Victorian England attitudes towards sexuality and have shown a notable reluctance to use condoms (UNAIDS, 2002b). Russian respondents were the least likely to place together words on the second dimension: "sex." This may reflect a relative reluctance to moralise in a society where there has been considerable confusion about sexual relations following the end of communism and where the marked eroticisation of culture has been accompanied by considerable ambiguity about the rights and wrongs of sexual behaviour (Kon, 1995). At the same time, these Russian respondents demonstrated the greatest proximity between "Africa" and AIDS, with the analysis of the Russian data showing the strongest loading for Africa on the second dimension, "deadly disease." Such a finding suggests a potential psychological "distancing" in this country that may allow a sense of detachment from those perceived to be at risk. Such a detachment can have important implications for risk behaviours by encouraging a sense of personal invulnerability and may contribute to a pattern of high-risk behaviour. Our findings demonstrated the importance of the moderating impact of gender differences when looking at sexual behaviour and attitudes in these changing cultures. Gender differences in mean scores on the "sex" dimension were highest in Poland, whilst differences in reported sexual activity were greatest in Georgia. These findings are consistent with Bajos and Marquet's (2000) observation that differences in sexual behaviour are likely to be greatest in more traditional cultures.

One common representation of HIV/AIDS, reported in the United States, Africa, and South America, is that HIV/AIDS is something that happens only to "older strangers" and that relative youth and acquaintance with a partner provides immunity from the epidemic. Particular subgroups – drug addicts, homosexuals, and prostitutes – may be viewed by adolescents as the only groups at risk, although, among the poorest adolescents, a pervasive sense of fatalism may make them feel powerless to control their infection risk. In a further study in Russia, Georgia and the Ukraine (Goodwin, Kozlova, Nizharadze, & Polyakova, 2004), we focused on two groups of adolescents: school children (those living at home with family or relatives and attending school) and shelter children (adolescents living on the street but attending temporary shelter accommodation). Homeless children are likely to become sexually active at a younger age than their peers and are more likely to have had multiple partners. Because of the realities of street life, such children are more likely to use illicit drugs, and, because they are more economically dependent on sexual activity for obtaining food and shelter, they are also more likely to be sexually abused. Furthermore, because such children are often removed from traditional information sources, they usually receive only limited information about safer sexual practices.

Data for this study were collected from more than 1,500 adolescents aged 13 to 17 during the year 2002. Approximately one-third of them lived in temporary accommodations or on the streets and regularly visited sheltered accommodation. Respondents participated in structured one-on-one interviews with members of the research team and then separately completed confidential, anonymous questionnaires. The shelter children were more likely to be sexually active and to have injected drugs. As with their older counterparts, Russian adolescents were more likely to be sexually active, reporting levels of sexual experience similar to those recorded in other representative studies in this country. However, school children in Georgia (rather than their shelter counterparts) were the most likely to be sexually active and to inject drugs, and the Georgian children in general knew least about the HIV/AIDS epidemic. These findings demonstrate the importance of considering different societal subgroups when assessing the impact of particular epidemics on a changing society.

Finally, cultural differences amongst migrant groups may serve to mediate the ways in which HIV is discussed and tackled by family and friends. In the United States, Poppen (2004) reported significant differences between Latinos and Brazilians in their disclosure of HIV and subsequent risk-taking and psychological behaviours. Latinos in their study were significantly less likely to disclose than Anglos, particularly to their fathers. Poppen's research found that those who did disclose to their mothers or their main partners received more social support and consequently were less depressed. In the Brazilian community, however, a greater openness about sexuality and open and aggressive campaigns in Brazil meant a different approach to the problems. Here, disclosure to mothers had less impact on depression, as those infected displayed a greater willingness to talk to friends and partners.

SUMMARY

Whilst sexual practices and attitudes have undoubtedly evolved over time, particularly with the onset of modernisation and the "fluid sexuality" that this might have promoted, it is also clear that governments have had a direct impact on sexual practices and changing sexual relations. Much of this direct interference has stemmed from an apparent fear of modernisation as a force that undermines women's desire for children (namely, the prohibition of abortion) or that acts as a corruption of morality (hence, the regulation of sexual interactions). The acceptance of homosexuality in some countries of the world has been seen as an important step in the "deinstitutionalisation" of modern relationships, but much of this acceptance has been reluctant and opposed by religious bodies. Modernisation has also allowed for a greater movement of populations and the opportunities for the spreading of sexual diseases, which have fed into persisting notions of immorality and "unacceptable out-groups." All this has meant that sexual behaviour has become a major part of the wider discourse about relationship transitions around the world and their implications for changing societies.

CHAPTER 6

Marriage and the Family

THE FAMILY AND MARRIAGE

Writing more than 50 years ago, Murdock (1949) claimed that the nuclear family represents a basic unit of society across the world, with no society having yet found a suitable substitute for this form. Certainly, family and marriage have been central to the lives of individuals for centuries in most populations (Thornton & Young-Demarco, 2001). Also clear is that there is considerable emotional and political significance to the concept of the family. Indeed, the family is not only a core component of traditional and collectively oriented societies, but is also a key topic for debate in most world societies (Inglehart & Baker, 2000).

The association between the family and broader State affairs was recognised by the Greek philosopher Aristotle. He saw the family unit not only as a self-sustaining social organisation, but also as the basis of the village and the State. For thousands of years, marriage has been functional, serving myriad political, social, and economic functions (Coontz, 2004). This means that individual needs and desires were subservient to wider societal goals and the desires of the broader family members (ibid.). For the rich, marriage was a way of keeping and consolidating wealth. For the poor, marriage provided a means of acquiring new resources and skills. As I noted in Chapter 3, love was generally seen as a rather poor reason for partner choice. Instead, marriage was most often for economic and political reasons (Hird & Abshoff, 2000).

Rothenbacher (1998) differentiates between the impact of long-term and short-term social change on families in his analysis of families in Europe. Mirroring my earlier distinction between rapid and more gradual social change, he argues that households and families on this continent have been influenced by long-term transformations that have been ongoing since industrialisation. These include changes in social security regimes and the development of educational and employment systems and regulations. Other long-term demographic transitions have included the decline from preindustrial mortality rates and a reduction in the European birthrate since around 1965. Such changes in themselves have arisen from transformations in norms and values and the compression of the procreative phase for women as larger numbers entered the workforce. Notably since the 1980s, most of the jobs created in the European Union have been for women, with many of these part-time. There has also been a marked increase in flexibility of work contracts, allowing for new family arrangements for child care and at least a partial restructuring of gender roles. At the same time, even within one continent, families have been influenced by local historical events, such as the improvement of housing supply or educational facilities in a particular area. These have often taken place over a relatively short period of time, and they demonstrate the mediating effect of particular geographies and social groupings on family change. Furthermore, the directionality of many social changes in the family sphere is far from clear (Smock, 2004). Thus, for example, changes in gendered family roles can be seen as leading to economic changes as a result of greater female participation in the workforce. On the other hand, Goode (1963) suggests that it is changes in the broader society that structure the organisation of the family. Certainly, movement to the city has widely weakened the power of extended families to control conjugal family life around the world (Hirschfield & Minh, 2002).

DEBATING THE CHANGES

The value of such changes to the wider society has been fiercely debated. Indeed, marriage and family change have always been a "hot research topic" (Walker, 2004, p. 843), with concerns about marital decline and its impacts on society discussed for the last two centuries, much of this part of an overtly moralising debate about social change in general (Amato, 2004; Lewis, 2003). For some students of social change, such as LaPiere (1965), the family has been a major bulwark against change. Indeed, for them it is only when local clans, tribes, or families become disorganised that there has been major social change

(p. 333). From this perspective, families often seem to act as largely conservative institutions, preserving the status quo, with the extended family in particular serving to restrict both physical and social mobility. Early American colonials reported their worries that families were disintegrating, with troubling implications for the broader society (Douglas, 2003). Burgess (1926) noted how the urbanised family had moved from a social to a private, companion-based institution. He claimed that since around 1900 industrialisation and urbanisation had weakened marriages' institutional basis in the United States, leading to less practical reliance on each other. Cutler (1916) was concerned with new transitions in women's role in the family, writing in the *American Journal of Sociology*:

Every considerable change in life conditions in the past has resulted in a change in the sex division of labour. It is the nineteenth century change in life conditions, which we now call the industrial revolution, that is producing now a new sex division of labour and is thus altering the status of women (cited in Smock, 2004).

Others stressed the family as an agent of change, a perspective particularly popular amongst social scientists in the late nineteenth and early twentieth centuries (Smock, 2004; Walker, 2004). Opponents of women's liberation at the turn of the twentieth century, in particular, expressed their fears about destroying the sanctity of the home, the "pollution" of women's purity, and the consequent neglect of children (Janes, 1891, cited in Smock, 2004; LaPiere, 1965). Later commentators, such as Popenoe (1988, 1993), have argued that an increased divorce rate and the decline of two-parent families, particularly since the 1950s, has led to the erosion of a whole way of life. From the marital-decline perspective (Amato, 2004), an increasingly individualistic culture has meant the end of commitment to such traditional institutions as marriage, with individuals no longer willing to stick together during difficult times and with commitment only temporary. A rise in individualistic values and a decline in religious influence (and greater plurality in religious influences) seemed to undermine commitment to lifelong marriage (Amato et al., 2003; Amato, 2004; Thornton & Young-Demarco, 2001). The family as a vital bulwark against an aggressive capitalist society has been compromised, leading to a decline in societal norms and trust between individuals and wider social groups.

Central to the "moral debates" about family change have been idealisations about the supportive extended family and its decline.

A desire for personal fulfillment, most notably that of women, has been seen as undermining the socialising role of marriage and is associated with a reduced ability for spouses to deal with conflict when it arises (Douglas, 2003). Males, too, have been seen as undermined by the loss of their "traditional bread-winning role" (Lewis, 2003). Beck and Beck-Gernsheim (2002) have argued that later and fewer marriages and increased divorce have made partnerships more diverse and fragile. Women are more likely to file for divorce, often dissatisfied with the lack of fulfillment provided by their family life. Individuals are now married for a lesser proportion of their lives during the twentieth century, partly because of demographic changes and partly because divorce or nonmarriage has become more acceptable (Coontz, 2000). In the United States and Canada, divorce rates quadrupled in the last three decades of the twentieth century (Huston & Melz, 2004; Le Bourdais & La Pierre-Adamcyk, 2004). The probability of a U.S. marriage ending in divorce doubled during the 1960s and 1970s (Bengtson, 2001). Consequently, despite recent decreases in divorce rates in the United Kingdom and the United States, around 40 percent of marriages beginning at the start of the twenty-first century in those countries are anticipated to end in divorce. It is also apparent that there have been significant changes in family structures, with, for example, nearly half of the children born in the United States expected to spend some time in a "nontraditional" family as a result of being born outside marriage or as a consequence of divorce (Lewis, 2003), Even within marriages and families, individuals lead more independent lives, doing less together than in previous generations (Amato et al., 2003).

As women's opportunities for independent economic success have increased, there is evidence that this has led to some retreat from marriage. The result has been a diminished family, which has a weaker role in socialisation (Bengtson, 2001). In many industrialised countries, there are particular fears about the ability of the family to socialise children appropriately. This has led to debates over a supposed rise of criminality as the result of a lack of family stability (Lewis, 2003). For others, a marriage based on psychological gratification fails to provide stability, with a "cancerous" individualism and a desire to "get ahead" invading the private family world and with obligations and commitments replaced by notions of full and honest communication between self-actualised individuals (for example, Bellah et al., 1985). Individuals thus invest only in themselves and not in their families (Popenoe, 1988). Love, if it exists at all in such relationships, is a romanticised notion that fails to provide real stability, as we saw in the earlier discussion on modern intimacy. The result has been a general pessimism about the family (Amato et al., 2003).

Given the above, it is unsurprising to find that if there is any area of relationships in which the State has intervened actively, it has been in the area of the family (Lewis, 2003). Indeed, it is here that we can probably see the most direct impacts of the effects of social change on relationships. Moghadam (2004) makes this clear:

Nowhere is the family free of State regulation. This intervention takes various forms: Apart from marriage registration, ... there is family law. ... [T]here are also laws pertaining to reproductive rights, contraception, and abortion. There may or may not be legal codes regarding the provision of care within families and the responsibilities of family members to each other. There may or may not be legal codes pertaining to domestic violence, child abuse, wife battering, or spousal rape. There are invariably laws pertaining to family disintegration. ... Far from being an enclave, the family is vulnerable to the state, and the laws and social policies that impinge upon it and undermine the notion of separate spheres (p. 140).

When Britain colonised Basutoland (Lesotho) in 1868, it issued a series of proclamations that affected the marriage system and family life. It created a dual system with Christian or civil marriage, which was set against the customary laws in the country (Modo, 2001). In Hong Kong, the 1971 law forfeited the legal status of concubines, indicating a significant change in the social status of extramarital affairs (Kung, Hung, & Chan, 2004). The National Socialists in Germany after 1933 introduced a series of measures to decrease female employment, although these were changed again shortly afterward due to rearmament in the Second World War (Beck & Beck-Gernsheim, 2002). More recently, new legislation in Britain regarding paid paternity leave and the father's right to ask for flexible working has helped address the perceived needs of working parents. Changes in legislation on paternity leave may then have effects on other parts of family life and on the emotional commitment of the father to rearing and taking care of his children (Smit, 2001). Divorce rates in England and Wales tripled since the Divorce Reform Act (1969), which allowed for the possibility of "irretrievable breakdown" as a qualitative judgement leading to the end of marriage (Allan, 2001). I discuss further examples of such State interference in more detail below.

HISTORICAL INTERPRETATIONS

Some of these dire prognoses about the family and marriage arise as a result of specific interpretations of the historical data on family structure and activities. For this reason, Coontz (2000) argues that a historical perspective on the family is vital. A number of commentators have noted how historians have often drawn from dated sociological treatises on modernisation and industrialisation. This has led to erroneous conclusions about the extent to which these processes led to the end of the "traditional" family (for example, Coontz, 2000; Hareven, 2000). Moghadam (2004) notes that, although there has been no "golden age" of the family, myths about such an age are easy to construct, especially during times of rapid social change elsewhere in society. The close-knit family described by Burgess and Locke in 1953 reflected probably only a short period (Douglas, 2003; Lewis, 2003). During the years immediately following World War II, marriage became of increasing importance, with marital rates higher in the United States than earlier in the century and with the average age at marriage dropping from 26 for men, 23 for women, at the start of the century to 22 and 20, respectively, by 1960 (Cherlin, 2004). Kiernan (2004) describes the 1950s and 1960s as a "golden age" in Western marriage, with nearly universal marriage and with marriage seen as the predominant setting for children. This was accompanied by a marked increase in birthrates. As with comparisons of social capital across time, a focus on the ideal 1950s family in North America is particularly atypical. It was only during that decade that, for the first time in 80 years, the age of marriage fell sharply, fertility increased, and the proportion of never-married decreased. Figures of unmarried women aged over 18 in 1998 are actually more similar to those of 1900, compared to those of the 1950s (Coontz, 2000). Hence, it is misleading to focus on what seemed to be a temporary state that followed World War II (ibid.). This postwar optimism was evident elsewhere, even in societies where the outcomes of that war had led to severe economic challenges. During the 1950s and 1960s in Western Germany, the family was also placed at the centre of society, enshrined in the West German constitution and given State protection (Beck & Beck-Gernsheim, 2002).

Hareven also suggests that despite myths about extended, closely bonded families, high mortality rates in previous generations means that the "great extended family" of the past was rarely evident. Data from England and France show that in the preindustrial period, age at marriage was much later than is generally assumed (Hareven, 2000). Households were far more malleable in structure than often alleged (Rothenbacher, 1998). In the United States, for example, the traditional family often included nonfamily members such as lodgers, boarders and – in richer families – servants (Coontz, 2000; Rothenbacher, 1998).

Several authors have noted that there is evidence that the family has been nuclear in form since the sixteenth century (for example, Hareven, 2000). As Rothenbacher (1998) notes, whilst for agrarian populations the extended family may have been the normative model, in reality a high adult mortality rate and a short life expectancy meant that nuclear families were often far more dominant amongst the poor. Indeed, extended families were more significant amongst the richer classes, who could afford such a family network. In the cities, urban living conditions (most notably a shortage of housing) restricted the extended family, and lone parents were rather common in the second half of the nineteenth century due to a high illegitimacy rate. LaPiere (1965) argues that familism amongst the European peasantry waxed and waned at different times according to different circumstances. Thus, even during the Middle Ages families unable to maintain economic self-sufficiency became fragmented, with workers moving to find work outside of the family setting. Later, industrialisation actually increased extended family coresidence in some areas for quite functional reasons (Coontz, 2000). Certainly, family membership has also changed over time and within different classes (ibid.). Thus, for example, the nineteenth century white middle-class family existed alongside families with child labour in the fields and factories and extended families in particular labour-intensive trades.

Hird and Abshoff (2000) claim that even considering the family to be "natural" is a "distinctly modern discourse" (p. 347). Certainly, the notion of motherhood as a social role for women, rather than a sexual reproductive role, is relatively recent. The very notion of childhood as a period requiring protection and nurturance by parents is also relatively recent (Aries, 1960; Hareven, 2000). Traditionally, childhood was not a long period of innocence, as currently championed in many postindustrial societies, and women were not expected to devote themselves to their children as in contemporary times. Instead, procreation was more about producing heirs for economic survival, rather than following modern parenthood desires. For the poor, little time was spent caring for children, with older siblings responsible for this, whilst for the wealthy, wet nurses, servants, and teachers looked after offspring (Hird & Abshoff, 2000). Two-parent provider families have been the norm throughout most of history. Consequently, exclusive child care by mothers is historically rare: It has been much more common for women to work and to attend to their children at the same time (Coontz, 2000).

In other cases, what appears new in family life is often rather traditional (Coontz, 2004). Many of the new family forms evident across Europe (such as people living alone, lone parenthood, unmarried cohabitation) had all existed in earlier times. Stepfamilies were more common in the past than now, and the divorce rate was higher in 1940s Malaysia than in the modern United States (ibid.). Cohabitation was relatively common in early twentieth-century England, following informal marital separation or widowhood (Lewis, 2003). In many countries, individuals might live in nuclear households for parts of their lives, but with extended kin or nonrelatives at others, meaning that simplistic family life cycles are rarely generalisable (Hareven, 2000). Reports that U.S. parents spend less time with their children since the 1970s fail to allow for the fact that in the colonial United States families often sent children to live in other people's homes as servants (Coontz, 2000). Indeed, research comparing the 1920s to the 1970s found that parents spent more time with their children in the 1970s than 50 years previously.

A further part of the family decline debate has concerned the role of the family in supporting ageing populations. Greater physical separation from parents, diminished family sizes, and an increase in individualistic attitudes have reduced the role of children as an insurance policy for the parents' old age (Coontz, 2000). The growth of more comprehensive social security systems has partly replaced some family functions and helped permit a greater individualism in family relationships (Rothenbacher, 1998). However, Bengtson (2001) argues that in the twenty-first century multigenerational family bonds have become more important as a result of the greater number of years of shared lives among generations and the increasing importance of active grandparents and other family members in supporting the different generations. Indeed, in some cases these multigenerational bonds replace nuclear-family functions. In the United States today, a 20-year-old is more likely to have a grandmother alive than a similarly aged person would have had a *mother* alive 100 years previously (ibid.). These intergenerational relationships are becoming increasingly diverse due to changing family structures and new intergenerational family forms. In Asian societies such as Korea and Japan, multigenerational household sharing is decreasing, with a greater dependency on State provision (ibid.). In Latin America, an increased life expectancy has led to more women entering widowhood at an advanced age. This has led to new adjustments being required. Examining different marital patterns in Brazil and Mexico, Gomes da Conceição (2002) notes that Mexicans enjoy longer marriages because of their increased longevity; over the last 50 years, life expectancy for couples living together rose from 17 to 41 years. In Brazil, a formal pension system means that most take this pension; in Mexico, the limited availability of State support means greater dependency on emigration and support from relatives overseas.

MARITAL SENTIMENT OVER TIME

Accompanying these debates over family structure have been questions about the supposed decline in family attachments (Cherlin, 2004). As noted above, several commentators have seen a decline in adherence to the family values promoted by traditional societies (Inglehart, Norris, & Welzel, 2003). As discussed in earlier chapters, in the nineteenth century bonds of sentiments were far less central to marriage. Between the mid-nineteenth century and the mid-twentieth century, marriage was seen as mandatory, so that even in the 1950s emotional satisfaction was centered around the nuclear family. Whilst many of the "modern" economic and ideological changes in family sentiments were in fact noted by Burgess as early as the 1930s (Burgess & Cottrell, 1939), most commentators suggest that the importance of marriage began to noticeably diminish in the 1960s (Cherlin, 2004; Kiernan, 2004). Higher levels of women's education and employment made marriage a union based on an emotional bond, with individuals seeking to fulfill their inner needs (Beck & Beck-Gernsheim, 2002). Writing in the mid-1960s, LaPiere (1965) described incongruence in family organisation, where the monogamous family system was seen as having lost much of its traditional functional value but where, at the time, there was yet to be a sufficient liberalisation of divorce laws and settlements that acknowledged this. He described the United States at the time as a society in a state of incongruence, "fraught with conflicts and contradictions. ... [E]verything has a quality of uncertainty and instability" (p. 199). This led to a variable and erratic socialisation and the development of contradictory personality traits, with men in particular feeling uncomfortable in their revised social roles.

This time of uncertainty can be seen as followed by a period described by Cherlin (2004) as "the deinstitutionalization of marriage, ... the weakening of the social norms that define people's behaviour in a social institution such as marriage" (p. 848). During the 1970s, the family began to be seen in increasingly bipolar forms, represented either as an instrument of repression or as a "haven" against the realities of a harsh outside world (Lasch, 1977). Several anthropologists and psychologists started to question the cosy image of the nuclear family, whilst many feminists challenged the structural inequalities and normative gender-based roles inherent in the traditional family (Amato, 2004; Bengtson, 2001; Gillies & Edwards, 2005; Lewis, 2003). Such commentators proposed that it was only stigmatisation and prohibitive divorce regulations that kept divorce rates relatively low in the past, and they welcomed the greater freedom of choice and equality in modern marital relationships (Amato, 2004; Thornton & Young-Demarco, 2001). The darker sides of the traditional family were exposed in a new way, with its unpleasant and exploitative nature more to the fore (Goodwin & Cramer, 2002). The traditional family was seen as overvalued: In a great deal of premodern and early modern times, men controlled women and threatened them with violence. In contrast, modern relationships insist on a greater dialogue: Marriage continues on the basis of how well the couple get on together rather than representing an unquestioned "state of nature" (Giddens & Pierson, 1998, p. 136). Self-development, negotiated gender roles in the relationship, and communication and openness became increasingly significant, with social norms and laws declining in their significance as regulators of family life (Cherlin, 2004). Nonfamilial organisations play an increasingly large role in our daily lives. Bengtson (2001) proposed that a narrow family decline argument has focused too much on coresidence and failed to recognise the extended lives between generations and the support this can offer.

In recent decades, low fertility and greater longevity mean more opportunities for women to work outside their families and marital home. Since the 1960s, there has been a rise in the age of marriage and an increase in the ideal age at marriage. Real options emerged for women for solitary living in modern Western societies (Coontz, 2004). New opportunities also arose for both women and men through their work activities. South, Trent, and Shen (2001) in the United States examined features of the social structure that might influence marital breakdown. They considered the relative number of attractive marital partners in the environment, using a two-wave panel survey of interviews conducted in 1987–1988 and 1992–1994 of 3,745 married couples, 11 percent of whom divorced or separated by wave two. They found couples more likely to divorce when they lived in geographic areas where there was a marked gender imbalance. They also found that couples were more likely to divorce when wives worked in occupations with a large number of men compared to women, although this did not influence the husband's divorce. The availability of spousal alternatives influenced divorce amongst both low-risk and high-risk couples.

Just as with discussions of modernisation and personal lives in general, not all commentators have so unquestionably accepted theses of radical family decline or have been so negative about such social changes in marital relationships (Amato, 2004; Gillies & Edwards, 2005). Instead, many have pointed to the complex set of countervailing forces that have both contributed to and detracted from marital happiness (Amato et al., 2003; Thornton & Young-Demarco, 2001). Recent evidence suggests that although there has been some retreat from marriage (in terms of numbers of those marrying), the institution is still highly valued in most cultures around the world (Huston & Melz, 2004): Despite a greater acceptance of divorce, there is still a very strong commitment in the United States to marriage, children, and family life. Indeed, Thornton and Young-Demarco (2001) note a persisting and relatively stable belief in marriage as important in the United States, consistent since the 1960s. Cherlin (2004) argues that marriage is still very popular because it represents "enforceable trust" (p. 854), entailing a public commitment in front of friends, family, and religious representatives. Even amongst those least likely to marry (for example, African Americans in the United States), there is a strong and symbolic reverence for marriage (Huston & Melz, 2004), as it represents an elusive, sought-after goal in often the poorest communities and a symbol of achievement amongst those who have few economic assets (Cherlin, 2004; Edin, Kefalas, & Reed, 2004). Whilst there was evidence of a greater approval of divorce up to the 1980s, there has been a flattening of this trend in the last decade, with the great majority believing that marriage is for life and should only be ended under extreme conditions. Indeed, although the divorce rate increased dramatically in the 1970s and peaked around 1980, it has actually decreased slightly (U.S. Bureau of Census, 2000), with a similar pattern evident in the United Kingdom (in England, the divorce rate in 2006 was at its lowest since 1984; National Statistics, 2007). Nationwide surveys also show that a high proportion of the population is pro-marriage, even in countries such as Sweden, where cohabitation is high. Furthermore, whilst there has been an increase in divorce, there is also evidence of greater remarriage (Amato et al., 2003).

There has also been little evidence of a decline over these decades in the desire for individuals to become parents. Most believe parenthood is fulfilling and maintain a commitment to marital ideals of family and children (Douglas, 2003; Thornton & Young-Demarco, 2001). Conservative discourse about the decline of marriage in many ways has emphasised the need for "conjugal perfection" (Gillis, 2004): In Gillis's words: "[M]odern families spend a great deal of time and money on the ritual and representations, on the special family times and places, that sustain our ideal of the perfect couple or ideal parent–child relationship" (p. 990). Hence, Cherlin suggests, "[W]hat has happened is that although the practical importance of being married has declined, its symbolic importance has remained high, and may even have increased. ... It used to be the foundation of adult personal life, now it is sometimes the capstone" (Cherlin, 2004, p. 855). The proportion of unhappy marriages has also not necessarily increased, although leaving such marriages has become more likely (Amato et al., 2003). Whilst wives' job demands and increased premarital cohabitation may have increased the likelihood of divorce, greater equality in decision making, increased family income, and later marriage have decreased relationship dissatisfaction (ibid.). Indeed, Amato finds that means for marital happiness and divorce proneness in the United States were nearly identical in 1980 and 2000. An emphasis on different qualities in a partner and a greater emphasis on economic and moral autonomy have also not necessarily meant a decline in commitment to the partner (Lewis, 2003). Using data from the World Values Survey, Diener et al. (2000) found that, overall, married people were more satisfied with their lives than those living with a significant other, with the relationship between marital status and subjective well-being very similar across the world.

The result has also been something of a confusing set of dialogues (Beck & Beck-Gernsheim, 2002), with little agreement about the state of the "traditional family" – although all sides of the debates cite empirical, usually demographic, data (ibid.). "Families of choice," greater diversity in personal relationships, and the detraditionalisation of marital life have freed people from previously constrained roles and unconditional, sometimes problematic ties. At the same time, the search for love and intimacy is ever greater, but maybe harder to attain (Gillies & Edwards, 2005). Thus, many in modern industrialised societies remain uncertain of their attitudes to marriage: Whilst they value the freedom to leave bad marriages and to find new partners, they are also concerned about social stability and its impact on children (Amato, 2004). Amato summarises it thus:

The clash between these two concerns reflects a fundamental contradiction within marriage itself: that is, marriage is designed to promote both institutional and personal goals (p. 962).

GENDER ROLES AND THE ROLE OF FATHERS

According to revised modernisation theory (Inglehart, 2003), modernisation brings certain predictable changes in gender roles, family, and marriage. Beck and Beck-Gernsheim (2002) differentiate between several stages of family development. In a preindustrial marital relationship, couples performed mainly material tasks as part of common, shared economic activities. During a later bourgeois family period, couples carried out a mixture of material and emotional tasks, with the man having financial responsibility and the woman performing "emotion work." This they see as still evident amongst older-generation couples. Now, however, "a radical change is altering women's education, career opportunities, fertility rates, sexual behaviour and worldviews" (Inglehart & Norris, 2003, p. 159). Cultural changes have laid the basis for mass mobilization through women's movements, and these in turn accelerate the social change process (Inglehart & Norris, 2003). This has signaled a systematic movement "away from traditional values and toward more egalitarian sex roles" (p. 9). Industrialisation has meant that a deference to authority, absolute family values, and the rejection of divorce and abortion have been replaced by a greater emphasis on gender equality, despite the determined resistance of some elites (Inglehart & Norris, 2003). Thus, although women are more supportive of gender equality in every society, there are marked differences in gender values between traditional agrarian cultures and egalitarian postmodern societies.

Inglehart and his colleagues provide empirical evidence for these trends through their analysis of the World Values Survey, a continuing data collection that took place in four waves between 1981 and 2001, with a large pool of countries and participants (Inglehart, 2003). Changes in gender roles correspond to movements along two major dimensions in cross-cultural variation identified in the survey. The first movement sees a transition from traditional to secular-rational values. This they see as mirroring a decline in the traditional family. The second has witnessed a transition from survival to self-expression values, which challenges traditional gender roles. In their analysis, high levels of economic insecurity characteristic of preindustrial society lead to an emphasis on traditional authority, strong leadership, and communal ties and obligations. The family is characterised by a traditional two-parent family, there is strong sexual division, and social norms support traditional family values. Childbearing and child rearing are seen as the major female roles, with the large extended family an important source of protection and support for parents in old age. In poorer and developing societies, both men and women accept these different gender roles as natural; it is not simply a case of men actively repressing women. The rise of capitalism and the industrial revolution led to more women entering the paid market-place and attaining greater legal rights (such as the right to vote). Fertility rates and family size fell, with large families no longer so important as other schemes arose (such as insurance policies). There was also a related move from the extended to the nuclear family.

Postindustrialisation brings a greater sense of security, greater affluence, and an increased emphasis on quality of life and self-expression. During the late twentieth century, gender equality has become a major issue in affluent Western societies, with the rejection of many traditional cultural beliefs and values about women. These egalitarian and liberal values are particularly strong amongst women, the young and well educated, and those who are less religious. They are also more prominent in societies with greater human and democratic development (Norris & Inglehart, 2003). Consonant with these post-modern values is a rise in gender equality as women move into management and gain political influence, with this equality evident at home as well as in the workplace. In postmodern societies, roles have been reevaluated as women work outside the house and self-expression and individualisation of marriage became more significant. Women have new opportunities to initiate divorce and support themselves and their children if they are not satisfied in their marital relationships (Coontz, 2004). Thus, whilst 30 percent of American women worked in 1950,

55 percent did so in 1986. Similarly, 28 percent of married women with children between ages 6 and 17 worked in 1950, but this rose to 54 percent in 1986 (Turiel, 2002). Changes in women's earning potential have had a major impact on marriage patterns in postindustrial society, with the increasing significance of women's earning potential in determining marriage prospects (Sweeney & Cancian, 2004). England (2004) argues that this may be so for a number of reasons: Men can now gain more from a woman with high earnings, and the shift in cultural preferences has made women's employment more accept-able. Press (2004) suggests that as women have more money through earnings, they need money from men less. This may mean that they turn to other aspects of a man's attractiveness (such as his appear-ance or housework skills) in evaluating mate fitness.

Men and women in the United States now hold less traditional views about marriage, such as who should be homemakers. Collating data from five large-scale data sets, with data in particular from the last four decades, Thornton and Young-Demarco (2001) found that between the 1960s and the mid-1980s both men and women demon-strated more positive attitudes and beliefs towards egalitarian decision making, the involvement of women in previously male roles, and the subsequent implications of maternal employment for children and families. This egalitarian attitude continued into the 1990s, although in the late 1990s there was evidence of some leveling off in these atti-tudes. There has been a decrease in the work performed by wives in the household and a (small) increase in husbands' participation (Amato et al., 2003), although there is considerable variation in this and little agreement about what should be done across cultural groups (Cherlin, 2004). These new work roles and opportunities for women have improved the family's economic situation, but they have also increased the potential for work-related conflict (Amato et al., 2003). Some have argued that this new role for men has led to confusion over their bread-winning role and the "need to act like a man" in a world where giving women economic benefits can be resented (Goldberg, cited in Giddens, 1992).

Some of the challenges for women in these postindustrial societies are summarised in Beck and Beck-Gernsheim's (2002) analysis of the current, complex situation of many women in modern Germany. In the nineteenth century, German women had few chances to shape their lives. Since the 1960s in Western Germany, in common with most postindustrial societies, there has been a sharp increase in female employment, and women – as they were released from direct family ties – gained new opportunities. Changes in their education, work, and public life have brought their "normal life story" closer to that of men. Women now enjoy greater opportunities to enter the educational system and greater equality of treatment in the workplace. They no longer see marriage as a goal to be achieved as soon as possible, but aim for greater satisfaction from their work lives, although those who have monotonous and poorly paid work may still see family life as their area of greatest satisfaction. Greater financial freedom allows for greater autonomy and power to assert themselves over their environment and from the family that relies on their income. This allows for new contacts and experiences, greater physical mobility, and new internalised models of living. But despite all this, social inequalities still exist and tend to increase during times of economic problems. Whilst women have became less defined by their family roles, there is also no clear model that defines women's life prospects. Although men have changed many of their views on gender roles, they have been slower to change than women in terms of actual practice, with the conflicts that arise over housework reflecting issues of identity and esteem for both genders. New patterns of living create new decisions that can encourage insecurity and disappointment, whilst continuing sexism amongst employers and the lack of nursery provision still present many challenges for the working woman.

Revised modernisation theory recognises that these social changes are moderated by a number of factors and that not all societal modernisations lead to greater opportunities for women: "although economic prosperity is *one* of the factors that [is] most strongly associated with [the] existence of an ethos of equality, . . . it is far from the whole story" (Inglehart & Norris, 2003, p. 35). Indeed, privatisation processes often lead to greater gender inequalities (Inglehart & Norris, 2003). Moderating factors for the influence of modernisation on gender roles include cultural heritages, with Latin American countries such as Colombia more egalitarian than postcommunist countries. Scarcity factors are likely to be important, too: A greater availability of men in the early years of the United States allowed women greater independence in their personal lives (LaPiere, 1965). Inglehart and Norris also recognise the existence of further moderators, including education, marital status, and generation. Thus, while there are few generational differences in these views in agrarian societies, there are substantial generational gaps in views on gender roles between those countries with sustained economic growth (such as Japan) or rapid economic growth (such as South Korea). In economically developing societies, the young are more egalitarian in their attitudes towards sex roles, whilst the generation gap is particularly large for women. Furthermore, values rarely change immediately: Adults usually retain childhood norms. Thus, in Western nations the interwar generations are more insecure, holding for a clearer demarcation in the division of household and parental responsibilities. Those born postwar exhibit more postmaterial values, with a rapid rise in egalitarian views of those born in the relative security of the 1950s, 1960s, and 1970s.

One particularly significant moderating factor for the impact of modernisation on gender roles is religion. Religion is generally seen as an important socialiser of moral values and social norms regarding gender equality, with religious organisations such as the Catholic Church seeking to reinforce traditional social norms in some countries (Inglehart, 2003). Industrial societies are generally only moderately religious, and postindustrial societies are markedly less so. Increased education and greater workforce participation correlate with large decreases in women's religious observance, although it is unclear whether it is women's life experiences that lead to less religiosity or whether it is their religious values that help influence their workplace choices. One notable exception to this is in the United States, where around 45 percent attend a religious service every week, a pattern similar to that in 1939 (www.worldvaluessurvey.org). In this country, some 80 percent of respondents claimed that they received strength and comfort from religion (ibid.).

Political changes, however, can have a profound impact on the influence of religious doctrine in a country and its implication for gender roles. Huntingdon (1996) claims that there has been a sharp "clash of civilisations," with different "core" civilisations defined largely by religion. He argues that there are sharp differences in core political values between those sharing Western Christian heritage and beliefs elsewhere, particularly in the Islamic world. These religious differences can lead to global conflict between nation states. Using the World Values Survey, Norris and Inglehart (2003) maintain that although there are many similar attitudes towards democracy in the West and in the Islamic world, the divide between the West and Islamic societies is strong in the domain of gender values. After the 1979 Iranian Islamic revolution that brought Ayatollah Khomeini to power, restrictions were placed on dress, reading materials, and contacts between men and women. Women were seen as at service to their men and were not allowed to leave home without their husband's permission (Turiel, 2002). In Kenya, increased education for women has combined with changing gender expectations and the influence of Christianity to lead to a marked decline in polygamous marriages. This figure stood in 1977 at 30 percent for Kenyan women, but it declined to 16 percent by 1998 (Wilson, Ngige, & Trollinger, 2003). Land use change and the scarcity of livestock similarly combined with gender role changes and Christian disapproval in leading to a decrease in the payment of bride-wealth (Wilson et al., 2003).

Inglehart and his colleagues at the World Values Survey are primarily interested in value change across cultures, and they provide important international data on this subject taken from an impressive range of societies. However, an important issue is the extent to which these values actually relate to behaviours similarly across cultures. Cultural habits and beliefs may add another layer to the translation of values into actual behaviours. Although it is of course possible to observe relatively noncontentious indicators of gender relations such as age at marriage or the number of women in employment, it is far more difficult to ascertain gender equality in the privacy of the home or family. Unfortunately, we have far more international data on values than actual behaviours, an important omission that should be addressed by future workers in this field.

The Role of Fathers

In Western societies at the start of the twentieth century, images of the male as breadwinner were very much part of the "fabric" of society (Lewis, 2003). Assumptions of full male employment were seen as underlying stable "natural" families, where homemaking wives supported their husbands. This echoed long-established concerns over men's obligations and the assumption that men needed family responsibilities to "civilise" them. However, by the 1980s social research increasingly noted the effects of a bad marriage on children. At the same time, a retreat from marriage was seen as threatening the maintenance of social order, with particular concerns about the impact of absent fathers on their offspring.

LaRossa et al. analysed fatherhood in the United States over six decades, from 1940 to 1999, using data from 490 Father's Day and Mother's Day comic strips (LaRossa et al., 2000). They argued that, on the one hand, an increase in dual-earner families has meant that more fathers are spending quality time with their children. On the other hand, a rise in divorce has meant that many fathers have only limited contact with their offspring. Their analyses revealed that the culture of fatherhood has changed over the years, but not in a simple way. In general, there had been an increase in the number of comic strip characters who are parents. There was also evidence that during the 1970s fathers were less likely to be mocked than in later decades. There was evidence for the supportive "new father" in the 1980s and 1990s, although many of the discussions of such fathers echoed previous debates dating back six decades. Overall, they claim, "fluctuation is the mode" (p. 386), with little evidence of a long-term acceptance of fathers in any particular role during these decades.

This theme of the "more expressive" role of fathers is taken up by Smit (2002) in South Africa. In this country, there has been a move from male-dominated affairs over the last few decades. Women now have a greater role in a more egalitarian and companion-based relationship. The "new" man in this situation identifies himself not only as a bread-winner but as a more active child-carer, too. Furthermore, although men may only be playing a small part in domestic tasks, Smit argues, they are doing more "emotional" work – but this may be moderated by social class and occupation. In his analysis, Smit interviewed 400 respondents from Guanteng province in South Africa. All were married men from an urban area, Afrikaans or English mother-tongue speakers, and members of dual-earning families where at least one residing child was not older than 13. Smit found that men in higher professional roles in particular did less domestic work, as their careers required a greater time commitment.

In the contemporary United Kingdom, there is only limited support for stereotyped notions of the mother as the family carer and the father as the prime worker outside the home (Dex, 2003). In fact, the typical family has both parents working, but sees the family as their priority. Both sexes dislike weekend working, seeing this as disruptive to their responsibilities at home. Perhaps unsurprisingly, those couples that do put their work needs ahead of their children tend to exhibit greater stress and higher divorce rates.

Gender Roles and Fertility Rates

Changing gender roles have been closely related to a decline in fertility rates. There is evidence of a fertility transition from higher to lower fertility in nearly all the countries of the world. For example, in the 1950s the average woman in Africa, Asia, and Latin America had around six children; by 1999, this was down to three (Townsend, 2003). This has been influenced by decisions to delay sex and marriage, to space out births, and to avoid unwanted pregnancies. It has also been affected by a move towards the use of contraceptives, with around 50 percent of married women now using contraceptives, compared to one-fifth of that 50 years ago (ibid.).

This decline in birthrates has become a particular issue of debate in Western societies (Beck & Beck-Gernsheim, 2002). Several factors have contributed to this, including women's drive for emancipation, the reduced influence of the Church, and the greater cost of children. The reproductive revolution, spearheaded in particular by the contraceptive pill, has transformed the taken-for-granted relationships between marriage, sex, conception, childbirth, and parenting, and it has allowed for new marital goals that do not include children (Coontz, 2004). As women are no longer limited to unpaid child rearing, but move towards more egalitarian work roles, childlessness has increased markedly since the 1970s in many postindustrial countries: "Women without children" thus no longer becomes a "contradiction in terms" (Hird & Abshoff, 2000). In New Zealand, Britain, and Canada, it is estimated that 20 percent of women currently of reproductive age will remain childless, although these societies still value childbearing. As women's identities continue to stretch beyond motherhood, we would expect this proportion of childlessness to rise (ibid.). In Latin America, as in much of the the rest of the world, greater education for women has been positively correlated with increased contraceptive use, later age at marriage, and fewer children (Schvaneveldt, 2003). Family formations have increasingly been compressed into a shorter time, between the end of a period of extended study and career development and the physiological limitations placed by the "biological clock" (Rothenbacher, 1998). Unsurprisingly, perhaps, there has been an almost universal increase in out-of-wedlock births in industrialised countries (De Mino, 2000).

It is important not to see the rise of modern and postmodern societies as leading to a complete rejection of the value of children. There are large numbers of people waiting to adopt children or to have the reproductive treatment sometimes necessary to enable children to be born to older parents (Beck & Beck-Gernsheim, 2002). Indeed, there is little evidence that "career women" do not wish to have children (ibid.). Furthermore, while modernisation is often seen as leading to declining fertility rates, it is actually in those European countries where economic development is less intensive and fewer women are in the workplace that we see the strongest evidence of a decline in fertility. Italy is one example of this trend (Polini, Quadrelli, & Rapari, 2004). In such countries, the great majority of births are in wedlock, and children are seen as optional and planned for when the economic conditions are right. The choice for a family is often made for when there is a stable parental presence in the home, usually the mother. In these families, quality of life is seen as important, rather than normative expectations for a child, and low fertility can be viewed as the result of the complexities involved in fulfilling multiple life projects.

THE RISE OF COHABITATION

In ancient Rome, differences between cohabitation and legal marriage were often subjective. For more than a millennium, the Catholic Church accepted that if a man and woman claimed that they had exchanged consenting vows, they were married regardless of where those vows took place (Coontz, 2004). Historically, living together in Latin America has been very common, partly because of a lack of funds to pay for the documentation and the ceremony required and also because of the Catholic Church's negative view on divorce. This left may still legally married to former partners with whom they no longer resided (Schvaneveldt, 2003).

However, the last decades have seen a marked growth in cohabitation in Western societies, beginning in most industrialised societies in the 1970s and accelerating in the 1980s and 1990s. In both the United States and Britain, this rise in cohabitation was initially amongst those whose first marriages ended in divorce – as a step towards remarriage – then spreading to those not yet married (Seltzer, 2004). In the United States, 0.4 million households were maintained by cohabiting heterosexual couples in 1960. By 2004, this number was nearer 4.6 million, with the greatest increase in these households occurring since the 1970s (ibid.). In the United Kingdom, only 5 percent of those who married for the first time between 1965 and 1969 lived together first. By the year 2000, more than half of the marrying couples lived together first (Allan, 2001). Similar figures are also reported for the United States (Huston & Melz, 2004).

For some, cohabitation has provided an important indicator of "the deinstitutionalisation of marriage" (Cherlin, 2004; Huston & Melz, 2004). Certainly, cohabitation has moved from a peripheral phenomenon to an accepted alternative to marriage in some countries, rather than just a "trial marriage." The proportion of U.S. cohabitations ending in marriage dropped from 60 percent in the 1970s to around one-third in the 1990s. Indeed, much social science research has moved from analysing simply the marital future of those who previously cohabited to studies of the children of those who have decided to only cohabit (Walker, 2004). There are a number of different reasons why a couple may cohabit, and these are likely to reflect both social class and individual differences (Lewis, 2003). Some may cohabit as a principled move, others as a trial marriage, whilst yet others see cohabitation as a "rational" response to difficult circumstances, often in a situation with low male wages and economic uncertainty. Those in the United Kingdom who do not marry but cohabit are likely to be less educated and to have experienced parental separation or divorce. Those who cohabit with children are likely to be young and poor and have only low levels of education. Cohabitation may also follow divorce, whereas economic or emotional barriers may restrict a wish to remarry.

Legislation has both followed and helped influence such trends. This reflects a movement in many States to recognise marriage more as a lifestyle than as a social institution (Allan, 2001). Kiernan (2004) has talked of "redrawing the boundaries of marriage," with marriage increasingly moving towards a ceremony confirming a union, rather than one at the commencement of this union. Whilst cohabitation has traditionally been seen as a less "committed," private arrangement, involving lesser investment and less likelihood of long-term investment (Cherlin, 2004), new laws have reflected the need to protect weaker family members who may have cohabitated for some time (Kiernan, 2004). There are, however, important cultural variations in this, even within Europe. In Scandinavia, distinctions between marriage and cohabitation seem relatively slight (Cherlin, 2004); in other countries, such as in the European Mediterranean, cohabitation is still a relatively fringe phenomenon. In Québec, Canada, cohabitation is seen as a reasonable basis for family life (Le Bourdais & Lapierre-Adamcyk, 2004), but in the remainder of the country it is more likely to be viewed as a childless prelude to marriage. These differences may have their origin in attitudes towards religion: Until the 1960s, Québécois society was heavily influenced by the Catholic Church, but it moved sharply away from this influence and the institution of marriage in subsequent decades. In other countries, however, cohabitation remains illegal, even though normatively there may a growing acceptance of it, particularly amongst the younger generation. Hence, in China cohabitation is still prohibited (Xu et al., 2007): However, Li and Xu (2004) found that more than half of their participants agreed that cohabitation is acceptable – if the couple intend to marry.

TECHNOLOGY AND THE FAMILY

Many of these family changes have been discussed in the light of technological change. Technology has had an important influence on the time a couple has available to perform various household tasks, which interact with other factors, such as the changes in gender roles discussed below. As an Institute for Social and Economic Research report (2004/2005) revealed, the way men and women spent their leisure time 40 years ago was very different from today. At that time, for women, "free days" – such as Sundays – were at least half occupied with domestic duties. Technology helped relieve both sexes of some of this burden. For women, work outside the home also led to changes in the division of tasks. Work patterns for men and women have become increasingly similar, with men doing less paid work and more unpaid work and women having more paid work and less unemployment.

Politicians have frequently scapegoated the mass media for the supposed decline in family life (Douglas, 2003). Just as there were earlier concerns about the influence of the romantic novel on nineteenth-century women, television is seen as helping shape expectations about modern relationships, providing "a consensual reality" (p. 12). However, whilst the media present a strong *sense* of change, this is more often inferred than observed in media outputs. Content-based media studies have shown that conversations on television still tend to follow traditional gender-based models, where husbands offer advice to their wives and children. Such studies also demonstrate that children in the media are increasingly dependent on their parents, not only for instruction, but also for mutual supportiveness and openness. At the same time, viewer-based studies indicate that such parent–child and sibling relationships are frequently problematic. One reason for this may be that the challenging situations often presented by TV dramas serve to emphasise potential problems in the parent–child interaction.

The impact of the internet on the family has also been increasingly examined. As with the earlier discussion of the effects of technology on personal lives, there is evidence of both positive and negative takes on the ways in which the internet and other new technologies interact with daily family life (Chesley, 2005). Some argue that the advent of the personal computer and other technological developments permits too great a permeability between work and family boundaries. From this perspective, work spillover leads to negative outcomes, promoting overwork and allowing employers to have employees "on call" at all times. Others see the advantages of increased ease of communication in the workplace as well as at home. From their viewpoint, work spillover permits flexibility and the reduction of work versus family conflict (ibid.). Using longitudinal data from the Cornell Couples and Career Study, Chesley suggests that it is communications technology rather than just computer use per se that is linked to negative spill-over. In these data, negative spillover occurred for both men and women, particularly evident with the use of mobile phones for work purposes, which were linked to higher distress and lower family satisfaction.

There are similar debates over the impact on the family of teen-agers' internet usage (Wang, Bianchi, & Raley, 2005). Wang in the United States argues that whilst some parents appreciate the role of the internet in helping their children with their schoolwork, others are concerned about the possible isolating effects of heavy computer use, its impact on the fitness of their children, and the risks associated with exposure to unsuitable strangers or pornography. Parents may also feel isolated and unable to relate to a medium where their children know more about the technology than they do. Using data from the Pew Internet and American Life Project, Wang finds that there are important subgroup/socialisation moderators in how the internet influences the family, with the parents' own technological experiences and internet usage related to the rules imposed on wider internet use in the family (Wang et al., 2005).

RAPID CHANGE: SOME EXAMPLES

The above provides a summary of some key debates in the sociological and psychological literature over family change. Most of these data were collected in Western nations, in particular the United States, and it is not clear the extent to which many of these putative changes have occurred in other parts of the world. As I argued in Chapter 1, the pace and types of responses to cultural change vary by culture and a family's adaptation to local conditions and constraints. Furthermore, many of the changes discussed above occurred over a relatively long period of time and, in terms of the model I introduced in Chapter 1, were influenced by a gradual change in values and beliefs. Many more direct political interferences and unexpected events have also had impacts on marital relationships. These can take several forms and are often an amalgam of policies and programmes: They might include the provision of early-childhood care or education such as in kindergartens, changes in parental-leave policy, and subsidies for those who have (or do not have) children or live as marital partners (Rostgaard, 2004). I consider these in more detail now in a review of some of the dramatic changes that have occurred over the last decades in three major world regions – Eastern Europe, Asia, and the Middle East – and their implications for marriage and family across the lifespan. I then consider the direct impact of war and migration on family relations.

Eastern Europe

A considerable number of political transitions occurred in the early 1990s across the former communist nations of Eastern and Central Europe. Real wages dropped more than 25 percent in Poland during 1990, and food prices increased 1,200 percent in Bulgaria that year. Particular groups, such as elderly women (who retire early and live longer than men), were especially at risk of poverty (Einhorn, 1993). A 1992 survey across Central Europe showed considerable dissatisfaction amongst a range of social groups with the changes then occurring in the region (ibid.).

A major concern has been the impact of the economic and political transitions on employment (in particular, women's employment) and the related effects of political uncertainties on fertility rates. According to Engels (1884), it was essential for women to play a major part in production, and they were to be distracted only to a minor extent by their domestic duties. Marxist ideology emphasised the importance of equal participation in the workforce and sought mechanisms to encourage (and enforce) this. In contrast to the existing religious practices of some constituent states of the Soviet Union before 1918, the Soviet Family Code (1918) viewed marriage as a union of equal partners that either could dissolve. The former centrally planned governments of Eastern Europe guaranteed employment rights for all of their working-age populations, with high rates of labour force participation for women. Thus, some 80 percent of women worked in these communist countries, helping address "the woman question" (Rostgaard, 2004). Full-time work for all was encouraged by government propaganda, in addition to the real material need for a family to earn two salaries in these low-wage economies. Working mothers were particularly strongly supported after the late 1960s due to low fertility rates. Employed mothers with children under 16 were allowed shorter hours. Inexpensive child care and after-school care were provided, and special allowances were paid for single mothers or families with many children. Government policies helped women combine family and paid work, with men in the GDR more likely to put family first when changing jobs (Trappe & Rosenfeld, 2000). Thus, in East Germany the government aimed to keep women fully employed – in contrast to further west in Germany, where full-time mothering was encouraged and where there were greater incentives to stay at home (ibid.). By the end of the 1980s, nearly 75 percent of women earned the full 43.75 hours a week, compared to only 30 percent of West Germans working full time (ibid.). These long hours of work did not make the lives of women at this time particularly easy. Alongside the traditional double burden of full-time work and domestic and child care duties, women in these countries often had the additional burden of expected participation in local committees and organisations. Few communist regimes recognised the persistence of sexual inequalities and were quick to reject Western feminist critiques as interference from unwelcome outsiders.

Whilst there was some evidence of rejection of Marxist gender roles and a return to the traditional attitudes towards the family even before 1989 in some countries, the harsh economic demands that followed the collapse of communism, coupled with a change in ideological demands, located women back at the centre of the family (Einhorn, 1993; Moghadam, 2004). Women left the workforce (Rostgaard, 2004) for several reasons. These included an acceptance of the need for "professional mothers," coupled with a new climate of child rearing, the unwillingness of employers to hire women (in particular to provide part-time jobs), and a decline in day care, with women with young children having little alternative but to stay at home (ibid.). A sharp rise in unemployment following the transitions in most of these countries meant that by the early years of the new millennium employment rates amongst women had dropped markedly, particularly in the new private-sector economies. Many previous low-level bureaucratic jobs staffed by women were now eliminated. Men's jobs were now particularly important in dictating job movement at a time when the new market forces conspired to favour the employment of men and when women were seen as "unreliable" workers who required child care leave (Einhorn, 1993; Trappe & Rosenfeld, 2000). Most post-communist regimes provided few new possibilities for women to protest against their employment status (Haskova & Krizkova, 2003). Indeed, any such protest was seen as threatening a new national identity. In the Czech Republic, for example, major political parties such as the Christian Democratic Union strongly opposed what they saw as measures to undermine traditional family values and roles. Despite the ascension to the EU and the implications of this for the adoption of new pan-European gender equality regulations, equal-opportunities legislation was largely viewed as a Western European import that could threaten a traditional Czech belief in the comple-mentary roles of men and women. Despite some concessions on pay discrimination and domestic violence, new emphasis was placed on individual rights, seen as representing a genderless liberal ideology but often ignoring the increasing economic inequality between the sexes (ibid.).

In this post-Soviet world, media images rejected the grim heroic determinism of the communist woman, replacing her with a new, glamorous woman who reflected the position of her husband or father (Einhorn, 1993). Mothers came to be portrayed in near mythological terminology, with many of these changes accompanied by pro-natalist policies, as a result of pressure from religious groups and conservative parties (ibid.). Thus, women's reproductive/nurturant roles were seen as central to the survival of a new national/ethnic sense of community and as a reaction against old State Socialism and statism, which was viewed as undermining the family and was blamed for high rates of divorce and other social ills (ibid.). Whilst this pressure did lead to some improvement in terms of maternity or paternity leave, it was accompanied by a strong emphasis on encouraging women to stay at home, partly as an attempt to ease labour market pressures (Rostgaard, 2004). Indeed, the traditional family model was now seen as a focus for a new self-determined identity and for new postcommunist values. Thus, whilst market economics was sending women back into the home, nationalists were telling them to have babies (Einhorn, 1993). Writing at this time of transition, Einhorn (ibid.) summarises this well:

The image of the female tractor driver is out, as is Superwoman wearing a hard-hat on a building site. Cinderella of fairy-tale fantasy and dreams is back. ... She works ... but only in the household, so that her feminine qualities are not marred by the fatigue and premature ageing incurred by the hardships of the double burden. This picture may be pretty, but it signals a nineteenth-century model of domesticated women with no claim to citizenship rights in society (p. 216). ... [I]n the current period of chaos and complexity, there is resort to the "feminine principle" as the solution to the nation's ills (p. 218).

Birthrates were an issue of some concern, both during the communist era and following the collapse of this system. Family allowances and parental leave were relatively generous during the communist system. In the GDR, for example, the 1950 Act for the Protection of Mother and Child and the Rights of Women allowed for the creation of State child care facilities, maternity grants, and relatively generous paid maternity leave (Einhorn, 1993). Heavily subsidised meals for children provided at least some social security for poorer families. The region as a whole displayed a comparatively low age at marriage, a high marriage rate, and a high percentage of married people compared to the West (Rothenbacher, 1998). The economic reforms of the 1990s led to the abandonment of simple pro-natalist policies of supporting larger families, as well as the removal of many benefits for larger families, which were viewed as inconsistent with the principles of a market economy (Rostgaard, 2004). The abolition of nurseries or kindergartens provided by employers led to a marked drop in the assistance traditionally available for poorer women (Haskova & Krizkova, 2003). In the days of the GDR, for example, the family represented a private refuge from the State and played an important part in people's lives. Although East German women were strongly job-oriented, viewing their work not only as financially important but also as a mark of esteem and social recognition, cutbacks in the government's provision for children, and high levels of unemployment meant that they had to deal with a market economy and could not risk being single mothers. Increased economic pressures also led to a decline in family allowances as a share of GDP, with growing economic uncertainties making young couples anxious about the costs of rearing children (Beck & Beck-Gernsheim, 2002). Perhaps unsurprisingly, this resulted in postcommunist Europe producing some of the lowest fertility rates in the world (Rostgaard, 2004). The decline was most marked in the Christian Orthodox countries, such as Latvia, which exhibited a 40 percent decline in its total fertility rate over a period of little more than a decade, and a decline in the Eastern German birthrate of 60 percent between 1989 and 1994. In Poland, the fertility rate (total births per woman) was 2.08 in 1989 but had fallen to 1.40 in 1999. In Russia, the decline was from 2.01 to 1.25 in the same period (Svejnar, 2002). Whilst the political and social changes occurring at the time should not be seen as the sole cause of this fertility decline (a general decline in fertility in the industrialised world was also evident during this time), the speed of these changes does appear remarkable (Rostgaard, 2004). The changes were accompanied by an increase in births outside of marriage, resulting in a general, if largely unplanned, movement to a pattern more representative of countries further West.

Divorce rates increased rapidly during the State Socialism period, with Czechoslovakian, Hungarian, Soviet, and East German divorce rates amongst the highest in the world (Einhorn, 1993). Despite the persistence of strong romantic ideals, it was often very hard to live in tiny apartments, which were frequently shared with parents. In addition, due to a chronic shortage of housing, many marriages were organised rapidly in order to move up the list of available housing stock. The interpersonal impacts of the postcommunist transformations would seem to have done little to secure the institution of marriage. This is demonstrated in Hraba, Lorenz, and Pechacova's (2000) study of family stress during the Czech transformation. Economic problems, with high rates of inflation and a decline in guaranteed employment, had been a feature of this country since the late 1980s. In a panel survey of 4,000 Czech households, Hraba and colleagues examined three waves of Czech data. They found that the family economic pressures evident in 1994 led to a dynamic relational process that threatened marital stability for both husbands and wives. Economic pressures made both partners irritable, which increased other problems, such as drinking and depression. Irritability in 1994 was directly related to spousal hostility in 1995 and later marital instability. A similar picture is painted in Vannoy and Cubbins's (2001) analysis of Russia, which they claim to be "a curious mixture of ideology and attitudes." They argue that despite equality in employment, education, and income during communism, there was evidence of a strong and persisting patriarchal tradition in the country. As noted above, the economic and social transformation in Russia in the late 1980s and the

1990s led to a greater emphasis on traditional gender stereotypes and a stronger adherence to models of the "traditional family." Using data from a multistage cluster probability sample in urban Moscow in 1996, Vannoy and Cubbins (ibid.) found that economic expectations interacted with gender expectations, so that women who earned more than their husbands were perceived by wider society as "deviant," – and indeed reported lower levels of marital satisfaction. Rates of egalitarian marriages decreased from 46 percent in 1989 to 37 percent in 1995. The authors see this reversion to traditional marital arrangements as a result of the difficult economic problems faced by Russian citizens. In another interview study of nearly 1,000 couples in Moscow and rural Pskov and Saratov (Vannoy et al., 1999), Vannoy again found evidence of the persistence of traditional gender attitudes in all three locations. In each sample, women had the main responsibility for child care, and this had led to notable dissatisfaction amongst the wives. A possible exception to the above can be found in the Georgian Republic during the 1990s (Sumbadze, 2006). Sumbadze suggests that the economic challenges of this time actually increased the opportunities for women because they were perceived as offering labour that was more adaptive to the labour market than their male counterparts'. Women's ability to provide vital resources during this time of transition undermined some of the traditional authoritarianism of their husbands – a liberation that parallels some of the movement towards egalitarianism heralded by Giddens and his colleagues and discussed above. Sumbadze suggests that these findings demonstrate some of the particular characteristics of Georgian society and underline the significance of culture as moderator in the relationship between rapid economic transition and family relations.

For all this, there is little evidence that the economic transformations of the 1990s in Eastern Europe actually destroyed marriages (Svejnar, 2002). Rather than increasing divorce, the insecurity of this period probably contributed to a decline in divorce rates in many countries. In Georgia, the divorce rate declined from 9,000 in 1990 to 1,600 in 1999, as couples maintained their relationships to help deal with the difficulties of the time. In Central Europe, divorce rates per 1,000 inhabitants were almost identical in 1989 and 2000; in the Baltic States and in the Commonwealth of Independent States of Russia, Ukraine, and Kazakhstan, they actually fell (from 4.0 to 3.1 in Russia). In contrast, these figures rose in the United States, the United Kingdom, and Germany during that same period (ibid.).

Asia

Birthrate

The high birthrate in Asia – and attempts to curb this fertility – have been a major topic of discussion for researchers interested in social change. While imbalanced sex ratios are frequently found in different populations, in China and some other parts of Asia (for example, India and Bangladesh), these ratios are particularly marked (Secondi, 2002). In these countries, there are considerably more men than women.

In Chinese society, males have generally been more highly valued (Liu, 2006; Secondi, 2002). Rural families, in particular, may treat the sexes as worthy of different investments. Although traditionally any dowry (paid by the woman's family) and bride-price (paid by the man's family) might be similar in size, only the son could carry the family line and reputation and pay homage to the family's ancestors. Male agricultural labour may be particularly valued, with sons traditionally living in the same village and contributing to the household for a longer period of time. In contrast, females might join the family of the husband. Parents also expect greater support in old age from sons. In interviews conducted in 1999, Liu (2006) notes how the daughter is seen as less reliable once she marries outside the family. The one-child policy, introduced in China to deal with the country's high fertility rate in 1979, allowed urban families in China just one child – or two in the countryside if the first child was a girl, usually following a five-year wait. Failure to follow this ruling could lead to a range of punishments, including fines, confiscations, and dismissal from work (Hesketh, Li, & Xing, 2005). It is important to note that this legislation applied to only a minority of mainland Chinese, as 70 percent of the population live in rural locations (Ding & Hesketh, 2006; Hesketh et al., 2005). In fact, there are a number of exceptions to this: In Zhejiang, for example, a couple is exempt from this policy if the first child has defects, if in a remarriage one partner has no previous child, if the couple belongs to specified occupational groups, or if both partners are from one-child families (Hesketh & Zhu, 1997). In addition, third and fourth children are allowed for some ethnic minorities and in areas of underpopulation (ibid.). The policy was reinforced by new financial incentives introduced in 2007 involving annual payments for parents in the countryside when they reach the age of 60 – if they have one child or two girls.

The effects of this policy on abortion practices, child rearing, and wider gender and family relations have spurred considerable debate in China and further afield. Certainly, the total fertility rate (mean number of children per woman) fell from 2.9 in 1979 to 1.7 in 2004, with one child now predominant in urban areas and two in rural residences (Hesketh et al., 2005). There is also evidence that most women desire small families, with the great majority wanting no more than two children (Ding & Hesketh, 2006). There have also been large decreases in fertility in other Asian countries at this time – in fact, the most dramatic fall in fertility in China was during the 1970s (that is, before the introduction of the one-child policy). Of particular concern has been whether the one-child policy has led to an increase in female infanticide, with parents thought to resort to either abortion or the killing of the newborn girl to ensure that they have a boy. In particular, the ability to identify a foetus's gender gives parents the opportunity to abort the foetus, whilst others may attempt to conceal a female birth or give up a newborn girl for adoption to have another chance at having a son (ibid.; Hesketh et al., 2005). Parents may also, consciously or subconsciously, differentially allocate nutrients and health care to boys and girls, influencing the child mortality rates of the two sexes (Secondi, 2002). Where selection takes place, it is more likely to be with the first child in urban areas, the second child in rural locations (Ding & Hesketh, 2006).

To test the direct impact of the one-child policy, Secondi examined the 1988 Chinese Household Income Project, a survey conducted by researchers in 1989, with more than 13,000 children aged 1 to 14 included in the survey. The data showed an average sex ratio of 111.5 – very high by Western standards. However, the analysis also suggested that a bias in the sex ratio actually occurred prior to the one-child policy, with a balanced sex ratio achieved at a time when the policy was most strictly enforced, when concealing births became more difficult. However, the data also demonstrated that when looking only at first-born children, lower-income parents were more likely to have a higher ratio of surviving sons to daughters. The desire to have sons is widespread amongst both rich and poor families, but first-born girls may present a luxury that only richer families feel they can afford.

The impact of the large imbalance in sex ratios has led to a number of concerns in China about the social disruption that can occur when men are unable to find a partner (Ding & Hesketh,

2006). This has led the Chinese government to mount a number of campaigns to encourage the valuation of women, and there is indeed evidence that a preference for boys may be declining. Thus, a national planning survey found that 37 percent of women had no sex preference for their child and 45 percent claimed that an ideal family had both a boy and a girl (ibid.).

In Singapore, different governments and economic conditions have differentially encouraged large families (Yun, 2004). Despite some persistence in traditional Chinese family patterns, there is a great deal of evidence for the impact of industrialisation and urbanisation over the last four decades in this country. When industrial development started in the 1960s, childbearing couples were told that "two is (more than) enough," and preference was given for housing to small families. However, a labour shortage in the 1980s meant that selected educated groups were encouraged to have larger families. Tax incentives were given to increase reproduction amongst those with higher incomes, with the slogan "three or more, if you can afford it." There are, however, considerable religious differences in birthrate in Singapore: The Muslim population has more children (3.1) compared to the Chinese (2.5) and Indian ethnic groups (2.4) (2000 Census of Singapore). Wisendale (2000) in Vietnam examined the large and unexpected population growth in this country in recent decades. Because of this growth, the government has encouraged delayed marriages and an ideal family size of two children. Those who meet government guidelines get a week's holiday in a seaside resort, a month's salary, and early workplace promotion. Wisendale argues that there are some signs that this is helping steady the population increase.

As family size in general declines, one hypothesis is that the husband–wife relationship will become more emotive, partially replacing the parent–child bond (Koh & Tan, 2000). Koh and Tan examined parent–child relationships amongst middle class Chinese in Singapore. Evidence from their interviews suggested that, far from a decline in the parent–child bond, this bond is actually getting stronger. Thus, family relationships are changing so that "emotionality becomes central not only in conjugal relationships but also in parent–child relationships" (p. 526). The result is a general "emotional nucleation" of the family (p. 527), a theme I return to again below.

Family and Residence Arrangements

The Chinese family has traditionally been seen as a functional, stable, and effective unit, with clear social roles (LaPiere, 1965). The ideal Chinese family contained several generations, but, as was the case in many other countries, this pattern was largely confined to wealthy families (Fukuyama, 1995). Fukuyama describes a cyclical evolution of families, from nuclear to stem to joint and back to nuclear over time. The permission for wealthy men to take multiple wives or concubines, coupled with jealousies between brothers or their wives, often undermined family stability, leading to some fractures in the family household. More recently, urbanisation and geographical mobility have weakened lineages, with large joint or extended families being replaced by conjugal ones. Indeed, even in rural China the norm is for nuclear households with between three and six members (Xu et al., 2007). Ironically, the family has now reconstituted itself in something of its patrilineal form, with the "traditional family" seen as the only trustworthy organisation set against a changing society and a vital provider of stability and certainty for old age. Self-sufficient peasants have now been given a chance to return to traditional bonds and former family enterprises (Fukuyama, 1995). These closer family structures have often been complemented by the search for common demonstrated descent (ibid.). These descent lines demand lesser loyalty than the immediate family, but they can provide the basis for trust and allow for the expansion of a family business. These and other presumed lineages may be of particular significance for modern Chinese businesses in the Pacific Rim, where lineages continue from those established on the mainland.

Residence patterns have changed quite markedly over the last few decades in some Asian countries, such as Japan and the Philippines (Logan, Bian, & Bian, 1998). However, national and local politics have had a significant impact on family residence in China, which has actually led to a relatively stable residence situation. Fei Xiaotong (1982, cited in Logan et al., 1998) found that whilst 49 percent of rural Chinese households included a parent with married children in 1936, this figure had decreased by only 6 percent by 1981. Thus, residence patterns were consonant with a traditional family that appeared to have disappeared half a century beforehand. Logan argues that here behaviours do not necessarily follow values, but may simply be a result of responses to daily needs and living circumstances. In Chinese society, restraints imposed by the State and local government officers on housing policy and public services for children and the elderly have had a notable impact on family life. For example, a greater construction of housing in Tianjin meant an increase in living space for young couples, who were then more likely than their counterparts in Shanghai to be offered their own place to live (Logan et al., 1998). At the same time, some traditional gender preferences in living arrangements have persisted. For example, some families have tried to arrange homes for married sons when the housing stock was scarce, although a lack of adequate child care has often meant coresidence with the family to help support the working woman. Parents are more likely to live with a child if they have a son rather than only daughters; similarly, a daughter with a brother is less likely to live with parents. Younger married couples rarely lived with the wife's parents, and married couples are more likely to live with the wife's parents if she has no brothers. Education had little impact on these patterns. Logan et al. conclude that State policies have combined with traditional gendered practices to help shape residence patterns in contemporary China.

Pimentel and Liu (2004) examined life histories of coresidence with wives' parents in urban China for cohorts married during the Cultural Revolution, its aftermath (1966–1979), and the early reform period (1980–1991). Coresidence opportunities during the Cultural Revolution were affected by families being sent to the countryside or to labour reform camps. A chronic lack of housing supply and the reliance on bicycles for transportation limited the development of new suburbs. During the reform period, the 1980 Marriage Law allowed men to marry at age 22 and women at 20. This led to a rush of younger marriages in the early 1980s. But because this group was less likely to have qualified for its own housing, there was an increase in coresidence. Although labour laws did allow young adults more mobility and new business opportunities, a massive increase in living expenses in urban settings still meant that coresidence with parents was an important option.

Pimentel and Liu (2004) also consider the modernisation hypothesis that increased education, free mate choice, older age at marriage, and urban residence decrease parental control over younger generations and reduce the likelihood of young people living with their parents after marriage (Goode, 1963). They argue that freedom of mate selection allows for an increased relationship power for women, meaning that it may be the woman's parents rather than the husband's who are now preferred for residence. Education (of both the couple and their parents) may be a further factor in encouraging a breaking with tradition. The availability of housing stock and the length of the working day are additional major factors in residence patterns. Yi (2001) underlines this in an analysis of Chinese family household structure, using 1982–1995 census data. There have been high degrees of coresidence in urban areas, primarily due to the long waiting lists for government apartments. Furthermore, although there has been a decrease in family size since the 1970s, there is little evidence of an increase in one-person households, with most families living in small family households. Although there is a preference amongst both the young and the old for independent living, housing shortages are having an important impact. Thus, "Contrary to the expectations of the influence of industrialization and urbanization, the changes in Chinese family households in the 1980s and in the first half of the 1990s are chiefly the outcome of direct government intervention" (p. 31).

Divorce across Asia has been growing in the last few decades (Wisendale, 2000), and Chinese attitudes towards divorce have changed markedly in the last half-century. Divorce doubled following the introduction of the 1980 Marriage Law, which made absence of love a primary criterion for relationship breakdown. A failure for the partner to "deliver" in the more materialistic 1980s led to an increase in marital dissatisfaction and a rise in divorce (Honig & Hershatter, 1988). Although divorce rates were low by Western standards, they did increase substantially in the 1980s, especially in urban areas. However, rates of remarriage are also very high, with more older people now remarrying: Ninety-six percent of divorcé(e)s remarry, 83 percent within five years (Yi, 2001). Notably, however, some of the declared relationship status statistics are a direct result of registration demands: Yi observes that changes in household registration booklets around 1990 led many to declare themselves as single in order to get particular rations. Divorce rates also vary by geographic regions: In 2004, the highest rates were in Shanxi, the lowest in Tibet (Xu et al., 2007).

The development of free trade provided new temptations for mobile businessmen – "astronauts" – working for long periods overseas. Mainland China's acceptance of free trade in the 1980s led to most manufacturing industries in Hong Kong opening up on the mainland. By the mid-1990s, around 25,000 Hong Kong factories had moved, and large enterprises opened Chinese offices. Many single men in Hong Kong were attracted by mainland Chinese women, and the women themselves were tempted by the relative affluence of Hong Kong men. Often these men lived apart from their families for long periods, and this, of course, created opportunities for them to have extramarital affairs or take new wives in mainland China (Kung et al., 2004). Needless to say, these relationships were often strained when their new wives moved to Hong Kong, with husbands forced to adjust to their new responsibilities.

Gender and Employment

For a thousand years in China, men were more likely to work outside the home, women inside the home (Lu, Maume, & Bellas, 2000). Indeed, until 1911 most women had bound feet and rarely worked in fields or factories. However, with the establishment of the People's Republic in 1949 and the Great Leap Forward in 1958, many women entered the workforce. As in other communist societies, labour force participation was key to gender equality. Thus, in the early 1990s 90 percent of urban Chinese aged 16 to 54 were employed.

Lu et al. (2000) examined data from the 1991 Household Survey of the China Health and Nutrition Study. In this study of more than 14,000 individuals, they found that urban husbands spent more time on household labour than rural husbands and were more likely to do so if they had employed wives, more education, and earnings more similar to their wives'. However, their data also showed that although most Chinese women worked, the vast majority of the housework was done by the wives. They argue that although there is some progress evident towards greater equality in doing housework chores, as in most societies across the world full equality has yet to be achieved. There is some evidence, however, to suggest a gradual increase in parity in women's decision making and gender role equality in the home, as well as some sharing of household burdens (Xu et al., 2007). Indeed, a study of more than 19,000 Chinese participants from a wide range of provinces suggests that most believe that husbands and wives should share household responsibilities (ibid.).

Traditionally, women in Taiwan were more likely to leave work after marriage and childbirth than their mainland counterparts. However, the development of export zones during the 1960s and

1970s meant that many middle-aged married women joined unmarried women in the workforce, with the most notable increases taking place between 1966 and 1973. There has been a steady decline in continuous employment as females' age cohort progresses, with older women more likely to participate in the informal sector as family or agricultural workers. Full-time participation in outside work leaves little time to do housework. And if this work is of high status, then others are also hired to deal with child care or house management tasks (Fukuyama, 1995). Yi and Chien (2002) examined employment and gender and familial role demands in Taiwan, Tianjin, and Shanghai. The massive economic changes that occurred in the late 1970s in mainland China meant that new gender roles emerged in rural areas, reminiscent of earlier times. Men frequently took employment elsewhere, and women stayed to manage farms. As in postcommunist Europe, privatisation of industries meant that women were the first to lose their jobs, whilst the State promoted an ideology of women returning to the family to deal with unemployment pressures. However, the impact of this depended on rural or urban location. In Tianjin, there is evidence of a feminisation of the farming business in the rural areas. In contrast, economic reform in the large cities led to nonconventional work for females outside the family residence, as well as longer periods of continuous employment.

Yun (2004) noted that fewer than 20 percent of married women were in the labour force in Singapore in the late 1960s. However, by 1999 women constituted 56 percent of the workforce. Young women, especially the more educated, increasingly valued their personal independence and autonomy and were often unwilling to give this up for their husband or child, which often led to struggles with their husbands. These women, however, received little support from a Singaporean State that persisted in promoting patriarchy and traditional family values. In Vietnam, families have tried to navigate the tricky path between egalitarian socialism, which had begun in that country in the 1940s, and a policy of free-market capitalism, *do moi*, adopted in 1986 (Wisendale, 2000). The 1959 Marriage and Family Law removed cultural barriers that had stopped women from working in "male jobs," leading to significant improvements in female literacy and education. State provision was introduced for women to help keep them in the workforce – for example, through the provision of child care facilities. In addition, legislation was introduced to protect the basic rights of both men and women for freedom from abuse and oppression at home. In 1986, legislation reiterated equality between husbands and wives and the rights and duties of parents, grandparents, children, and grandchildren. However, there is evidence that the move to a free-market society has led to greater gender inequality, with a decline in child care facilities and a downsizing of government jobs, where many women were employed. Although there are still relatively high levels of female economic activity, there have also been cuts in maternity leave.

Kwon et al. (2003) examined marital relationships following the Korean economic crisis of the late 1990s. They drew on Boss's family stress model, which views economic conditions as providing important external contextualising variables for families. A stressful economic context can lead to families cutting down on food, clothing, housing, medical care, and educational expenditures, with economic stresses also increasing emotional stress in the family. Traditional normative gender roles can also become challenged, as wives blame their husbands for incompetence in being unable to support the family financially. As couples experience economic difficulties, they become frustrated, angry, and emotionally distressed. Kwon also found a direct pathway between economic pressure and marital conflict, with consequent impacts on marital satisfaction. Unlike in U.S. studies, however, there was little evidence of family resilience through husbands' emotional expression, with a direct effect between economic pressure and marital conflict in Korea. These data are supported by court records in Korea, showing that following the crises there was an increased number of divorces arising from family financial problems.

The Middle East

Marriage
Marriage has traditionally been seen as a fundamental obligation for both men and women in the Arab world. However, increased work and education have made it possible for women to be important contributors to the financial status of their family, reducing the pressures for early marriage. Indeed, there has been a notable increase in age at marriage in recent decades, with the average age at marriage in some Arab countries amongst the highest in the world (Moaddel & Azadarmaki, 2003). This has

questioned the presumed universality of marriage in Arab Muslim countries. In addition, there is evidence of greater independence amongst conjugal couples, reflecting some Western notions of separation and individuation (Cohen & Savaya, 2003).

In Kuwait, the percentage of single women aged over 15 almost doubled from 1965 to 2000, whilst the percentage currently married dropped from 67 percent to 56 percent. Similarly, the percentage of women single at age 29 rose from 5 percent (1965) to 23 percent (2000) (Moaddel & Azadarmaki, 2003). The formation of relationships has also changed in Kuwait. Greater employment has allowed a large number of women the opportunity to meet potential suitors in the workplace. Polygamy has decreased with the increase in literacy and educational level and increased intolerance of wives for polygamy and the higher cost of maintaining multiple families. There has also been a decline in consanguineous marriage (marriage with a relative), from more than 50 percent in 1983 to 35 percent in 1999 (ibid.).

Divorce rates are generally low in the Arab world. Cohen and Savaya (2003) examined the reasons given for divorce by Muslim Arab men and women in Israel, interviewing 312 Muslim citizens of Israel who had divorced between the mid-1980s and 1997. Sixteen percent of their sample suggested conflicts over traditionalism and modernity as a reason for their divorce. Almost all women complained that their ex-husbands had been too traditional, while men were divided: Half complained that their ex-wives had been too traditional, half that they had been too modern. Cohen and Savaya interpret this finding as indicating that modernisation has affected Arab men in Israel in a complex manner, with some preferring the better-educated, more independent partner.

Gender
Cohen and Savaya (2003) claim that the traditional Arab family is authoritarian, patriarchal, and hierarchical. The man is seen as "master of the household," with the wife having sole responsibility for household duties and expected to obey and satisfy her husband. Women are viewed as repositories of family honour; as a result, there has been strict gender supervision and separation in some Arab nations and restrictions on women's behaviour, especially on dress and contact with men outside the family. A relatively extreme example is under the Taliban in Afghanistan, but there are also strict

laws concerning women's dress in Iran and some sanctioning of honour killings in Jordan (Moghadam, 2004). In Sudan, tribes and nomadic groups have maintained a high degree of patriarchy. In Egypt, poor families live in a patriarchal system where the wife is expected to be loyal and respectful to her husband. Although she may be critical of her spouse, particularly when defending her children's interests, the woman will also accept the greater freedom of her spouse in the relationship (Wikan, 1996). Traditional gender norms in Egypt favour the man by giving him a greater allocation of resources (such as education). Although there are gender changes in these norms, with women demonstrating more egalitarian beliefs and autonomy, women are still more dependent on their spouses for major family decisions than those in the West (Severy et al., 2003). Data from 1995 and 2000 national surveys note that three-quarters of women do not select their own spouses, violence in marriage is not rare, female clitor-dectomy circumcision is wide-spread, and boys continue to have greater educational opportunities than girls, although the latter differentiation is decreasing.

There is evidence, however, of challenge to these patterns in some Arab settings. Women's education and participation in the labour force have gradually made the maintenance of patriarchal hierarchy and restrictions on Arab women harder to justify (Cohen & Savaya, 2003). Arab Palestinian women in Israeli society are increasingly educated and work more now outside the home. This can be relatively disruptive for traditional family and gender relations, while the mass media and contact with the Israeli Eurocentric Jewish population have had impacts on values and patterns of life via education. The *hamula*, the traditional Arab kinship network, has decreased in size, its economic power has been reduced, and the status and authority of elders have been undermined. Adult sons employed in the Israeli economy have become increasingly more economically independent of their families of origin, and they are less likely to continue to cohabit with their families of origin.

The United Arab Emirates (UAE) is a federation of seven states that formed an Arab nation in 1971. Oil was discovered in Abu Dhabi in 1958, which contributed to a very rapid economic development. Schvaneveldt examined matched pairs of daughters and mothers in these states in a questionnaire study (Schvaneveldt, Kerpelman, & Schvaneveldt, 2005). Consonant with most modern-isation theorists, daughters were less traditional in their attitudes towards early marriage than mothers and were more likely to want to choose their own husbands. They also desired fewer children and greater equality in child care roles.

Family

The modern Muslim view sees family as the fundamental unit of society and stresses the mother's role in the socialisation of children (Moghadam, 2004). Yet at the same time, the family has also become a powerful signifier and index of social change, reflecting current debates within Islam. Indeed, in Moghadam's words, "Muslim family law has become a field of contestation amongst feminists, fundamentalists, and the state" (p. 157). Whilst extended-family households have become less prevalent and the patriarchal extended family has been weakened by migration, particular policies have formally reinforced patriarchal systems. Moghadam identifies three conflicting trends in the Middle East and North Africa: (1) an expansion of industrialisation, urbanisation, proleterianisation, and State-sponsored education, which undermines tribes, extended family units, and patriarchal family authority; (2) the retention of Muslim family law, which legitimises prerogatives of male family members over females; and (3) women's demands for greater civil, political, and social rights on the basis of global discourses and conventions.

A number of contemporary trends in Arab societies illustrate these tensions. In Turkey, there has been continuing debate about the relationship between religion, state, and family since Ataturk replaced the existing Family Law with a secular law in 1926. In the early days of Islam in the UAE gender roles were more egalitarian than at present, with the more restrictive roles for women evident with the reemergence of Neolithic, pre-Islamic traditions (Schvaneveldt et al., 2005). In Tunisia, reforms in the 1950s abolished polygamy and unilateral male divorce; in Yemen in the late 1960s and early 1970s, there were similar reforms to bolster women's family position. However, in the 1970s and early 1980s the growing political power of Islamist movements led to conservative revisions of family laws in Algeria, Egypt, and Iran and in the early 1990s revisions in Yemen and in Afghanistan (Moghadam, 2004). In discussing the Palestinians in Israel, Cohen and Savaya (2003) argued that there has been little change amongst this group compared to some other societies in the region. Here, the family is still seen as a central social institution, and commitment to the family and family honour is strong. Parents and in-laws still have an authoritative role, and the status of Arab wives is relatively low. Cohen and Savaya argue that this may reflect the importance to this Arab minority of maintaining what they consider to be their traditional family heritage and gender roles in response to this group's wider marginalisation within Israeli society. It may also suggest an increase in a conservative form of Islam that rejects modern Western values as corruptive.

It is important to note, however, that the impact of religion has not always been straightforward, with religious practices interlaced with existing cultural norms. In Iran, which has been dominated since the Islamic Revolution in 1979 by a religious fundamentalist regime, there are more pro-modern values than in Egypt or Jordan (Moaddel & Azadarmaki, 2003). Using data from the World Value Survey, the ideal number of children is four in Jordan, just two in Iran (ibid.). While there is strong support for marriage across the region (95 percent of respondents support marriage in Egypt, 87 percent in Jordan, and 67 percent in Iran), 17 percent in Iran claim that this is an outdated institution. Iranians are also less likely to agree that a woman needs to have children to feel satisfied (89 percent agreed in Egypt and Jordan, but only 45 percent in Iran) and are more likely to hold that a working mother can have an intimate relationship with children in the same way as a non-working mother can (40 percent vs. 19 percent of Egyptians and 23 percent of Jordanians). Finally, only 24 percent of Iranians, but 47 percent of Egyptians and 42 percent of Jordanians, held that a woman should always obey her husband.

In many Middle Eastern and North African countries, urban/rural residence, education, and socioeconomic status heavily determine the number of children in the family (Moghadam, 2004). A woman's lower status has tended to mean less education or fewer employment opportunities and higher fertility. Education has been associated with more knowledge about and use of contraceptives, although available family planning opportunities are also important. Both young men and young women may delay marriage prior to the attainment of educational qualifications. However, for agricultural populations high fertility is advantageous to the family and is often further justified on cultural or religious grounds. During a period of urbanisation, a large supply of cheap workers might also be useful for the provision of capital, with poor urban migrants needing children to enable them to survive town life.

War and Migration

War

Wars around the world have had dramatic impacts on individuals and their families and communities. Somasundaram (1996) in Sri Lanka questioned refugees exposed to aerial bombing. Following the bombing, respondents reported little social support and 19 percent reported interpersonal relationship problems. Communities and extended families were particularly disrupted by the displacement that followed the attacks.

Rape and violence against women is common during war, even in refugee camps, with women often seen as the property of men (Murphy, 2003). Extreme cases, such as the use of rape as a form of ethnic cleansing in Serbia, make headlines, but there have been surprisingly few studies directly tracking the impact of war on personal and family relationships.

Cohan, Cole, and Davila (2005) examined the effects of being a captured soldier in Vietnam on later marital transitions. The National Vietnam Veterans Readjustment Study indicated that men with higher war zone stress were more likely to report subsequent marital problems. Cohan notes that this stress is unlikely to affect all couples equally: Those with greater communication skills may have a chance to deal with it constructively, but the separation implied in war stress is still likely to be challenging. Cohan et al. argued that war-related stress is a combination of the threats to which an individual was exposed and the resources to cope with such stress. In particular, war-related problems were likely to be more pronounced amongst servicemen who were younger when captured, were less educated, were from a lower socioeconomic status, had a less hardy personality, and had suffered previous traumas.

In their study, Cohan et al. (2005) compared marital outcomes 20 years following repatriation of Vietnam War prisoners and a matched comparison group of Vietnam aviators who were not captured. Their results showed that, consistent with similar studies, former prisoners of war had higher rates of divorce than a comparison sample of aviators, with the greatest risk for divorce in the two years after repatriation. Prisoners of war were more likely to divorce when they were younger, had shorter marriages, and had wives with lower marital satisfaction and greater financial stresses.

During the Lebanese civil war (1976–1989), 7 percent of the Lebanese population were killed and more than 10 percent were seriously injured. A quarter of the population was displaced, and more than a third emigrated, whilst many hundreds of thousands also lived in fear, hiding from bombing and the threats of snipers. Saxena, Kulczycki, and Jurdi (2004) studied the impact of the civil war on the mean age at first marriage and the singulate mean age at marriage as a consequence of the civil war, comparing marriage cohorts from 1958 to 1964, 1975 to 1989, and 1990 to 1996. They found that, compared to other Middle Eastern countries, a large percentage of Lebanese were still single at the ages of 30 to 34. Looking across cohorts, the number of single women almost doubled after 1970, with 47 percent of women aged 25–29 still single in the later cohort. Similar figures were evident for those aged 30–34, with singulate rates increasing from 14 to 30 percent. Delayed marriage and an increase in the proportion of never-marrying females reflected the "marriage squeeze" that resulted from a low availability of suitably aged men following the war. In similar work, Jabbra (2004) studied family change in Lebanon's Biqa Valley as a result of the civil war, focusing on the small town of 'Ain al-Qasis (population approximately 2,500, primarily Melkite Greek Catholics). During the war, economic disruption led to high levels of unemployment. These economic conditions contributed to low marriage rates and an increased age at marriage, with couples opting for small families for primarily economic reasons.

Ismael (2004) notes how women and children are often disproportionately affected by the traumas of war. The distress of losing loved ones and economic strains can combine with increased workloads and family stresses. The 1971 Constitution of Iraq and National Action Charter affirmed the nuclear family, but it subordinated the family to the State in return for security functions, such as health care and education. The Ba'ath regime encouraged women's education and work. Following the 1991 war, however, and the increasingly harsh economic conditions that followed it, State-funded nurseries and kindergartens began to close (ibid.). As noted above, in other parts of the world large-scale unemployment led to a policy of encouraging women to return to the home. Forms of polygamy were revived as a result of large-scale male deaths and emigration, whilst the postinvasion concentration of troops led to new demands for prostitution. This was accompanied by a return to greater social conservatism and religious orthodoxy (such as in women's wearing of the *hijab*, rarely seen in decades prior to the sanctions).

Migration

Around 2 percent of the world's population live in countries other than those in which they were born (Townsend, 2003). A major impact of wars has been forced migration. Migration, of course, also occurs for economic reasons. Some 75 percent of those from Swaziland have at least one household member in wage labour in South Africa (Smit, 2001). Migration also occurs as a result of legal restrictions that enforce separation (such as the expulsion of the Asians from Uganda under Idi Amin). Both the host society and the immigrants' beliefs about the family have a notable influence on immigration practices (Settles, 2001), with substantial differences between situations where a migrant is wanted only as a temporary worker or student (where their family may be denied entrance) and those who obtain political asylum. Ethnic origin and culture are also important factors in predicting how immigration is experienced, as are immigrants' attitudes towards their own families (Darvishpour, 2002).

Smit (2001) examined the impact of labour migration on African family life and relationships. Under apartheid in South Africa, city policies, based on racial lines, controlled the movement of people, making it difficult for a family to migrate as a unit. The Natives (Urban Areas) Act of 1923 and the Native Laws Amendment Act (1937) prevented Africans from owning land or buying houses in urban areas. When apartheid ended, there was still a substantial labour migrant system in place due to housing shortages in urban areas and high unemployment that discouraged rural Africans from settling in urban areas. As a result, many preferred to work as migrant labourers, with circular migration between rural and urban areas. Ironically, given that migration was usually aimed at helping the family, it often served to exaggerate already existing strains and provided new problems with parental absenteeism and infidelity. Migrant workers were mostly absent during the critical early years of marriage and child rearing, often leading to a decline in marital quality. In most hostels, families were excluded, with married men living as bachelors; as with migrants elsewhere, this often led to an unofficial polygamy. The formation of second families overseas led to further problems for the original family, as there was then less money available to send home.

Similar patterns have been observed in Lesotho, where some 40 percent of the young male labour force moved to South Africa to work (Modo, 2001). As a result, nearly every Lesotho household depends either directly or indirectly on remittances from South Africa. Modo argues that this has both positive and negative effects: Whilst such work can provide money for the family, the separation of partners, children, and friends may have a long-lasting, deleterious impact (ibid.). Unemployment and hunger have led many married women to establish economically supportive *nyatsi* relationships, where a married woman takes a male "friend." High levels of out-migration in Botswana have also substantially changed marriage timing, with marriages now delayed until the man is in his thirties and has the financial resources to establish a family home (ibid.). Sekhar (1996, cited in D'Cruz & Bharat, 2001) examined Indian male migration to the Middle East. Women back home had to take on new responsibilities, which led them to making a number of new adaptations. This often served to increase the self-confidence and esteem of these women. However, on the husband's return, the wife was keen to maintain at least partly her decision-making influence, although the man would often still play an important part in executing these decisions.

In India, D'Cruz and Bharat (2001) noted that international migration can often mean the performance of dangerous jobs, creating considerable anxiety amongst those left back home. In the absence of fathers, families may re-form, with two mother/children family units forming woman-headed households. Children of male migrants may be separated from their fathers for more than half their childhood years. And with his absence, the father loses much of his patriarchal authority, making it difficult for him to readjust when returning to his family. In other situations, grandparents may raise the children. Whilst this may allow for the development of strong kinship relationships, poverty may restrict the opportunities for these extended family members to nourish, clothe, and educate the children. Sometimes both spouses may work in the labour migration process. Women may work as domestic labourers, often living with their employers due to a lack of housing. Such women have little opportunity for regular contact with their families. Whilst persisting collectivist cultural values may aid basic survival and make sure that the traditional family persists, poverty has reduced the wider sharing of resources. Internal migration may be particularly stressful for both partners. Here, migrants may earn relatively little extra money, whilst the wife has to combine family, domestic, and earner roles (ibid.).

The existence of established family networks can make a major difference to a new migrant to a country. In the United States, Bastida (2001) notes how extended family households can ensure that new U.S. arrivals gain support in the new country. Such extended families can also provide crucial services to nonresident kin. Marriage may also be promoted by selective migration and a U.S. immigration policy that promotes family reunification (Oropesa & Landale, 2004). Some 95 percent of the Mexican immigrants in 2002 were admitted under family-sponsored schemes or were the immediate relatives of U.S. citizens (ibid.). Binational networks on the United States–Mexico border help undocumented workers incorporate into the informal economy. Extended-family households, while not common in Mexico, may be used as an adaptive process following migration, although men and women in the same family may sometimes use the same resources for different purposes. As human capital increases, migrants then become less reliant on these kinship networks (Bastida, 2001).

The values and practices of the host country plus the economic situations of the new migrants may significantly influence the demographics of this group. Oropesa and Landale (2004) argue that the divorce culture in the majority U.S. population is having a major influence on the migrant Hispanic population and their descendents. Consistent with the experiences of the majority community, Latin migrants may come to prefer a greater individualism in personal affairs and a lessening of obligations to their partner (Bellah et al., 1985; Oropesa & Landale, 2004). Furthermore, economic necessities – particularly unemployment – may encourage cohabitation rather than marriage, and welfare programmes may reduce the financial gains of staying married. Thus, single mothers may fare better in the United States than back in Mexico, as they are less economically dependent on extended families and less subject to stigmatisation.

The experience of migration may also challenge traditional sex roles in the marriage, leading to a revision in roles and responsibilities (Oropesa & Landale, 2004). Darvishpour (2002) notes how

Iranian immigrants to Sweden enter a new social context in which family structures and relations have changed dramatically over recent decades. In this relatively "feminine" society (Hofstede, 2001), men may have particular difficulty adjusting to their new partnership roles. Women may have access to new power resources and support networks beyond those of their families. They enjoy greater legal opportunities to challenge unhappy marriages. Thus, many women will change the way they have lived their relationships after time in their new society.

Marriage is now a major form of migration into Western countries (Reniers, 2001; Tzeng, 2000). Reniers (ibid.) examined the postmigration survival of traditional marriage patterns, in particular consanguineous marriages amongst Turks and Moroccans in Belgium. Most research sees demographic characteristics such as educational level and socioeconomic class as negatively correlated with contemporary consanguineous marriage. However, migration can both accelerate social factors related to modernisation (by, for example, placing a greater reliance on wage labour rather than family property) whilst reinforcing other aspects of traditional authority (for example, when family solidarity encourages "adaptive" kin marriage practices that allow migration). In addition, a family that can arrange for a marriage of their kin to someone from the country of origin can increase its own status. Perhaps unsurprisingly, therefore, there is a higher frequency of consanguineous marriages amongst Turks and Moroccans in Belgium than there is in their countries of origin.

The likelihood of marrying outside your ethnic group increases as the availability of your own group diminishes (Hooghiemstra, 2001). Increased social interaction amongst individuals from different backgrounds can also promote intergroup interactions that can result in intermarriage (Tzeng, 2000). The availability of more spouses from Latin America in the United States has led to greater intermarriage: Following a relaxation of U.S. immigration policy towards Latin America in 1970, intermarriage rates increased between Mexican and non-Hispanic whites from 19 percent in 1970 to 29 percent in 1990 (Rosenfeld, 2002). Important moderators in this process are religious preferences and length of residence (Roy & Hamilton, 2000). Socioeconomic status is also significant: Those with higher socioeconomic status are more likely to be attractive to members of both the in- and the out-group and are more likely to be open to marrying those from outside their group. Tzeng in Canada finds that the Asian communities' relatively high educational achievement and work opportunities facilitate marrying outside the group. In particular, those more "unconventional" couples (where, for example, the wife is older, more educated, and with higher labour force participation) are more likely to intermarry. Language ability is an important related characteristic: It is hard to progress from an initial interaction to a deeper relationship without the appropriate means of communication (Tzeng, 2000).

Second-generation migrants – often referred to as "bicultural individuals" – are often caught between cultures (Lalonde et al., 2004). The relationship experiences of groups such as South Asians in a more individualistic Western country can be challenging, with considerable opportunities for tensions when an older first-generation cohort tries to promote arranged marriages in a generation brought up in a new country. In a study of a large Hindu Gujarati community in central England, we found an ethnic group where the institution of marriage is still highly regarded and where support from the family plays a valuable role in married life (Goodwin & Cramer, 2000). Consistent with the collectivist values of Hindu societies, marriage is seen as a process of linking families: The majority of the marriages amongst our respondents are arranged by the family or by other community members. Although some generational differences were evident, with the greater number of self-introduced marriages amongst the younger generation, fears about the loss of identity did not emerge as a major theme in our interviews. Indeed, our respondents demonstrated a number of compromises and accommodations typical of acculturating communities in many parts of the world (Berry, 1994). Our respondents could be best seen as choosing an integrationist strategy, combining the maintenance of cultural and social identity with the retention of good relationships with the white community and some adaptation of behaviours in line with the prevalent majority community norms. Thus, our respondents saw their marriages as combining the benefits of living in a traditional community with those associated with the individual fulfillment of personal desires. Personal attractions and bonds were demonstrated by the large number of respondents who stressed the role of love in their marriages, alongside a moral belief that marital commitment is sacrosanct. This combined with considerable community pressure that underlined the importance of long-term commitment and formed a strong barrier to relationship breakdown.

In all societies, long working hours and particular working times (such as weekends) can have negative impacts on family life (Dex, 2003). An interview study of ethnic minority businesses in the United Kingdom found that the trust between family members was crucial in starting up businesses and establishing enterprises in an economic manner (Basu & Altinay, 2003). The provision of labour, money, and social capital was accepted by the wider family as a natural extension of family activities. Domestic support was often provided to allow family members' commitment to the long hours frequently worked by new entrepreneurs. However, a lack of a boundary between family and work left some feeling dissatisfied. Family hierarchies were also carried forward into the business arena, leading to some resentment. Working patterns were partly moderated by ethnic group, with East African Asian entrepreneurs more likely than their Indian, Bangladeshi, Pakistani, or Turkish Cypriot colleagues to involve family members in establishing their businesses and providing labour, finances, and information. East African Asians also worked longer hours and were more dissatisfied with the limited time that remained for them to spend at home.

RESILIENCE

Previously, I have discussed some of the changes that have occurred following relatively rapid changes in Eastern Europe, Asia, and the Middle East. Yet it is clear that not all are equally affected by these socioeconomic and political changes. Resilience can be defined as "a dynamic process encompassing positive adaptation within the context of significant adversity" (Luthar, Cicchetti, & Becker, 2000, p. 543) – and it is evident that some are more resilient than others. Some stay healthy in the face of risk and adversity; others are affected and suffer both psychological and physiological disorders (Patterson, 2002; Settles, 2001). Individuals and families act as key mediators in this process (Settles, 2001).

Patterson (2002) discusses both normative and nonnormative events and their subsequent strains on a family. Normative risks are those that commonly lead to dysfunctional behaviour or symptoms (ibid.). Living in poverty, in crime-ridden areas with few community resources, places families at high risk. Marital conflict is more likely to emerge under such difficult social conditions. Poor adults are less likely to marry, as this can undermine economic security. Those having a poor-quality home life, perhaps with impoverished parents, face stresses that encourage the use of authoritarian or inconsistent parenting. This in itself can contribute to later adult problems (Seccombe, 2002). At the same time, however, many poor couples do not express these patterns of behaviour and have well-adjusted children (ibid.). According to family stress theorists, families balance family demands (everyday family strains and hassles, as well as stressor events) with existing family capabilities (Patterson, 2002). Particular psychological resources, tangible (physical) assets, and coping behaviours help overcome the stresses. Parental education, family cohesiveness, good health, and education services can act as "protective factors" (ibid.), at least until the demands of a crisis exceed capabilities. Seccombe (2002) identifies three moderating factors in helping families face poverty. Individual traits and personality resources mean that those with good communication skills and stronger mental resilience can tackle poverty by believing they can help overcome obstacles. Warm, affectionate families provide support for each other that allows the family to endure stressful situations. The wider community, too, can help encourage greater resilience amongst both the youth and the adults in the community, often through the encouragement of teamwork and good leadership skills. Such communities also provide opportunities to help others and for peers and other adults to work together.

During challenging events, such as floods and tornados, the appraisal a family makes of their situation is likely to be particularly important. Families' shared meanings – about the situation, their identity as a family, and their view of the world – are likely to be critical to their response and vulnerability (Patterson, 2002). Cohesiveness and flexibility are likely to be key resources in allowing for the development of effective communication that helps the family accomplish its core functions in times of stress (ibid.). Following major changes within a society, a family may be faced with several possibilities: to blend in with a more powerful group or to stand in opposition. Its choice of action may depend on its reliance on the established political/economic system for employment, as well as its position within existing community infrastructures (Settles, 2001). Mobility for the family may be aided or abetted by the relative attachment of families to their home and culture, as well as how their shared worldview affects their ability to negotiate opportunities for such mobility (ibid.).

One large study of family resilience examined the impact of economic decline in the rural Midwest of the United States during the late

1980s. Conger and Conger (2002) conducted a five-year panel study with yearly assessments (1989–1993) of children from the seventh grade onward. They proposed that family resilience would change over time and that a range of events or conditions might have adverse affects on individuals and their families. In their model, hardships (such as low income) acted to create economic pressures on the family. These pressures had particular meanings for the family – for example, they limited their ability to buy basic necessities, such as food. They may also have effects on the emotional health and the relationships of parents. Parental distress then affected parenting and on child and adolescent development. Particular economic pressures were seen as exacerbating harsh and inconsistent parenting, but those parents who avoided hostile and angry parenting also reduced the risk of their adolescents internalising their problems. Moderators of this stress included biological, psychological, and social resources. For example, money from the extended family helped them cope with economic problems and acted as a buffer. Wives and husbands in a highly supportive relationship would show little or no increase in emotional distress as a result of economic pressure. An individual sense of mastery or control also acted as an important psychological resource in dealing with stressors. Mastery compensates for the direct effects of economic pressure on depressive symptoms and allows parents to deal with their economic problems more effectively.

Zotovic (2004) provides a further example of resilience in a large-scale study of the impact of stress on the mental health of children. This study followed the bombing of the Serbian towns of Vrbas and Novi Sad during the Balkan conflicts of the late 1990s. She questioned a total of 629 12-, 15-, and 18-year-olds in these two cities, again viewing stress as a process that involves numerous external processes (such as social support) as well as internal processes (including personal characteristics). Her findings suggest that a year after the bombing there were significant levels of post-traumatic stress amongst approximately 60 percent of the children she questioned. Specific coping strategies were important, with those who were the most stressed seeking social support from others. However, such support was not particularly effective given the broad sharing of distress amongst all of those living in the cities. In contrast, the use of avoidant coping styles was relatively effective in predicting lower post-traumatic stress. Her findings suggest that the simple provision of support for those suffering from stress may be less effective when this stress is widely experienced. These findings are consistent with those reported by Hobfoll and London (1986) in their study of Israeli women whose partners or relatives were engaged in the 1982 Israel-Lebanon war. Their work found that turning to others suffering similar anxieties could lead to an exaggeration of the dangers faced by these men, only helping perpetuate rumours and increasing anxieties.

PATTERNS OF ADAPTATION

In the preceding sections, I described some major changes that have occurred in marriages and families and the ways in which individuals may or may not be resilient to such changes. From a functionalist perspective, the family can be seen as a unit with a series of interrelated roles, each dependent on the other (LaPiere, 1965). Changes in these roles can have a complex effect on the whole family system, but in time this system is likely to readjust. According to Amato et al., "[M]arriage appears to be an adaptable institution" (2003, p. 21); for Rothenbacher, families and households can be seen as "adaptive social units" (1998, pp. 10ff). Furthermore, whilst at times the family seems to succumb to large social pressures, at other times it has helped dictate patterns of change. Thus, the nepotistic family in preindustrial societies helped prevent the very formation of modern economic institutions (Fukuyama, 1995). Kinship networks were vital for the increased migration that followed the industrial revolution, with a geographically stretched migration contributing to the formation of new kinship functions. Kin ties provided stable and long-distance networks, giving bidirectional assistance and helping members adapt to the industrial system. These ties helped both kin and their employers, too, initiating and socialising young and new immigrants and acting as recruiters for the industrial employers (Hareven, 2000). In the absence of welfare functions, kin provided a primary source of support, and even during the apparent disruptions of industrialisation the family continued to see itself as a work unit.

Hareven (2000) argues that the above analyses "call into question the linear view of social change advanced by modernization theory" (p. 22). Instead, "modernization at the workplace did not automatically lead to the 'modernization' of family behaviour" (p. 23). Although the family adapted to the new industrialised environment, this adaptation was not as rapid as often thought, as the family both maintained traditions and encouraged the adaptation. The family thus provided important continuity whilst making significant decisions (such as whether to send children to the workplace).

We can see these patterns of adaptation in a number of modern industrialising economies. Vincent (2000) examined family relations in rural Peru after the economic crisis that followed the emergence of capitalism. She described the manner in which households and communities interacted with the wider political and economic processes of Peruvian society. Vincent argued that, faced with raw economic challenges, individual family members developed new interests that diverged from previous family patterns. In particular, after 1980, when stable jobs became rare, men took new short-term contract jobs, such as picking coffee or tropical fruit in the jungle. Economic uncertainties meant that they also lived at home with their parents from time to time. Children would stay away from school to participate in farm work, whilst migration increased the importance of child labour to compensate for missing household members. Women's roles changed, too, with young women now looking for work. Waged work in the cities, in particular, allowed women to survive without husbands and to gain greater independence. Overall, however, generational roles continued to complement each other. The family might no longer have worked together on one agricultural project, but ties between family members stayed close, even if their roles were new ones that had evolved to meet particular economic and social challenges. Working children in the cities sent money back to their parents in the village, whilst parents sent children agricultural produce, helping maintain a sense of family belonging. The economic crisis thus led to a strong reliance on kinship support ties, with the family important not only for economic reasons but for emotional help during a difficult period.

Similarly, Hirschman and Minh (2002) argued that in northern Vietnam "family and household living arrangements are not static representations of cultural continuity, but adapt and change over time in response to internal pressures and external influences" (p. 1064). Goode (1963) argued that modernisation would lead to the strengthening of conjugal ties and the weakening of extended-family obligations. Above, I reviewed evidence to suggest that residence patterns have echoed changes in the provision of housing stock in many Asian cities. However, it is also clear that strong sentiments for intergenerational living remain. Hirschman and Minh examined the incidence and duration of intergenerational coresidence between the 1950s and the 1990s and found little evidence of a reduction in patrilocality.

Their later data showed that around one in every four married couples lived with the groom's parents after marriage, although the duration of coresidence had decreased. This, they claim, demonstrates the continuing social pressure to conform to intergenerational residence expectations.

In China, Xu et al. (2007) claim that although families still represent a "cornerstone" of support, they are getting smaller and are reformulating as "networked families." However, these smaller units retain strong reciprocal ties. Unger (1993) in urban China suggested that although families might live apart, they maintain close contact and strong intergenerational networks. In India, D'Cruz and Bharat (2001) also considered Goode's (1963) hypothesis that industrialisation and urbanisation will lead to a nuclear or conjugal family system, greater freedom of mate choice, older marriages, egalitarian spouse relations, neolocal residence, and greater divorce and remarriage. However, D'Cruz and Bharat argue that, in fact, this may have only happened in a small number of cases, mainly amongst upper-caste groups. They note that a wide range of family forms exist and have always existed in Indian society, including joint families, nuclear families, single-parent families, dual-earner families, and adoptive families. While structural changes seem to have occurred, "functional jointness" may continue, with changes signifying not a total family system breakdown but adaptations that make change and continuity simultaneous. D'Cruz and Bharat recognise that this is not, of course, without its challenges. Children are raised with a combination of modern and traditional values, as well as with a combination of loving and more authoritarian mothering roles, which may sometimes induce anxiety in the children. Furthermore, the existence of only limited role models for the nuclear family may make finding a stable model for the family difficult. Further west, in Italy, Polini et al. (2004) conclude that industrialisation did not necessarily lead to the nuclearisation of the family. Instead, the extended family developed into a modified extended family in which family organisation based on several households linked together on an egalitarian basis.

How does this fit in with my earlier description of new, post-industrial (and largely Western) societies? As I noted above, whilst there may be little evidence to suggest that the family is simply fragmenting, there is some suggestion that it is taking on new historical forms. Beck and Beck-Gernsheim (2002) report that traditional rhythms of life are now being questioned and the "normal biography" of marriage and family has become disrupted. Giddens (1992) suggests that whilst kin relations have not been completely destroyed by modern institutions,

In the separating and divorcing society, the nuclear family generates a diversity of new kin ties. ... [T]he nature of these ties changes as they are subject to greater negotiation than before. Kinship relations used often to be taken for granted on the basis of trust; now trust has to be negotiated and bargained for, and commitment is as much an issue as in sexual relationships (p. 96).

The evidence suggests, however, that this "negotiation" does not mean that affectional ties have weakened. Indeed, there are data to suggest *affectional stability* even in the most "post-postindustrial" society. Coontz (2000) argues that although family affections may take a different form and meaning in the present day, "people in the past were probably not more or less caring than they are today" (p. 284). Smock (2004) suggests that a "long view" of family change allows us to "see twists and turns on the family landscape" and that although "close relationships are continually being defined and redefined" they are not "losing their deeply felt value" (p. 971). As discussed above, there is evidence in North America to suggest that in the 1990s a good marriage and family life has gained increased importance and that there is a strong ideological commitment to these institutions (Thornton & Young-Demarco, 2001). There is also evidence of strong bonds across generations. Bengtson (2001) examined a longitudinal study of more than 2,000 three-generation couples in California from the 1970s to 1996. Using nationally representative samples, he reported a variety of intergenerational family relationships, ranging from the tight-knit family (emotionally close, with frequent interaction and high levels of support) to the more detached (less close, with little interaction). He argued that all of these types are present in contemporary American society, with the most common being tightly knit, sociable families. Furthermore, he argued, North American families continue to socialise across generations, even when the parents are divorced. Georgas (2004) examined emotional distance between family members in a European cross-cultural sample of some 6,000 participants. His study examined a range of variables, including geographical proximity, the number of family visits, and the frequency of phone calls to family members. The family was shown to have universal expressive and instrumental roles. Affluence was not a predictor of either nuclear or extended-family emotional distance. Across the sample, the closest relationships were maintained with mothers, followed by siblings, fathers and grandparents, and uncles and aunts.

Many of these adaptations can be summarised from an ecocultural perspective. This work has been influential in explaining adaptations in family patterns (Lee, 1987). From this viewpoint, individuals and broader populations adapt biologically and culturally to their habitats (Berry, 2004; Berry & Poortinga, 2006, pp. 59ff). The family both adapts to the ecological situation and helps transmit cultural messages (Berry & Poortinga, 2006). Ecological variables (such as the percentage of people working in agriculture, religion, and affluence) interact with and influence structural variables, such as where people live and family roles. These subsequently influence psychological variables (Georgas, 2004; Van de Vijver, 2004). Working within this perspective, Kağitçibaşi (2004) presents her General Family Model. In this model, cultural living conditions (urban or rural, and level of affluence) influence both family structure (the family type, flow of wealth, family ties, fertility, and women's status) and family values (loyalties, emotional or material investments, independence or interdependence values, the valuing of children, and son preference). Family values and structure then have an effect on family interaction and socialisation patterns, such as parenting style and child-rearing orientation. This family interaction and socialisation also impacts on the development of the self and relationships with others.

Kağitçibaşi (2004, 2006) describes three family patterns. In the traditional family, there is total interdependence among family members, both material and emotional. This family pattern is particularly characteristic of poorer families living in rural agrarian and subsistence communities in the majority world. These family patterns are similar to the preindustrial societies described by Inglehart. In these families, the child is interdependent with the family, contributing to the family whilst still relatively young (primarily by working in the fields) and later on in life providing old-age security for parents. In such societies, there is typically a strong emphasis on high fertility, and parents value children, particularly sons, for their economic potential. Wealth in the family usually flows towards the parents. These societies are usually patrilineal; the child's independence is not valued and may even be seen as a threat. As a result, parenting styles are predominantly authoritarian, with the obedience of the child emphasised alongside the expected family and group loyalties.

This contrasts with a more independent, individualistic family model. This is characteristic of the wealthier "individualistic" urban family and more consistent with the atomistic view of society described by Bauman and others. Here, the separate functions and autonomy of family members are stressed. In this model, there is little evidence of either material or emotional dependency on the family. Individual loyalties are primary, and there are relatively high levels of emotional and material investment in the child, with independence values encouraged. There is no particular preference for sons, with children highly valued and wealth flowing towards them. Family structure is nuclear so that wealth flows towards children. There is low fertility, whilst women enjoy high status. Parenting is relatively permissive, and autonomy and self-reliance are emphasised for child rearing. There is a strong emphasis on familial independence and the development of a separate self.

Despite increased affluence and urbanisation, Kağitçibaşi argues, in many societies we see evidence of a weakening in material interdependency, but rather less evidence of a decline in psychological interdependence or separation. Instead, however, we can witness the development of a new "emotional/psychological interdependent" pattern for family life. This typically emerges within a culture of relatedness (in other words, in primarily collectivistic societies) marked by increased urbanisation, industrialisation, and affluence. She sees this new family type as not incompatible with urban living conditions, but well adapted to suit the modern environment of many developing, collective-oriented cultures. In addition, she sees this pattern as explaining both ethnic variations in family patterns in immigrant groups in Western countries and the emergence of postmodern values amongst majority populations in Western postindustrial societies. This interdependent family stresses both autonomy and relatedness, with authoritative parenting and socialisation patterns that mix the development of this autonomy along with control. Socialisation values stress a combination of family and group loyalties as well as individual loyalties. The self that emerges, she describes as "autonomous-related." There is emotional investment in parents and both emotional and material investment in the child. There is a decrease in son preference, whilst women have increased status. The family structure is "functionally complex": While wealth flows towards children, there are both nuclear and kin ties. Such a synthetic societal mixture she sees as an optimal one for human development.

These changes in child rearing are mirrored in the new way in which children are valued across cultures and the legislation that reflects this valuation. Children in a postmodern world are no longer desired for simply economic reasons; indeed, the prohibitive costs of having a child in Western countries mitigates against this (Giddens & Pierson, 1998). Kağitçibaşi (2004) compared data across the multinational Value of Children study, which covers the years 1975 to 2003 and includes data from China, Germany, India, Indonesia, Israel, Korea, South Africa, and Turkey. Although the actual and desired number of children has fallen, it is clear that children are now differently valued than in previous decades. In more recent years, mothers have been less likely to see their children as simply economic aids or merely as assistance to help around the house when parents age. Rural parents are less likely now than in 1975 to expect financial help from their sons or daughters. Instead, mothers are now more likely to desire children simply in order "to watch them grow," to view them as people who are "fun to have around," and as individuals to love and care for. According to Giddens, children have obtained a "semimythical" status, with the maltreatment of children a topic of major concern in many countries. Democratisation of the family has developed to include the development and enshrinement of children's rights (Giddens & Pierson, 1998), even if there are cultural differences in the interpretation of these rights (Murphy-Berman, Levesque, & Berman, 1996).

SIMPLY ADAPTING?

Ecocultural models are primarily functionalist accounts, describing adaptive changes that usually occur during the space of several generations. They do, however, go beyond the simpler functionalism in recognising the importance of material circumstances in helping to frame the ideas and beliefs that underlie relationship behaviour. They also contrast with the more pessimistic assessments of sociological theorists of postmodern society that describe the "chaos of love" (Beck & Beck-Gernsheim, 1995) and the alienation of "de-intimatised" societies. Yet, for some, functional accounts downplay the stresses that may occur in transitional societies, even when they do recognise the time lags in adaptation that occur when societies transform rapidly and unexpectedly. As a result, these models can appear rather optimistic. Kennedy and Kirwil (2004) argue that the unintended interpersonal consequences of apparently rational transitions are often missed in changing societies, downplaying the impact of conflicting allegiances. Hareven (2000), in her historical analysis, claims that there should be no surprise in this: "Patterns of family timing in the past were often as complex, diverse, and erratic as they are today" (p. 314). From this perspective, the family has not always smoothly adapted to contemporary social and cultural changes.

Some problems with adaptation can be located in the gap between cultural ideals and beliefs and economic and political realities. Riley, Kahn and Foner (1994) use the term "structural lag" to describe the mismatch between changes in lives and transitions in social structures. Hareven (2000) distinguishes between structural and cultural lag. Cultural lag concerns the myths and stereotypes in a society about what is "normal" and what is "deviant" in family relations and forms. These myths have a strong impact on individuals, institutions, and policies. This, however, may conflict notably with the economic and structural realities of a society. Thus, nineteenth-century ideals about the role of motherhood and homemaking in the United States were at odds with contemporaneous developments in society. Notions of privacy handicapped family interactions with wider social institutions, restricting the ability of the family to deal with social change and to influence public agencies. This led to the isolation in particular of older people and a lack of flexibility within families when dealing with change. Women in work, particularly those from poorer families, had to deal with poor child care facilities whilst notions of female domesticity continued to restrict progress at work.

A more recent example can be found in a study of the changing reproductive attitudes of three generations of women in Limpopo, South Africa (Spjeldnæs, Peltze, & Sam, 2006). These researchers examined continuity and change in attitudes in a society that had abolished its racial family planning programmes but was faced with a large-scale HIV/AIDS epidemic. Unlike other countries experiencing a decrease in fertility, South Africa is unusual in that this decline is not evident in young women, with a third of all births being to women under age 18. Spjeldnæs and colleagues examined whether teenage girls (averaging 14 years of age) wanted children, the age at which they wanted children, and how this compared to the age at which their mothers and grandmothers actually gave birth. They found that whilst the young girls preferred to have their children later and to have fewer children than their mothers or grandmothers, these preferences were in stark contrast to national statistics on reproduction and fertility. Thus, aspirations and actual behaviours appear to be quite distinct.

A further example can be found in the conflicting messages concerning women's role in postcommunist societies, described in more detail above. As economic downturns in the 1990s led to women losing jobs and returning to housework ahead of men, there was considerable dissatisfaction amongst educated women in particular and little evidence of functional adaptation for these well-trained – but now unemployed – workers. The disruptions of these times might be evidenced in the dramatic increase in alcoholism and drug abuse during the early 1990s and an associated sharp decrease in life expectancy (Bobak et al., 1998; Jenkins, Klein, & Parker, 2005). This "maladaptation" can also be seen in growing relationship violence in Russia (Vannoy, (1998). Perhaps unsurprisingly, several surveys have shown that the majority of those questioned in the early 1990s thought they had lost more than they had gained in the years since the end of communism (Reykowski, 2004; Svejnar, 2002).

SUMMARY

Changes in marriage and the family are at the forefront of many contemporary debates in relationship studies and, indeed, in the broader social sciences. Such changes are rarely viewed in a dispassionate manner, with many researchers relating these either to positive forces for egalitarianism and freedom or (more frequently) to negative declines in morals and social behaviour, particularly amongst the vulnerable young. However, as Coontz (2000) notes, to be either optimistic or pessimistic about these changes is likely to be misleading. Thus, for example, just as women gained new protection and status as wives or mothers at the end of communism in Eastern European societies, there was also an increased prejudice against these women in participating in public life and the workforce. Indeed, in those societies that have undergone relatively rapid changes and those where war and economic conditions have led to both internal displacement and large-scale migration, new uncertainties in family roles and responsibilities can have unexpected and challenging implications. At times, these can lead to serious relationship problems in marriages and consequent deleterious impacts on marital stability; at other times, the evidence suggests that couples may be less likely to divorce during periods of social upheaval (for example, in Eastern Europe following the end of communism). In such circumstances, models of adaptation and resilience need to be refined in the light of the considerable social and economic transformations that have affected substantial proportions of the world's population.

CHAPTER 7

Modelling Social Change and Relationships

Social change is occurring at psychological, economic, and political levels in all societies, albeit at difference paces. In this book, I have argued that rapid changes have had direct impacts on the relationship lives of at least portions of the populace, but must be set against a backdrop of more gradual transitions that follow alongside any broader process of modernisation or economic development. Changes are often far from smooth and can be subject to considerable resistance. Families and wider social groups may be keen to retain traditions and norms, which may serve valuable functions in allowing individuals to adjust or may inhibit relationship equality or personal freedoms. Thus, the link between economic transformations and relationship behaviours and beliefs is invariably complex.

I have also argued that it is too simple to portray social change and its implications for close relationships as simply positive or negative. Change is likely to have differential impacts on different individuals, groups, and cultures. Economically independent and "structurally powerful" women and their male counterparts may now seek similar qualities in a mate. Individuals – and cultures – high on fatalism and distrust may be unwilling to provide the close friendships and support networks so psychologically important in times of civil unrest. Religious beliefs in a culture may serve to limit the availability of contraception and the practise of abortion and influence responses to sexual diseases such as HIV/AIDS. These moderating factors are rarely studied in the analysis of close relationships, but they are particularly significant when we consider more rapid social transitions. Here, change that may lead to a simple and positive adaptation for one family may seriously disrupt the lives of others. At times, societal change may lead to relationship patterns that seem at first perverse: Modernisation may make individuals reluctant to make a commitment to a relationship and to delay their marriage, but it may also promote the idealisation of this relationship, even if divorce figures suggest it may prove short-lived. Rapid social change can discourage individuals from marrying, but it also may inhibit divorce. Understanding these findings requires us to attempt to comprehend the *meaning* of a transition for the actors involved and the significance these changes have for their individual daily activities and relationships.

ON CHANGING AND NONCHANGING RELATIONSHIPS

For many, the formation of close relationships is universal, meeting needs shared by all humankind (for example, self-determination theory, Deci & Ryan, 2000). However, the extent to which these relationships are malleable is unclear: What kinds of relationship activities and behaviours are most liable to change? Systematic comparative studies here are very rare, but the fragmentary evidence suggests some possible clues.

One potential way to examine this is to differentiate between core and peripheral relational emotions and cognitions. Core emotions and cognitions would be likely to meet evolutionary demands and may be less likely to fluctuate with short-term political and economic changes in a society. Intense affectional bonds, for example, are not merely governed by culture and socialisation but represent neurochemically mediated processes resulting from our mammalian heritage (Diamond, 2003). These bonds are important for initial mating rituals and help offspring develop in their environmental context. They are likely to be only weakly correlated with individual or cultural values. A desire for a healthy partner is universal; this partner should also be "beautiful," but with beauty defined within local norms. Core relational characteristics also include strongly emotional love styles, such as eros (romantic and passionate love, which is heavily influenced by physical attraction) and mania (obsessive and dependent love) (Lee, 1973; Neto et al., 2000). Romantic acts related to sexual relations and intimacy can also be included here, as can relationship *ideals* about sexual relations and intimacy – often as opposed to realities. In addition, there may be further core behaviours that are moderated by personality and other individual differences in a similar manner in each culture. These may arise from differential upbringings (in particular, attachment experiences), which have a universal impact on an individual's internalised "working model" of relationships. Examples are in the distribution of resources between groups (where the collectivist or individualist nature of a society influences this distribution; Hui et al., 1991) or where fatalistic beliefs tend to be associated with lower levels of social support across cultures (Goodwin et al., 2002). When changes occur, they are slow, depending on relatively long processes, such as the complex transitions to modernisation described in my opening chapter.

Other behaviours, cognitions, and affects, however, may be more susceptible to local ecological demands and temporal changes. These are likely to be correlated with relevant culture-level values and beliefs or axioms and are less likely to be consistent across situations. These might include actual (rather than ideal) behaviours in a relationship, "realistic" partner preferences that meet environmental and cultural demands, or love styles such as "pragma" (logical, practical, "shopping-list" love; Lee, 1973). It is also possible to include here romantic acts that express commitment rather than more romantic idealism. These are all likely to be context dependent, as are emotions dependent on local expectations and networks, such as loneliness (Suh et al., 1998). In this book, I hope to have shown that many of the choices made in the face of social changes are attempted adaptations to environmental conditions, even if these adaptations are sometimes at a considerable cost to individuals and their families.

Another way to consider this issue is to examine the different "levels of analysis" at which social change can occur. Unfortunately, psychologists usually tend to focus on their own pet level of analysis to the exclusion of all others – be it social, personality, evolutionary, or the like. Very little work has been done to integrate psychological findings across theoretical domains (Van Hemert, 2003): In Van Hemert's words, "There is a clear need for systematizing the vast amount of cross-cultural studies and for developing models explaining cross-cultural differences in psychology" (2003, p. 9). However, some typologies for understanding this do exist. Van de Vijver and Poortinga (1990) suggest a framework based on genetic and cultural transmission. They identify five psychological domains – psycho-physiological, perceptual, cognitive, personality based, and social behavioural – and argue that cultural variation increases as we progress from the psychophysiological to social behaviour. Van Hemert (2003) conducted a meta-analysis and found culture to be more important than other psychological domains in explaining social-psychological behaviour. Doise (1986) identifies four levels of analysis: psychological/intrapersonal, interpersonal/intrasituational, social position/status, and ideological/cultural. The psychological/intrapersonal includes, for example, Piaget's work on cognitive development and the traditional study of intelligence. Interpersonal/intrasituational work concerns the dynamics between individuals. Research that focuses on social position includes attribution work studying group memberships. Finally, work at the ideological level considers cultural norms, systems of beliefs and values, and norms within a culture/society. Doise recognises that there may be further levels that can be added. My own tentative framework that builds on this is offered in Table 1. This can also be organised, of course, as a set of concentric circles or can use other such diagrammatic aids according to taste. For the purposes of clarity, I illustrate these levels with a fictional example of a traveler making an international journal by aeroplane.

At the most fundamental level, we have evidence for the role of physiology in relationship interactions. Our physical abilities are likely to shape many of our everyday conversations; for example, individuals who find hearing difficult are more likely to stand closer to interact than those with excellent hearing. On an aeroplane, we might lean over to hear a conversation or may be prevented from boarding quickly due to a physical disability. Societal or political changes are unlikely to have any direct impact on this, although, of course, disclosures occurring at very close proximity may arouse suspicion in some situations (for example, in a State where such interactions are closely monitored). Other microenvironmental conditions may reflect other situational factors. Markus and Kitayama (1994) refer to these as the "immediate social environment" (p. 573), resulting mainly from local norms, practices, and institutions. In this, we might include seating arrangements, important, of course, for the exhibition of some nonverbal behaviours, as well as for the performance of more minor pro-social behaviours. On our aeroplane, a traveler might be more likely to provide others with easy assistance (such as bending down to pick up a dropped item) when she is close to the person who dropped the item and where the physical environment (for example, the seating arrangements) allows for this. Again, major societal changes are unlikely to have a profound impact on these social performances, provided again that daily interpersonal relations are not greatly disturbed by these new regimes.

An individual's personality may also be relatively unchanged by major societal events, although there is relatively little longitudinal evidence on this topic. Intriguingly, the meaning of and relationship

Table 1. Level of Analyses, Relationships, and Social Change

Level	Behaviour is dependent on ...	Relationship examples	Impact of social change
Physiological	Physical abilities of individuals	Interpersonal proximity as a result of hearing ability	Negligible
Microenvironmental	Immediate social environment	Some nonverbal behaviours and minor altruistic acts	Small
Individual values and personality	The individuals' values or personality type	Perception of social support; confidence in relationship formation	Small to moderate
Role relationships	Relationships within the immediate environment	Power relations in marriage; relationships at work	Moderate to large
Social position and work structure	Social structure; work routine; and daily activities	Opportunities for social interaction; the development of friendships; child socialisation	Moderate to large
Cultural beliefs, values, and representations	Cultural beliefs	Relationship beliefs; actual (rather than perceived) social support	Moderate
Adaptational environment	Cultural history and climate	Eagerness to cooperate	Small to moderate
Evolutionary pressure	Universal obligations	Procreation	Negligible

between personality and values might be historically mediated (Kemmelmeier et al., 2003). Kemmelmeier and his associates demonstrated that the relationship between authoritarianism and individualism was negative only in postcommunist societies, where authority and individual determination were seen as incompatible. Individual values and beliefs may be more malleable: Traumatic life events can challenge an individual's "assumptive world" undermining implicit but fundamental beliefs and values (Janoff-Bulman, 1989). Verkasalo, Goodwin, and Bezmenova (2006) compared the values of matched groups of Finnish school children and university students before and after the 9/11 terrorism attacks and found significant increases in security values. Our traveler may be unwilling even to board her plane to meet her fiancé if political events have increased her concerns over security. As mentioned in Chapter 4, the values of benevolence or egalitarianism towards others may be particularly challenged when a regime appears actively to punish citizens for holding these values.

Typical daily role relations have been rather undervalued by social psychologists, but they may be more important than acknowledged (Bond, 2004; Smith & Bond, 2003). For our traveler, the decision as to the class in which to travel and the preference for seat allocation (does she give seating preference to her elderly employer?) are all likely to be influenced by considerations of social norms and role relations. These rules and roles can, of course, be suspect to major political and economic interference: New societal groupings and classes can predominate following social change, and relationships with a new elite may take on a very new tenor. Work routines, as Kohn et al.'s work (1990) has demonstrated, can have a profound impact on the values of their workers, and these in turn may have profound impacts on child rearing and daily social interactions. Within a relationship, power relations in marriage may be influenced by broader societal stresses and new norms, as demonstrated by work on changes in marriage (see Chapter 6). Social beliefs, axioms, and cultural values can play a valuable bridging role in linking the individual to the wider culture. These may provide valuable "frames" for relationship interactions, although the permeability of these frames may in itself be culturally variable and such beliefs and values are not necessarily overt (Markus & Kitayama, 1994). Bond (2004, p. 75) notes how "the same outcome may be mediated by different psychological processes in different cultures," with group norms playing an important mediating role in linking cross-cultural variations to behavioural outcomes. Thus, relationship beliefs are more closely related to marital satisfaction in the more collectively orientated Republic of Georgia, compared to the more individualist Hungary (Goodwin & Gaines, 2004).

Climate and other physical delimiters are likely to form an important part of the adaptational environment. There is evidence of some

increase in attention to this in the cross-cultural psychological literature, although there have been few systematic attempts to link adaptational characteristics to close relationship practices (for a notable
exception, see Georgas et al., 2006). At a trivial level, our fictional
passenger may wrap up warmly on the plane as a result of her country
of origin, which is considerably hotter than the air conditioning at
30,000 feet. Van de Vliert has contended that respondents in increasingly demanding cold or hot climates value cooperativeness amongst
children if they live in richer societies, but "egoistic enculturation" if
they reside in poorer societies (Van de Vliert, 2006). This suggests
that environmental change interacts with resources of a society,
mirroring the framework provided in Chapter 1 that suggests that
individual or group resources help moderate the impacts of societal
change on relationship behaviour. This interaction approach again
recognises the importance of within-culture variability in helping
understand the impact of social change – be it political or climatic –
on both personal interactions and the values encouraged in future
generations.

Finally, at the level of evolution, particular universal drives may be
only partially mediated by the lower levels of this analysis. A strong
desire for survival may also mean that neither individual personality
nor personal role greatly influences the decision of our aeroplane
passenger to rush towards an exit when her plane is forced to make a
sudden landing. Reproductive activity represents "the first line of
evolutionary pressure" (Kenrick & Keefe, 1992, p. 75); Thus, sexual
activity of young people from this perspective can best be understand in terms of the fulfillment of reproductive interests (Thornhill
& Thornhill, 1987). Jealousy towards a mate may be relatively unaf-
fected by internal societal upheavals (Buss, 2000). However, the exact
exhibition and expression of behaviour may be considerably moderated by the attendant restraints that might accompany societal
change.

Of course, we must avoid the danger of excessive reductionism
in failing to consider other levels of analysis in the interpretations
of our data (Doise, 1986, p. 87). This framework suggests that
interpersonal behaviours may be considered most appropriately at
one particular level. Of course, there may be important cross-
cutting affiliations in any situation, and it is the interaction between
levels of analysis that is often of greatest interest. In particular,
the impacts of social change may be largest at the intermediate

levels in this model, suggesting the need for greater attention to social roles, daily work structures, and cultural beliefs and norms. Long-term projects that incorporate data from several levels of analysis are needed in order to examine more fully the impact of social change on relationship behaviours and processes.

LOOKING FORWARD

In the year 2000, around half of the world's population was under the age of 27. This suggests that we will continue to see substantial global population growth, even if family size decreases (Townsend, 2003). Populations are also increasing as a result of a rise in the average age of populations and the increased number of people living to over the age of 65 across the world. This number is predicted to treble between 1995 and 2050, with the greatest increases in East Asia and Latin America (ibid.).

These large population increases may require aid from unexpected sources if overpopulation is not to provide a serious challenge for many countries. Existing cultural systems, which may at first appear to be simple limiters to action, can provide important frameworks for debate about relationships and social change. Political and moral leadership is likely to be particularly significant (Wellings et al., 2006). Religious leaders in Iran, for example, may participate in helping reduce unwanted pregnancies to aid the family's health (Townsend, 2003). School-based education programmes are likely to be important in many countries to tackle problems such as sexual risk taking (Wellings et al., 2006). These programmes will need to recognise the importance of persisting daily routines and role behaviours whilst addressing key values and beliefs and exploiting important social networks (ibid.; Caramlau & Goodwin, 2007). Despite fears of increasing youth promiscuity, evidence suggests that school-based interventions are more likely to delay first sexual activity rather than encourage it (Wellings et al., 2006).

Considerable challenges need to be faced concerning the abuse of women or the lack of care of those vulnerable women most at risk. One-third of women worldwide have been beaten, coerced into sex, or subjected to extreme emotional abuse (Murphy, 2003). Fifty million abortions take place each year worldwide, ending one-quarter of all pregnancies. WHO considers two-fifths of these abortions to be unsafe, with most of these unsafe abortions occurring in developing countries. In a major WHO study, in more than half the countries studied a third or more of the women who had had sexual intercourse before the age of 15 had been coerced into it (Wellings et al., 2006). There is little evidence for substantial changes in these patterns, despite the apparent modernisation processes taking place in the economies of many countries. Levels of interpersonal trust and social capital are also being challenged by large-scale social movements and family reformulations (Edwards et al., 2003). Even where there is evidence of trust at the national level, it may be difficult to disperse this trust from the political elites and community leaders into wider communities (Maloney et al., 2000). Distrust between groups can often arise from oppositions in fundamental beliefs, such as the hostility of religion-based extremist groups to the dress code of some women or the meeting of unchaperoned single men and women of marriageable age. A belief in the "clash of civilisations" and the continued presence of terrorism threats, which appear to reinforce such beliefs, is rapidly changing our "risk society" to a "frisk society," where visible minority group members are liable to undergo extended scrutiny. Such developments hardly help in the development of smooth intercultural relationships and make the building of trust between groups a major challenge for large numbers of societies across the world.

What, then, is the prospect for personal relationships in the future? In this book, I hope to have stressed the difficulty for any simple prognosis. Global changes are clearly occurring at the economic, political, and relational levels, but simple formulae that see these as undermining intimacy – or leading to new freedoms and relational democracy – can miss the complex ways in which individuals, groups, and societies respond to these changes. Many of the changes that have occurred were not necessarily expected, representing the by-product of other economic or political transitions occurring in a society (Giddens & Pierson, 1998). Other apparent trends (such as a rise in early sexual experience) are less evident and internationally spread as is often assumed. Indeed, there is evidence of an increased delay in the onset of sexual behaviour for women in many developing nations (Wellings et al., 2006). "Flexibility" of analysis becomes a key word (Dex, 2003): Just as the opportunities for reciprocation in intimate relations may appear to be challenged by an increase in working hours for many, new ways of relating emerge, even if they do not necessarily always signify substantial behavioural shifts. Thus, new technology allows female professionals to maintain contact with their families when traveling for work, but those same women may still be likely to perform the majority of domestic work at home. Any "catchphrase sociological slogans," then, are likely to be misleading, as modernisation and traditionalisation motifs continue to coexist and as individuals struggle to make sense of the meaning for them of the continuing challenges and changes in their everyday lives.

References

Abu-Loghod, L. (1991). Writing Against Culture. In R. E. Fox, ed., *Recapturing Anthropology: Working in the Present*, pp. 137–162. Santa Fe, NM: School of American Research Press.

Adams, R. G. (2004). Friendship as a Source of Social Change. *SGI Quarterly*, 35. Retrieved from http://www.sgiquarterly.org.

Adler, N. E., Ozer, E. J., and Tschann, J. (2003). Abortion among Adolescents. *American Psychologist*, 58: 211–218.

Al-Thakeb, F. T. (1985). The Arab Family and Modernity: Evidence from Kuwait. *Current Anthropology*, 26: 575–580.

Allan, G. (2001). Personal Relationships in Late Modernity. *Personal Relationships*, 8: 325–339.

Allen, M. W., Ng, S. H., Ikeda, K., Jawan, J. A., Sridhara, A., Sufi, A. H., Waninara, W., Wilson, M., and Yang, K. S. (2004). "Cultural Value Change in Nine East Asian and Pacific Island Nations (1982 to 2002)." Paper presented at the seventeenth International Congress for Cross-Cultural Psychology, Xi'an, China.

Allen, M. W., Ng, S. H., and Leiser, D. (2004). Adult Economic Model and Values Survey: Cross-National Differences in Economic Beliefs. *Journal of Economic Psychology*, 26: 159–185.

Allik, J., and Realo, A. (2004). Individualism-Collectivism and Social Capital. *Journal of Cross-Cultural Psychology*, 35: 29–49.

Almond, B. (2006). *The Fragmenting Family*. Oxford: Oxford University Press.

Altman, I. (1992). A Transactional Perspective on Transitions to New Environments. *Environment and Behavior*, 24: 268–280.

Amato, P. R. (2004). Tension between Institutional and Individual Views of Marriage. *Journal of Marriage and Family*, 66: 959–965.

Amato, P. R., Johnson, D. R., and Rogers, S. J. (2003). Continuity and Change in Marital Quality between 1980 and 2000. *Journal of Marriage and Family*, 65: 1–22.

Amirkhan, J. H. (1990). A Factor Analytically Derived Measure of Coping: The Coping Strategy Indicator. *Journal of Personality and Social Psychology*, 59: 1066–1074.

Aries, P. (1960). *Centuries of Childhood*. London: Pimlico.

Arnett, J. J. (2002). The Psychology of Globalization. *American Psychologist*, 57: 774–783.

Bajos, N., and Marquet, J. (2000). Research on HIV Sexual Risk: A Social Relations–Based Approach in a Cross-Cultural Perspective. *Social Science and Medicine*, 50: 1533–1546.

Barber, N. (2004). Reduced Marriage Opportunity and History of Single Parenthood. *Journal of Cross-Cultural Psychology*, 35: 648–651.

Bardi, A., and Schwartz, S. (2003). Values and Behavior: Strength and Structure of Relations. *Personality and Social Psychology Bulletin*, 29: 1207–1220.

Barnett, T., Whiteside, A., Khodakevich, L., Kruglov, Y., and Steshenko, V. (2000). The HIV/AIDS Epidemic in Ukraine: Its Potential Social and Economic Impact. *Social Science and Medicine*, 51: 1387–1403.

Baron, S. (2004). Social Capital in British Politics and Policy Making: Families and Social Capital. (ESRC Research Group Working Papers, No. 7). London South Bank University. Retrieved from http://www.lsbu.ac.uk/families/.

Barrera, M. (1986). Distinctions between Social Support Concepts, Measures, and Models. *American Journal of Community Psychology*, 14: 413–445.

Basic Behavioral Science Task Force of the National Advisory Mental Health Council (1996). *American Psychologist*, 51: 22–28.

Bastida, E. (2001). Kinship Ties of Mexican Migrant Women on the United States/Mexico Border. *Journal of Comparative Family Studies*, 32: 549–569.

Basu, A., and Altinay, E. (2003). *Family and Work in Minority Ethnic Businesses*. York, England: Policy Press.

Bauman, Z. (2001). *The Individualized Society*. Cambridge, MA: Polity Press.
  (2003). *Liquid Love*. Cambridge, MA: Polity Press.

Baumgarte, R. (2002). Cross-Gender Friendship: The Troublesome Relationship. In R. Goodwin and D. Cramer, eds., *Inappropriate Relationships: The Unconventional, the Disapproved and the Forbidden*, pp. 103–124. Mahwah, NJ: Lawrence Erlbaum.

Beck, U., and Beck-Gernsheim, E. (1995). *The Normal Chaos of Love*. Cambridge: Polity Press.
  (2002). *Individualization: Institutionalized Individualism and Its Social and Political Consequences*. London: Sage Publications.

Beck-Gernsheim, E. (2002). *Reinventing the Family: In Search of New Lifestyles*. Malden, MA: Blackwell.

Bell, D. (1973). *The Coming of the Post-Industrial Society: A Venture in Social Forecasting*. New York: Basic Books.

Bellah, R., Madsen, R., Sullivan, W. M., Swindler, A., and Tipton, S. M. (1985). *Habits of the Heart: Individualism and Commitment in American Life*. Berkeley: University of California Press.

Bengtson, V. L. (2001). Beyond the Nuclear Family: The Increasing Importance of Intergenerational Bonds. *Journal of Marriage and Family*, 63: 1–16.

Berry, J. W. (1980). Social and Cultural Change. In H. C. Triandis and R. W. Brislin, eds., *Handbook of Cross-Cultural Psychology*, vol. 5, pp. 211–275. Boston: Allyn and Bacon.

(1997). Immigration, Acculturation and Adaptation. *Applied Psychology*, 46: 5–68.

(2004). Use of the Sociocultural Framework in Research with Family. Paper presented at the seventeenth International Conference for Cross-Cultural Psychology, Xi'an, China.

Berry, J. W., and Poortinga, Y. H. (2006). Cross-Cultural Theory and Methodology. In J. Georgas, J. W. Berry, F. J. R. Van de Vijver, C. Kağitçibaşi, and Y. H. Poortinga, eds., *Families Across Cultures: A 30-Nation Psychological Study*, pp. 51–71. Cambridge: Cambridge University Press.

Boase, J., and Wellman, B. (2006). Personal Relationships: On and off the Internet. In A. L. Vangelisti and D. Perlman, eds., *The Cambridge Handbook of Personal Relationships*, pp. 709–726. New York: Cambridge University Press.

Bobak, M., Pikhart, H., Hertzman, C., Rose, R., and Marmot, M. (1998). Socioeconomic Factors, Perceived Control and Self-Reported Health in Russia: A Cross-Sectional Survey. *Social Science and Medicine*, 47: 269–279.

Bond, M. H. (2004). Culture and Aggression – From Context to Coercion. *Personality and Social Psychology Review*, 8: 62–78.

Borisenko, K. K., Tichnova, L. I., and Renton, A. M. (1999). Syphilis and Other Sexually Transmitted Infections in the Russian Federation. *International Journal of STD and AIDS*, 10: 665–668.

Boudon, R. (1986). *Theories of Social Change*. Berkeley: University of California Press.

Bourdieu, P. (1983). Ökonomisches Kapital, kulturelles Kapital, soziales Kapital [Economic Capital, Cultural Capital, Social Capital]. In R. Kreckel, ed., *Soziale Ungleichheiten*, pp. 183–198. Göttingen, Germany: Otto Schartz and Co.

Bourdieu, P., and Wacquant, L. (1992): *An Invitation to Reflexive Sociology*. Chicago: University of Chicago Press.

Bowlby, J. (1969). *Attachment and Loss*, vol. 1: *Attachment*. New York: Basic Books.

Brown, R. A. (1994). Romantic Love and the Spouse Selection Criteria of Male and Female Korean College Students. *Journal of Social Psychology*, 134: 183–189.

Burgess, E. W. (1926). The Family as a Source of Interacting Personalities. *The Family*, 7: 3–9.

Burgess, E. W., and Cottrell, L. S. (1939). *Predicting Success or Failure in Marriage*. New York: Prentice-Hall.

Burgess, E. W., and Locke, H. J. (1953). *The Family*. New York: American Book Co.

Buss, D. M. (2000). *The Dangerous Passion: Why Jealousy Is as Necessary as Love and Sex*. New York: Free Press.

Buss, D. M., and Barnes, M. (1986). Preferences in Human Mate Selection. *Journal of Personality and Social Psychology*, 50: 559–570.

Buss, D. M., Shackelford, T. K., Kirkpatrick, L. A., and Larsen, R. J. (2001). A Half Century of Mate Preferences: The Cultural Evolution of Values. *Journal of Marriage and Family*, 63: 491–503.

Calves, A.-E. (2000). Premarital Childbearing in Urban Cameroon: Paternal Recognition, Childcare and Financial Support. *Journal of Comparative Family Studies*, 31: 443–461.

Caramlau, I., and Goodwin, R. (2007). Evaluating Health Promotion Leaflets' Impact on Young People in Romania. *Cognition, Brain, Behavior*, 11: 279–297.

Carballo-Diéguez, A., Miner, M., Dolezal, C., Rosser, B. R., and Jacoby, S. (2006). Sexual Negotiation, HIV-Status Disclosure, and Sexual Risk Behavior among Latino Men Who Use the Internet to Seek Sex with Other Men. *Archives of Sexual Behavior*, 35: 473–481.

Carbery, J., and Burhmester, D. (1998). Friendship and Need Fulfilment during Three Phases of Young Adulthood. *Journal of Social and Personal Relationships*, 15: 393–409.

Carver, C. S., Scheier, M. F., and Weintraub, J. K. (1989). Assessing Coping Strategies: A Theoretically Based Approach. *Journal of Personality and Social Psychology*, 56: 267–283.

Cha, J.-H. (1994). Aspects of Individualism and Collectivism in Korea. In U. Kim, H. C. Triandis, C. Kağitçibaşi, S.-C. Choi, and G. Yoon, eds., *Individualism and Collectivism: Theory, Method and Applications*, pp. 157–174. Thousand Oaks, CA: Sage Publications.

Cheal, D. (2002). *The Sociology of Family Life*. Cambridge: Cambridge University Press.

Cherlin, A. J. (2004). The Deinstitutionalization of American Marriage. *Journal of Marriage and Family*, 66: 848–861.

Chesley, N. (2005). Blurring Boundaries? Linking Technology Use, Spillover, Individual Distress, and Family Satisfaction. *Journal of Marriage and Family*, 67: 1237–1248.

Cicchelli, V., and Martin, C. (2004). Young Adults in France: Getting Adult in the Context of Increased Autonomy and Dependency. *Journal of Comparative Family Studies*, 35: 615–626.

Clarke, H. D., Kornberg, A., McIntyre, C., Bauer-Kaase, P., and Kaase, M. (1999). The Effect of Economic Priorities on the Measurement of Value Change: New Experimental Evidence. *American Political Science Review*, 93: 637–647.

Cohan, C. L., Cole, S., and Davila, J. (2005). Marital Transitions among Repatriated Prisoners of War. *Journal of Social and Personal Relationships*, 22: 777–795.

Cohen, O., and Savaya, R. (2003). Lifestyle Differences in Traditionalism and Modernity and Reasons for Divorce among Muslim Palestinian Citizens of Israel. *Journal of Comparative Family Studies*, 34: 283–302.

Cohen, S., and Syme, S. L. (1985). Issues in the Study and Application of Social Support. In S. Cohen and S. L. Syme, eds., *Social Support and Health*, pp. 3–32. New York: Academic Press.

Cole, M. (1990). Cultural Psychology: A Once and Future Discipline? In J. Berman, ed., *Nebraska Symposium on Motivation*, 1989, pp. 279–335. Lincoln: University of Nebraska Press.

Coleman, J. S. (1988). Social Capital in the Creation of Human Capital. *American Journal of Sociology*, 94: S95–S120.

(1990). *Foundations of Social Theory.* Cambridge, MA: Harvard University Press.

Collins, N. L., and Feeney, B. C. (2000). A Safe Haven: Support-Seeking and Caregiving Processes in Intimate Relationships. *Journal of Personality and Social Psychology*, 78: 1053–1073.

Comte, A. (1887). *System of Positive Polity.* London: Longmans, Green.

Conger, R. D., and Conger, K. J. (2002). Resilience in Midwestern Families: Selected Findings from the First Decade of a Prospective, Longitudinal Study. *Journal of Marriage and Family*, 64: 361–373.

Constable, N. (2003). *Romance on a Global Stage: Pen Pals, Virtual Ethnography, and "Mail-Order" Marriages.* Berkeley: University of California Press.

Coontz, S. (2000). Historical Perspectives on Family Studies. *Journal of Marriage and Family*, 62: 283–297.

(2004). The World Historical Transformation of Marriage. *Journal of Marriage and Family* 66: 974–979.

Corwin, L. A. (1977). Caste, Class and the Love-Marriage: Social Change in India. *Journal of Marriage and Family*, 39: 823–831.

Coyne, J. C., Wortman, C. B., and Lehman, D. R. (1988). The Other Side of Support: Emotional Overinvolvement and Miscarried Helping. In B. H. Gottlieb, ed., *Marshalling Social Support: Formats, Processes, and Effects*, pp. 305–330. Newbury Park, CA: Sage Publications.

Cummins, R. (1989). Locus of Control and Social Support: Clarifiers of the Relationship between Job Stress and Job Satisfaction. *Journal of Applied Social Psychology*, 19: 772–788.

(1990). Job Stress and the Buffering Effects of Supervisory Support. *Group and Organizational Studies*, 15: 92–104.

Da Conceição, M. C. G. (2002). Life Course, Households and Institutions: Brazil and Mexico. *Journal of Comparative Family Studies*, 33: 315–344.

Dalton, R. J., and Ong, N.-N. T (2004). Civil Society and Social Capital in Vietnam. In G. Mutz and R. Klump, eds., *Modernization and Social Change in Vietnam*. Hamburg, Germany: IFA. Retrieved from http://www.worldvaluessurvey.org.

Daneback, K., Cooper, A., and Mansson, S.-A. (2005). An Internet Study of Cybersex Participants. *Archives of Sexual Behavior*, 34: 321–328.

Danziger, R. (1996). Compulsory Testing for HIV in Hungary. *Social Science and Medicine*, 43: 1199–1204.

Darvishpour, M. (2002). Immigrant Women Challenge the Role of Men: How the Changing Power Relationship within Iranian Families in Sweden Intensified Family Conflicts after Immigration. *Journal of Comparative Family Studies*, 33: 271–296.

David, H. P., Dytrych, Z., and Matejcek, Z. (2003). Born Unwanted. *American Psychologist*, 58: 224–229.

Davis, D. W., and Davenport, C. (1999). Assessing the Validity of the Post-materialism Index. *American Political Science Review*, 93: 649–664.

Davis, D. W., Dowley, K. M., and Silver, B. D. (1999). Postmaterialism in World Societies: Is It Really a Value Dimension? *American Journal of Political Science*, 43: 935–962.

D'Cruz, P., and Bharat, S. (2001). Beyond Joint and Nuclear: The Indian Family Revisited. *Journal of Comparative Family Studies*, 32: 167–194.

De Golyer, M. E. (1995). What Is Politics in Hong Kong? Unpublished report for the Hong Kong Transition Project, Baptist University, Hong Kong.

De Mino, W. P. H. (2000). From Bastardy to Equality: The Rights of Nonmarital Children and Their Fathers in Comparative Perspective. *Journal of Comparative Family Studies*, 31: 231–262.

Deci, E. L., and Ryan, R. M. (2000). The "What" and "Why" of Goal Pursuits: Human Needs and the Self-Determination of Behavior. *Psychological Inquiry*, 11: 227–268.

Delmonico, D. L. (2003). Editorial: Cybersex: Changing the Way We Relate. *Sexual and Relationship Therapy*, 18: 259–260.

Demos (2003). London Calling: How Mobile Technologies Will Transform Our Capital City. Summary report edited by H. McCarthy and P. Miller. Retrieved from http://www.demos.co.uk.

Dex, S. (2003). *Families and Work in the Twenty-First Century*. York, England: Joseph Rowntree Foundation.

Diamond, L. M. (2003). What Does Sexual Orientation Orient? A Biobehavioral Model Distinguishing Romantic Love and Sexual Desire. *Psychological Review*, 110: 173–192.

Diener, E., Gohm, C., Suh, E., and Oishi, S. (2000). Similarity of the Relations between Marital Status and Subjective Well-being across Cultures. *Journal of Cross-Cultural Psychology*, 31: 419–436.

Diez-Nicolas, J. (2003). Two Contradictory Hypotheses on Globalization: Societal Convergence or Civilization Differentiation and Clash. In R. Inglehart, ed., *Human Values and Social Change: Findings from the Values Surveys*, pp. 235–263. Leiden, The Netherlands: Brill.

Ding, Q. J., and Hesketh, T. (2006). Family Size, Fertility Preferences, and Sex Ratio in China in the Era of the One Child Family Policy: Results from National Family Planning and Reproductive Health Survey. *British Medical Journal*, 333: 371–373.

Dion, K. K., and Dion, K. L. (1991). Psychological Individualism and Romantic Love. *Journal of Social Behaviour and Personality*, 6: 17–33.

——— (1993). Individualistic and Collectivistic Perspectives on Gender and the Cultural Context of Love and Intimacy. *Journal of Social Issues*, 49: 53–69.

Divale, W., and Seda, A. (2001). Modernization as Changes in Cultural Complexity: New Cross-Cultural Measurements. *Cross-Cultural Research*, 35: 127–153.

Doherty, R. W., Hatfield, E., Thompson, K., and Choo, P. (1994). Cultural and Ethnic Influences on Love and Attachment. *Personal Relationships*, 1: 391–398.

Doise, W. (1986). *Levels of Explanation in Social Psychology*. Cambridge: Cambridge University Press.

Donoghoe, M. C. (2003). HIV-1 in Eastern Europe. *Lancet*, 361: 1910–1911.

Douglas, W. (2003). *Television Families: Is Something Wrong in Suburbia?* Mahwah, NJ: Lawrence Erlbaum.

Duffield, J., Gavin, J., and Scott, A. J. (2004). Meet Me in the Real World: Self-Expression in Close Relationships Initiated through Online Dating

Agencies. Paper presented at the International Association for Relationship Research Conference, Madison, WI.

Dumont, M., Yzerbyt, V., Wigboldus, D., and Gordijn, E. H. (2003). Social Categorization and Fear Reactions to the September 11th Terrorist Attacks. *Personality and Social Psychology Bulletin*, 29: 1509–1520.

Dunkel-Schetter, C., and Bennett, T. L. (1990). Differentiating the Cognitive and Behavioral Aspects of Social Support. In I. G. Sarason, B. R. Sarason, and G. R. Pierce, eds., *Social Support: An Interactional View*, pp. 267–296. New York: Wiley.

Durkheim, E. (1951). *Suicide*. New York: Free Press.

(1982). *The Rules of Sociological Method*. New York: Free Press.

Edin, K., Kefalas, M. J., and Reed, J. M. (2004). A Peek inside the Black Box: What Marriage Means for Poor Unmarried Parents. *Journal of Marriage and Family*, 66: 1007–1014.

Edwards, R. (2004). Present and Absent in Troubling Ways: Families and Social Capital Debates. *Sociological Review*, 52: 1–21.

Edwards, R., Franklin, J., and Holland, J. (2003). Families and Social Capital: Exploring the Issues. Working Paper 1: Families and Social Capital ESRC Research Group. South Bank University, London. Retrieved from http://www.lsbu.ac.uk/families/.

Einhorn, B. (1993). *Cinderella Goes to Market: Citizenship, Gender and Women's Movements in East Central Europe*. London: Verso.

Elder, G. H. (1998). The Life Course as Developmental Theory. *Child Development*, 69: 1–12.

Elliott, A., and Lemert, C. (2006). *The New Individualism: The Emotional Costs of Globalization*. London: Routledge.

Engels, F. (1884). *The Origin of the Family, Private Property and the State*. Retrieved from http://www.marxists.org/archive/marx/works/1884/origin-family/index.htm.

England, P. (2004). More Mercenary Mate Selection? Comment on Sweeney and Cancian (2004) and Press (2004). *Journal of Marriage and Family*, 66: 1034–1037.

Etzioni, A. (1968). *Active Society*. New York: Free Press.

(1996). *The New Golden Rule: Community and Morality in a Democratic Society*. New York: Basic Books.

Etzioni, A., and Etzioni, E. (1964). *Social Change, Sources, Patterns and Consequences*. New York: Basic Books.

Feldman, K. (1994). Socio-economic Structures and Mate Selection among Urban Populations in Developing Regions. *Journal of Comparative Family Studies*, 25: 329–343.

Feldman, S. S., and Rosenthal, D. A. (1991). Age Expectations of Behavioural Autonomy in Hong Kong, Australia and American Youth: The Influence of Family Variables and Adolescent's Values. *International Journal of Psychology*, 26: 1–23.

Fernandez-Dols, J. M. (2002). Perverse Justice and Perverse Norms: Another Turn of the Screw. In M. Ross and D. T. Miller, eds., *The Justice Motive in Everyday Life*, pp. 79–90. Cambridge: Cambridge University Press.

Fevre, R. (2000). Socializing Social Capital: Identity, the Transition to Work, and Economic Development. In S. Baron, J. Field, and T. Schuller, eds., *Social Capital: Critical Perspectives*. Oxford: Oxford University Press.

Fieldhouse, E., and Cutts, D. (2006). Electoral Participation of South Asian Communities in England and Wales. York, England: Joseph Rowntree Trust.

Fine, B. (2001). *Social Capital versus Social Theory: Political Economy and Social Science at the Turn of the Millennium*. New York: Routledge.

Fox, G. L. (1975). Love Match and Arranged Marriage in a Modernizing Nation: Mate Selection in Ankara, Turkey. *Journal of Marriage and Family*, 37: 180–193.

Frankl, V. (1984). *Man's Search for Meaning*, 3rd ed. New York: Simon and Schuster.

Franklin, J. (2004). Social Capital: Critical Perspectives. Families and Social Capital ESRC Research Group Working Papers, No. 7. London: South Bank University. Retrieved from http://www.lsbu.ac.uk/families/.

Freud, S. (1914). On Narcissism. In *Pelican Freud Library*, vol. 7. Harmondsworth, England: Penguin.

Fukuyama, F. (1995). *Trust: The Social Virtues and the Creation of Prosperity*. New York: Free Press.

Furstenberg, F. F. (2005). Banking on Families: How Families Generate and Distribute Social Capital. *Journal of Marriage and Family*, 67: 809–821.

Gabrenya, W., and McCormack, A. (2004). Culture and Personality Predictors of Cybersex and Online Pornography Attitudes. Paper presented at the seventeenth International Conference on Cross-Cultural Psychology, Xi'an China.

Gabrenya, W., McCormack, A., Fehir, S., and Van Driel, M. (2006). Cybersex and Culture: Behaviors, Attitudes, and Values. Paper presented at the eighteenth International Conference on Cross-Cultural Psychology, Isle of Spetses, Greece.

Georgas, J. (2004). Implications of the Findings Regarding Family Change in Different Cultures. Paper presented at the seventeenth International Congress for Cross-Cultural Psychology, Xi'an, China.

Georgas, J., Berry, J. W., Shaw, A., Christakopoulou, S., and Mylonas, K. (1996). Acculturation of Greek Family Values. *Journal of Cross-Cultural Psychology*, 2: 329–338.

Georgas, J., Berry, J. W., van de Vijver, F. J. R., Kağitçibaşi, Ç., and Poortinga, Y. H. (2006). *Families across Cultures: A 30-Nation Psychological Study*. Cambridge: Cambridge University Press.

George, L. K. (1989). Stress, Social Support, and Depression over the Life-Course. In K. S. Markides and C. L. Cooper, eds., *Aging, Stress and Health*, pp. 241–267. Chichester, England: Wiley.

Gershuny, J. (2005). Busyness as the Badge of Honor for the New Superordinate Working Class. (ISER Working Paper 2005–09). Colchester, England: University of Essex. Retrieved from http://www.iser.essex.ac.uk.

Giddens, A. (1989). *Sociology*. Cambridge: Polity Press.

(1991). *Modernity and Self-Identity*. Cambridge: Polity Press.

(1992). *The Transformation of Intimacy*. Cambridge: Polity Press.

Giddens, A., and Pierson, C. (1998). *Conversations with Anthony Giddens: Making Sense of Modernity*. Cambridge: Polity Press.

Gillies, V., and Edwards, R. (2005). Secondary Analysis in Exploring Family and Social Change: Addressing the Issue of Context. *Forum: Qualitative Social Research*, 6: Article 44.

Gillis, J. R. (2004). Marriages of the Mind. *Journal of Marriage and Family*, 66: 988–991.

Goethe, J. W. von ([1774]; 1989). *Die Leiden des Jungen Werthers [The Sorrows of Young Werther]*. London: Penguin Books.

Goode, W. J. (1963). *World Revolution and Family Patterns*. Glencoe, IL: Free Press.

Goodwin, R. (1990). Dating Agency Members: Are They Different? *Journal of Social and Personal Relationships*, 7: 423–430.

(1995). The Privatisation of the Personal? Intimate Disclosure in Modern-Day Russia. *Journal of Social and Personal Relationships*, 12: 21–31.

(1999). *Personal Relationships across Cultures*. London: Routledge.

(2006). Age and Social Support in Central and Eastern Europe: Social Change and Support in Four Cultures. *British Journal of Social Psychology*, 45: 799–815.

(2007). Poles and Chinese in the United Kingdom. Keynote address at the European Association for Community Psychology: International Seminar on Migration. Seville, Spain.

Goodwin, R., Allen, P., Nizharadze, G., Emelyanova, T., Dedkova, N., and Saenko, Y. (2002). Fatalism, Social Support and Mental Health in Four Former Soviet Cultures. *Personality and Social Psychology Bulletin*, 28: 1166–1171.

Goodwin, R., and Cramer, D. (2000). Marriage and Social Support in a British-Asian Community. *Journal of Community and Applied Social Psychology*, 10: 49–62.

(2002). *Inappropriate Relationships: The Unconventional, the Disapproved and the Forbidden*. Mahwah, NJ: Lawrence Erlbaum.

Goodwin, R., and Gaines, S. (2004). Relationships Beliefs and Relationship Quality across Cultures: Country as a Moderator of Dysfunctional Beliefs and Relationship Quality in Three Former Communist Societies. *Personal Relationships*, 11: 267–280.

(2006). Terrorism Perception and Its Consequences Following the 7th July Bombings: A Four-Wave Study in London, England. Unpublished manuscript, School of Social Sciences, Brunel University, London.

Goodwin, R., and Giles, S. (2003). Social Support Provision and Cultural Values in Indonesia and Britain. *Journal of Cross-Cultural Psychology*, 34: 240–245.

Goodwin, R., and Hernandez-Plaza, S. (2000). Perceived and Received Social Support in Two Cultures: Collectivism and Social Support in Spain and England. *Journal of Social and Personal Relationships*, 17: 285–294.

Goodwin, R., Kozlova, A., Kwiatkowska, A., Nguyen Luu, L. A., Nizharadze, G., Realo, A., Kulvet, A., and Rammer, A. (2003). Social Representations of HIV/AIDS in Central and Eastern Europe. *Social Science and Medicine*, 56: 1373–1384.

Goodwin, R., Kozlova, A., Nizharadze, G., and Polyakova, G. (2004). HIV/AIDS amongst Adolescents in Eastern Europe: Knowledge of HIV/AIDS, Social Representations of Risk and Sexual Activity amongst School Children and Homeless Adolescents in Russia, Georgia and the Ukraine. *Journal of Health Psychology*, 9: 381–396.

Goodwin, R., and Kunowska, K. (2006). Culture and Attachment: How Culture Might Affect the Attachment Process. Paper presented at the International Association for Relationship Research Conference, Rethymno, Crete.

Goodwin, R., Nizharazde, G., Nguyen Luu, L. A., Kosa, E., and Emelyanova, T. (1999). Glasnost and the Art of Conversation: A Multi-level Analysis of Disclosure across Three Cultures. *Journal of Cross-Cultural Psychology*, 30: 78–90.

(2002). Social Support in a Changing Europe. *European Journal of Social Psychology*, 31: 379–393.

Goodwin, R., Realo, A., Kwiatkowska, A., Kozlova, A., Nguyen-Luu, L. A., and Nizharadze, G. (2002). Values and Sexual Behavior in Central and Eastern Europe. *Journal of Health Psychology*, 7: 45–56.

Goodwin, R., and Tang, C. (1998). The Transition to Uncertainty? The Impacts of Hong Kong 1997 on Personal Relationships. *Personal Relationships*, 5: 183–190.

Goodwin, R., Willson, M., and Gaines, S. (2005). Terror Threat Perception and Its Consequences in Modern Britain. *British Journal of Psychology*, 96: 389–406.

Graupner, H. (2000). Sexual Consent: The Criminal Law in Europe and Overseas. *Archives of Sexual Behavior*, 29: 415–461.

Green, S. K., Buchanan, D. R., and Heuer, S. K. (1984). Winners, Losers, and Choosers: A Field Investigation of Dating Initiation. *Personality and Social Psychology Bulletin*, 10: 502–511.

Greenberg, J., Solomons, S., and Pyszcynski, T. (1997). Terror Management Theory of Self-Esteem and Cultural Worldviews: Empirical Assessments and Conceptual Refinements. In P. M. Zanna, ed., *Advances in Experimental Social Psychology*, vol. 29, pp. 61–141. San Diego: Academic Press.

Gudykunst, W. B., Nishida, T., and Schmidt, K. L. (1989). The Influence of Cultural Variability and Uncertainty Reduction in Ingroup vs. Outgroup and Same vs. Opposite Sex Relationships. *Western Journal of Speech Communication*, 53: 13–29.

Gupta, S., Smock, P. J., and Manning, W. D. (2004). Moving Out: Transition to Non-Residence among Resident Fathers in the United States, 1968–1997. *Journal of Marriage and Family*, 66: 627–638.

Hamers, F. F., and Downs, A. M. (2003). HIV in Central and Eastern Europe. *Lancet*, 361: 1035–1044.

Hareven, T. K. (2000). *Families, History, and Social Change: Life-Course and Cross-Cultural Perspectives*. Boulder, CO: Westview.

Harrell, S. (1992). Aspects of Marriage in Three South-Western Villages. *China Quarterly*, 130: 323–337.

Haskova, H., and Krizkova, A. (2003). *Women's Civic and Political Participation in the Czech Republic and the Role of European Union: Gender Equality and Accession Policies.* Prague: Institute of Sociology, Academy of Sciences of the Czech Republic.

Hatano, Y. (1990). Changes in the Sexual Activities of the Japanese Youth. Paper presented at the International Conference on Sexuality in Asia, Hong Kong.

Hatfield, E., and Rapson, R. L. (1996). *Love and Sex: Cross-Cultural Perspectives.* Boston: Allyn and Bacon.

(2004). Emotional Contagion: Religious and Ethnic Hatreds and Global Terrorism. In Larissa Z. Tiedens and Colin Wayne Leach, eds., *The Social Life of Emotions*, pp. 129–143. Cambridge: Cambridge University Press.

Hazan, C., and Shaver, P. (1987). Romantic Love Conceptualized as an Attachment Process. *Journal of Personality and Social Psychology*, 52: 511–524.

(1994). Attachment as an Organizational Framework for Research on Close Relationships. *Psychological Inquiry*, 5: 1–22.

Headley, D. (1998). *HIV/AIDS in Russia.* London: Charities Aid Foundation, Russian Office.

Heer, D. M. (1965). Abortion, Contraception, and Population Policy in the Soviet Union. *Demography*, 2: 531–539.

Hesketh, T., Li, L., and Xing, Z. W. (2005). The Effect of China's One-Child Policy after 25 Years. *New England Journal of Medicine*, 353: 1171–1176.

Hesketh, T., and Zhu, W. X. (1997). The One Child Family Policy: The Good, the Bad, and the Ugly. *British Medical Journal*, 314: 1685–1687.

Higgins, B., and Higgins, J. (1963). *Indonesia: The Crisis of the Millstones.* New York: Van Nostrand.

Hill, R. (1949). *Families under Stress.* New York: Harper and Row.

Hillhouse, R. J. (1993). The Individual Revolution: The Social Basis for Transition to Democracy. Doctoral dissertation, Department of Political Sciences, University of Michigan, Ann Arbor.

Hingley, R. (2005). *Globalizing Roman Culture: Unity, Diversity and Empire.* London: Routledge.

Hird, M., and Abshoff, K. (2000). Women Without Children: A Contradiction in Terms? *Journal of Comparative Family Studies*, 31: 347–366.

Hirschman, C., and Minh, N. G. (2002). Tradition and Change in Vietnamese Family Structure in the Red River Delta. *Journal of Marriage and Family*, 64: 1063–1079.

Hitchner, R. B. (forthcoming). *The First Globalization: The Roman Empire and Its Legacy in the Twenty-First Century.*

Ho, D., and Chau, A. W. L. (1995). Transitional Hong Kong from a Psychological Perspective: Confidence in the Future. (Discussion Document No. 2) PATH Project, Hong Kong.

Hobfoll, S., and London, P. (1986). The Relationship of Self-Concept and Social Support to Emotional Distress among Women during War. *Journal of Social and Clinical Psychology*, 3: 231–248.

Hobfoll, S. E. (1988). *The Ecology of Stress*. Washington, DC: Hemisphere.
  (1989). Conservation of Resources: A New Attempt at Conceptualizing Stress. *American Psychologist*, 44: 513–524.
Hofstede, G. (2001). *Culture's Consequences: Comparing Values, Behaviors, Institutions, and Organizations across Nations*. Thousand Oaks, CA: Sage Publications.
Honig, E., and Hershatter, G. (1988). *Personal Voices: Chinese Women in the 1980s*. Stanford, CA: Stanford University Press.
Hooghiemstra, E. (2001). Migrants, Partner Selection and Integration: Crossing Borders? *Journal of Comparative Family Studies*, 32: 601–626.
Horenczyk, G., and Bekerman, Z. (1993). Calibrating Identities in the Fast Track of Immigration: Acculturation Attitudes and Perceived Acculturation Ideologies. Paper presented at the conference on Changing European Identities: Social Psychological Analyses of Social Change, Farnham Castle, Surrey, England.
Hortacsu, N. (1997). Family Initiated and Couple Initiated Marriages in Turkey. *Genetic, Social and General Psychology Monographs*, 123: 325–342.
  (2003). Marriage in Turkey. In R. R. Hamon and B. B. Ingoldsby, eds., *Mate Selection across Cultures*, pp. 155–171. Thousand Oaks, CA: Sage Publications.
Hraba, J., Lorenz, F. O., and Pechacova, Z. (2000). Family Stress during the Czech Transformation. *Journal of Marriage and Family*, 62: 520–531.
Hui, C. H. (1988). Measurement of Individualism and Collectivism. *Journal of Research in Personality*, 22: 17–36.
Hui, C. H., Triandis, H. C., and Yee, C. (1991). Cultural Differences in Reward Allocation: Is Collectivism the Explanation? *British Journal of Social Psychology*, 30: 145–157.
Huntingdon, E. (1924). *Climate and Civilisation*, 3rd ed. New Haven, CT: Yale University Press.
Huntingdon, S. P. (1996). *The Clash of Civilizations and the Remaking of World Order*. London: Simon and Schuster.
Huston, T. L. (2000). The Social Ecology of Marriage and Other Intimate Unions. *Journal of Marriage and Family*, 62: 298–320.
Huston, T. L., and Melz, H. (2004). The Case for (Promoting) Marriage: The Devil Is in the Details. *Journal of Marriage and Family*, 66: 943–958.
Ibn Khaldun (1987). *An Arab Philosophy of History: Selections from the Prolegomena of Ibn Khaldun of Tunis (1332–1406)*. Transl. by Charles Issawi. London: John Murray.
Iecovich, E., Barasch, M., Mirsky, J., Kaufman, R., Avgar, A., and Kol-Fogelson, A. (2004). Social Support Networks and Loneliness among Elderly Jews in Russia and Ukraine. *Journal of Marriage and Family*, 66: 306–317.
Inglehart, R. (1990). *Culture Shift in Advanced Industrial Society*. Princeton, NJ: Princeton University Press.
  (1997). *Modernization and Postmodernization: Cultural, Economic and Political Change in 43 Societies*. Princeton, NJ: Princeton University Press.
  (2003). *Human Values and Social Change: Findings from the Values Surveys*. Leiden, The Netherlands: Brill.

Inglehart, R., and Baker, W. E. (2000). Modernization, Cultural Change and the Persistence of Traditional Values. *American Sociological Review*, 65: 19–51.

Inglehart, R., and Klingemann, H. D (2000). Genes, Culture, Democracy and Happiness. In E. Diener and E. M. Suh, eds., *Culture and Subjective Well-being*, pp. 165–183. Cambridge, MA: MIT Press.

Inglehart, R., and Norris, P. (2003). *Rising Tide: Gender Equality and Cultural Change around the World*. Cambridge: Cambridge University Press.

Inglehart, R., Norris, P., and Welzel, C. (2002). Gender Equality and Democracy. *Comparative Sociology*, 1: 321–345.

Ingoldsby, B. B. (2003). The Mate Selection Process in the United States. In R. R. Hamon and B. B. Ingoldsby, eds., *Mate Selection across Cultures*, pp. 3–18. Thousand Oaks, CA: Sage Publications.

Inkeles, A. (1977). Understanding and Misunderstanding Individual Modernity. *Journal of Cross-Cultural Psychology*, 8: 135–176.

Inkeles, A., and Smith, D. H. (1974). *Becoming Modern: Individual Change in Six Developing Countries*. Cambridge, MA: Harvard University Press.

Institute for Social and Economic Research (2004/2005). Taking the Long View: The ISER Report 2004/5. University of Essex, Colchester, England.

Ismael, S. T. (2004). Dismantling the Iraqi Social Fabric: From Dictatorship Through Sanctions to Occupation. *Journal of Comparative Family Studies*, 32: 333–349.

Jabbra, N. W. (2004). Family Change in Lebanon's Biqa' Valley: What Were the Results of the Civil War? *Journal of Comparative Family Studies*, 32: 259–270.

Janoff-Bulman, R. (1989). Assumptive Worlds and the Stress of Traumatic Events: Applications of the Schema Construct. *Social Cognition*, 7: 113–136.

Jenkins, R., Klein, J., and Parker, C. (2005). Mental Health in Post-Communist Countries. *British Medical Journal*, 331: 173.

Jerusalem, M., and Mittag, W. (1995). Self-Efficacy in Stressful Life Transition. In A. Bandura, ed., *Self-Efficacy in Changing Societies*, pp. 177–201. Cambridge: Cambridge University Press.

Johnson, M. P., Caughlin, J. P., and Huston, T. L. (1999). The Tripartite Nature of Marital Commitment: Personal, Moral, and Structural Reasons to Stay Married. *Journal of Marriage and Family*, 61: 160–177.

Jones, G. W. (2005). The Flight from Marriage in South-East and East Asia. *Journal of Comparative Family Studies*, 36: 93–119.

Kachkachishvili, Y. (1999). Analysis of Sociological Survey on Reproductive Health Related Problems among Residents of Tbilisi. *New Paradigms*, 3: 125–129.

Kağitçibaşi, C. (1990). Family and Socialization in Cross-Cultural Perspective: A Model of Change. In J. Berman, ed., *Nebraska Symposium on Motivation*, 1989, pp. 135–200. Lincoln: University of Nebraska Press.

(1996). *Family and Human Development across Cultures: The View from the Other Side*. Mahwah, NJ: Lawrence Erlbaum.

(2004). A Theoretical Orientation to the Family and Family Change: Recent Evidence. Paper presented at the seventeenth International Congress for Cross-Cultural Psychology, Xi'an, China.

(2006). Autonomous-Related Self in Family and Culture: Toward a Healthy Human Model. Keynote address, International Conference on Personal Relationships, Rethymno, Crete.

Kahl, J. A. (1968). *The Measurement of Modernization: A Study of Values in Brazil and Mexico*. Austen: University of Texas Press.

Kalichman, S. C. (1998). *Preventing AIDS: A Sourcebook of Behavioural Interventions*. Mahwah, NJ: Lawrence Erlbaum.

Keller, H. (2002). Introduction: Developmental Psychology and Its Application across Cultures. *Cross-Cultural Psychology Bulletin*, 35: 6–9.

Kemmelmeier, M., Burnstein, E., Krumov, K., Genkova, P., Kanagawa, C., Hirshberg, M. S., Erb, H.-P., Wieczorkowska, G., and Noels, K. A. (2003). Individualism, Collectivism, and Authoritarianism in Seven Societies. *Journal of Cross-Cultural Psychology*, 34: 304–322.

Kennedy, M. D., and Kirwil, L. (2004). Guest Editors' Introduction: What Have We Learned from the Study of Social Change in Poland? *International Journal of Sociology*, 34: 3–14.

Kenrick, D. T., and Keefe, R. C. (1992). Age Preferences in Mates Reflect Sex Differences in Human Reproductive Strategies. *Behavioral and Brain Sciences*, 15: 75–133.

Kerr, C., Dunlop, J. T., Harbison, F. H., and Myers, C. A. (1964). *Industrialization and Industrial Man: The Problems of Labor and Management in Economic Growth*. New York: Oxford University Press.

Kiernan, K. (2004). Redrawing the Boundaries of Marriage. *Journal of Marriage and Family*, 66: 980–987.

Kobasa, S. C., and Puccetti, M. C. (1983). Personality and Social Resources in Stress Resistance. *Journal of Personality and Social Psychology*, 45: 839–850.

Koh, E. M. L., and Tan, J. (2000). Favoritism and the Changing Value of Children: A Note on the Chinese Middle Class in Singapore. *Journal of Comparative Family Studies*, 31: 519–528.

Kohn, M. L., Naoi, A., Schoenbach, C., Schooler, C., and Slomczynski, K. M. (1990). Position in the Class Structure and Psychological Functioning in the United States, Japan, and Poland. *American Journal of Sociology*, 95: 964–1008.

Kohn, M. L., Zaborowski, W., Mach, B. W., Khmelko, V., Slomczynski, K. M., Heman, C., and Podobnik, B. (2000). Complexity of Activities and Personality under Conditions of Radical Social Change: A Comparative Analysis of Poland and Ukraine. *Social Psychology Quarterly*, 63: 187–208.

Kon, I. (1995). *The Sexual Revolution in Russia: From the Age of the Czars to Today*. New York: Free Press.

Kotzé, H., and Lombard, K. (2003). Revising the Value Shift Hypothesis: A Descriptive Analysis of South Africa's Value Priorities between 1990 and 2001. In R. Inglehart, ed., *Human Values and Social Change: Findings from the Values Surveys*. Leiden, The Netherlands: Brill.

Kraaykamp, G. (2002). Trends and Countertrends in Sexual Permissiveness: Three Decades of Attitude Change in the Netherlands, 1965–1995. *Journal of Marriage and Family*, 64: 225–239.

Kraus, N., Liang, J., and Gu, S. (1998). Financial Strain, Received Support, Anticipated Support, and Depressive Symptoms in the People's Republic of China. *Psychology and Aging*, 13: 58–68.

Kryshtanovskaya, O. (1992). The New Business Elite. In D. Lane, ed., *Russia in Flux*. Aldershot, England: Elgar.

Kung, W., Hung, S.-L., and Chan, C. L. (2004). How the Socio-cultural Context Shapes Women's Divorce Experience in Hong Kong. *Journal of Comparative Family Studies*, 35: 33–51.

Kurzban, R., and Weeden, J. (2005). HurryDate: Mate Preferences in Action (2005). *Evolution and Human Behavior*, 26: 227–244.

Kwon, H.-Y., Rueter, M. A., Lee., M.-S., Koh, S., and Ok, S. W. (2003). Marital Relationships Following the Korean Economic Crisis: Applying the Family Stress Model. *Journal of Marriage and Family*, 65: 316–325.

Ladd, E. C. (1999). *The Ladd Report*. New York: Free Press.

Lakatos, I. (1970). Falsification and the Methodology of Scientific Research Programs. In I. Lakatos and A. Musgrave, eds., *Criticism and the Growth of Knowledge*, pp. 91–196. Cambridge: Cambridge University Press.

Lakey, B., and Cassady, P. (1990). Cognitive Processes in Perceived Social Support. *Journal of Personality and Social Psychology*, 59: 337–343.

Lalonde, R. N., Hynie, M., Pannu, M., and Tatla, S. (2004). The Role of Culture in Interpersonal Relationships. *Journal of Cross-Cultural Psychology*, 35: 503–524.

Lam Chiu, C.-Y., Lau, I., and Hong, Y.-Y. (1995). Social Identity of Hong Kong Adolescents. Paper presented at the workshop Countdown to 1997: Hong Kong in the Transition Workshop, Hong Kong.

Lane, D. (1992). *Soviet Society under Perestroika*. London: Routledge.

La Piere, R. T. (1965). *Social Change*. New York: McGraw-Hill.

La Rossa, R., Jaret, C., Gadgil, M., and Wynn, G. R. (2000). The Changing Culture of Fatherhood in Comic-Strip Families: A Six-Decade Analysis. *Journal of Marriage and Family*, 62: 375–387.

Lasch, C. (1977). *Haven in a Heartless World: The Family Besieged*. New York: Basic Books.

Laslett, P., and Wall, R. (1972). *Household and Family in Past Time*. Cambridge: Cambridge University Press.

Lau, I. Y., Chiu, C.-Y., Chau, A. W., Lee, H.-C., and Ho, D. Y. F. (1995). Psychosocial Correlates of Reactions to 1997. Paper presented at the workshop Countdown to 1997: Hong Kong in the Transition Workshop, Hong Kong.

Lau, S. (1981). Chinese Familism in an Urban-Industrial Setting: The Case of Hong Kong. *Journal of Marriage and Family*, 43: 977–992.

Lauer, R. H. (1977). *Perspectives on Social Change*, 2nd ed. Boston: Allyn and Bacon.

Lazarus, R. S. (1991). *Emotion and Adaptation*. New York: Oxford University Press.

Lazarus, R. S., and Folkman, F. (1984). *Stress, Appraisal and Coping*. New York: Springer.

Le Bourdais, C., and La Pierre-Adamcyk, E. (2004). Changes in Conjugal Life in Canada: Is Cohabitation Replacing Marriage? *Journal of Marriage and Family*, 66: 929–942.

Lee, G. R. (1987). Comparative Perspectives. In M. B. Sussman and S. K. Steinmetz, eds., *Handbook of Marriage and the Family*, pp. 59–80. New York: Plenum Press.

Lee, J. A. (1973). *The Colors of Love: An Exploration of the Ways of Loving*. Don Mills, Canada: New Press.

Leung, K., and Bond, M. H. (2004). Social Axioms: A Model for Social Beliefs in Multicultural Perspective. *Advances in Experimental Social Psychology*, 36: 119–197.

Lewis, J. (2003). *Should We Worry about Family Change? The 2001 Joanne Goodman Lectures*. Toronto: University of Toronto Press.

Li, G., and Xu, A. Q. (2004). *Youth's Mate Selection in the Marriage Market*. Shanghai: Shanghai Academy of Social Sciences.

Liebkind, K. (1996). Acculturation and Stress: Vietnamese Refugees in Finland. *Journal of Cross-Cultural Psychology*, 27: 161–180.

Liem, R., and Liem, J. (1978). Social Class and Mental Illness Reconsidered: The Role of Economic Stress and Social Support. *Journal of Health and Social Behavior*, 19: 139–156.

Lin, I.-F., Goldman, N., Weinstein, M., Lin, Y.-H., Gorrindo, T., and Seeman, T. (2003). Gender Differences in Adult Children's Support of Their Parents in Taiwan. *Journal of Marriage and Family*, 65: 184–200.

Linton, R. (1939). *The Individual and His Society*. New York: Columbia University Press.

Liu, D. L., Ng, M. L., and Chu, L. P. (1992). Sexual Behaviour in Modern China: A Report of the Nationwide Sex Civilisation Survey of 20,000 Subjects in China (in Chinese). Shanghai: SJPC Publishing Co.

Liu, L. (2006). Quality of Life as a Social Representation in China: A Qualitative Study. *Social Indicators Research*, 75: 217–240.

Logan, J. R., Bian, F., and Bian, Y. (1988). Tradition and Change in the Urban Chinese Family: The Case of Living Arrangements. *Social Forces*, 76: 851–882.

Lu, Z. Z., Maume, D. J., and Bellas, M. L. (2000). Chinese Husbands' Participation in Household Labor. *Journal of Comparative Family Studies*, 31: 191–215.

Lunin, I., Hall, T. L., Mandel, J. S., Kay, J., and Hearst, N. (1995). Adolescent Sexuality in St. Petersburg, Russia. *AIDS*, 9: S53–S60.

Luthar, S. S., Cicchetti, D., and Becker, B. (2000). The Construct of Resilience: A Critical Evaluation and Guidelines for Future Work. *Child Development*, 71: 543–562.

Maloney, W., Smith, G., and Stoker, G. (2000). Social Capital and Urban Governance: Adding a More Contextualized "Top-Down" Perspective. *Political Studies*, 48: 802–820.

Mamali, C. (1996). Interpersonal Communication in Totalitarian Societies. In W. B. Gudykunst., S. Ting-Toomey, and T. Nishida, eds., *Communication in Personal Relationships across Cultures*, pp. 217–236. Thousand Oaks, CA: Sage Publications.

Manderson, L. (1995). The Pursuit of Pleasure and the Sale of Sex. In P. R. Abramson and S. D. Pinkerton, eds., *Sexual Nature, Sexual Culture*, pp. 305–329. Chicago: University of Chicago Press.

Markova, I. (1997). The Individual and the Community: A Post Communist Perspective. *Journal of Community and Applied Social Psychology*, 7: 3–17.

Markova, I., Moodie, E., Farr, R. M., Drozda-Senkowska, E., Eros, F., Plichtova, J., Gervais, M.-C., Hoffmannova, J., and Mullerova, O. (1998). Social Representations of the Individual: A Post-Communist Perspective. *European Journal of Social Psychology*, 28: 797–829.

Markus, H. R., and Kitayama, S. (1994). A Collective Fear of the Collective: Implications for Selves and Theories of Selves. *Personality and Social Psychology Bulletin*, 20: 568–579.

Martindale, D. (1962). *Social Life and Cultural Change*. Princeton, NJ: D. Van Nostrand.

Martínez, M., and García, M. (1995). La perspectiva psicosocial en la conceptualización del apoyo social [Psychosocial Perspective in Conceptualizing Social Support]. *Revisita de Psicología Social*, 10: 61–74.

Marx, K., and Engels, F. (1932). *Manifesto of the Communist Party*. New York: International Publishers.

Maya Jariego, I. (2006). Mallas de paisanaje: El entramado de relaciones de los immigrantes. In J. L. Pérez Pont, ed., *Geografías del desorden: Migración, alteridad y nueva esfera social [Geographies of Turbulence: Migration, Otherness, and New Social Spheres]*, pp. 257–276. Valencia, Spain: Universidad de Valencia.

McClelland, D. (1961). *The Achieving Society*. New York: Free Press.

McCubbin, H. I., and Patterson, J. M. (1983). The Family Stress Process: The Double ABCX Model of Adjustment and Adaptation. *Marriage and Family Review*, 6: 7–37.

McKenna, K. Y. A., Green, A. S., and Smith, P. K. (2001). Demarginalizing the Sexual Self. *Journal of Sex Research*, 38: 302–311.

McKinney, C. V. (1992). Wives and Sisters: Bajju Marital Patterns. *Journal of Comparative Family Studies*, 31: 75–87.

Medora, N. P. (2003). Mate Selection in Contemporary India. In R. R. Hamon and B. B. Ingoldsby, eds., *Mate Selection across Cultures*, pp. 209–230. Thousand Oaks, CA: Sage Publications.

Medora, N. P., Larson, J. H., Hortacsu, N., and Dave, P. (2002). Perceived Attitudes towards Romanticism: A Cross-Cultural Study of American, Asian-Indian, and Turkish Young Adults. *Journal of Comparative Family Studies*, 33: 155–178.

Mehmet, K. A., and Mehmet, O. (2004). Family in War and Conflict: Using Social Capital for Survival in War Torn Cyprus. *Journal of Comparative Family Studies*, 35: 295–309.

Micklin, M. (1969). Urbanization, Technology, and Traditional Values in Guatemala: Some Consequences of a Changing Social Structure. *Social Forces*, 47: 438–446.

Mikulincer, M., Florian, V., and Hirschberger, G. (2003). The Existential Function of Close Relationships: Introducing Death into the Science of Love. *Personality and Social Psychology Bulletin*, 7: 20–40.

Mishra, R. C. (1994). Individualist and Collectivist Orientations across Generations. In U. Kim, H. C. Triandis, C. Kağitçibaşi, S.-C. Choi, and

G. Yoon, eds., *Individualism and Collectivism: Theory, Method and Applications*, pp. 225–238. Thousand Oaks, CA: Sage Publications.

Moaddel, M., and Azadarmaki, T. (2003). The Worldviews of Islamic Publics: The Cases of Egypt, Iran, and Jordan. In R. Inglehart, ed., *Human Values and Social Change: Findings from the Values Surveys*, pp. 69–89. Leiden, The Netherlands: Brill.

Modo, I. V. O. (2001). Migrant Culture and Changing Face of Family Structure in Lesotho. *Journal of Comparative Family Studies*, 32: 443–452.

Moghadam, V. M. (2004). Patriarchy in Transition: Women and the Changing Family in the Middle East. *Journal of Family Comparative Studies*, 35: 137–162.

Moghaddam, F. M., and Crystal, D. S. (2000). Change, Continuity, and Culture: The Case of Power Relations in Iran and Japan. In S. Rushton and J. Duckitt, eds., *Political Psychology: Cultural and Cross-Cultural Foundations*, pp. 201–214. New York: Macmillan.

Moreno, A. (2003). Corruption and Democracy: A Cultural Assessment. In R. Inglehart, ed., *Human Values and Social Change: Findings from the Values Surveys*, pp. 265–277. Leiden, The Netherlands: Brill.

Moscovici, S. (1961). *La psychoanalyse, son image et son public [Psychoanalysis: Its Image and Its Audience]*. Paris: Presses Universitaires de France.

Murdock, G. P. (1949). *Social Structure*. New York: Macmillan.

Murphy, E. M. (2003). Being Born Female Is Dangerous to Your Health. *American Psychologist*, 58: 205–210.

Murphy-Berman, V., Levesque, H. L., and Berman, J. J. (1996). U.N. Convention on the Rights of the Child. *American Psychologist*, 51: 1257–1261.

Nakoney, P. A., Reddick, R., and Rodgers, J. L. (2004). Did Divorces Decline after the Oklahoma City Bombing? *Journal of Marriage and Family*, 66: 90–100.

National Statistics (2007). Divorces. Retrieved from http://www.statistics.gov.uk.

Nauck, B., and Settles, B. H. (2001). Immigrant and Ethnic Minority Families: An Introduction. *Journal of Comparative Family Studies*, 32: 461–463.

Neto, F., Mullet, E., Deschamps, J.-C., Barros, J., Benvindo, R., Camino, L., Falconi, A., Kagibanga, V., and Machado, M. (2000). Cross-Cultural Variations in Attitudes toward Love. *Journal of Cross-Cultural Psychology*, 31: 626–635.

Nisbet, R. A. (1969). *Social Change and History*. London: Oxford University Press.

Norris, F. H., and Kaniasty, K. (1996). Received and Perceived Social Support in Times of Stress: A Test of the Social Support Deterioration Deterrence Model. *Journal of Personality and Social Psychology*, 71: 498–511.

Norris, P., and Inglehart, R. (2003). Islamic Culture and Democracy: Testing the "Clash of Civilizations" Thesis. In R. Inglehart, ed., *Human Values and Social Change: Findings from the Values Surveys*, pp. 5–35. Leiden, The Netherlands: Brill.

Ogburn, W. F., and Nimkoff, M. F. (1955). *Technology and the Changing Family*. Boston: Houghton Mifflin.

Onishi, M., and Gjerde, P. F. (2002). Attachment Strategies in Urban Japanese Middle Class Couples: A Cultural Theme Analysis of Asymmetry in Marital Relationship. *Personal Relationships*, 9: 435–455.

Oppong, C. (1980). From Love to Institution: Indications of Change in Akan Marriage. *Journal of Family History*, 5: 197–209.

Oropesa, R. S., and Landale, N. S. (2004). The Future of Marriage and Hispanics. *Journal of Marriage and Family*, 66: 901–920.

Owen, D. (1994). Spatial Variations in Ethnic Minority Group Populations in Great Britain. *Population Trends*, 78: 23–33.

Páez, D., Echebarria, A., Valencia, J., Romo, I., San Juan, C., and Vergara, A. (1991). AIDS Social Representations: Contents and Processes. *Journal of Community and Applied Social Psychology*, 1: 89–104.

Pahl, R. (2000). *On Friendship*. Cambridge: Polity Press.

Panok, V., Pavlenko, V., and Korallo, L. (2006). Psychology in the Ukraine. *Psychologist*, 19: 730–732.

Parsons, T. (1959). The Social Structure of the Family. In R. N. Anshen, ed., *The Family: Its Function and Destiny*, pp. 173–201. New York: Harper and Row.

—— (1966). *Societies: Evolutionary and Comparative Perspectives*. Englewood-Cliffs, NJ: Prentice Hall.

Patterson, J. M. (2002). Integrating Family Resilience and Family Stress Theory. *Journal of Marriage and Family*, 64: 349–360.

Pearlin, L., and Schooler, C. (1978). The Structure of Coping. *Journal of Health and Social Behavior*, 19: 2–21.

Phalet, K., and Schönpflug, U. (2001). Intergenerational Transmission in Turkish Immigrant Families: Parental Collectivism, Achievement Values and Gender Differences. *Journal of Comparative Family Studies*, 32: 489–503.

Philaretou, A. G., Mahfouz, A. Y., and Allen, K. R. (2005). Use of Internet Pornography and Men's Well-Being. *International Journal of Men's Health*, 4: 149–169.

Pillai, V. K., and Roy, L. C. (1996). Attitudes toward Sexual Behavior among Unmarried Zambian Secondary School Females. *Journal of Social Psychology*, 136: 111–112.

Pimentel, E. E., and Liu, J. (2004). Exploring Nonnormative Coresidence in Urban China: Living with Wives' Parents. *Journal of Marriage and Family*, 66: 821–836.

Polini, B., Quadrelli, I., and Rapari, S. (2004). Becoming Parents in a Context of Low Birth-Rate. Paper presented at the International Conference on the Future of the Family, Social Capital Foundation, Brussels.

Popenoe, D. (1988). *Disturbing the Nest: Family Change and Decline in Modern Societies*. New York: Aldine de Gruyter.

—— (1993). American Family Decline: 1960–1990: A Review and Appraisal. *Journal of Marriage and Family*, 55: 527–556.

Poppen, P. (2004). Mental Health and Disclosure of HIV-Status among Brazilian and Colombian Gay Men. Paper presented at the seventeenth International Congress for Cross-Cultural Psychology, Xi'an, China.

Press, J. E. (2004). Cute Butts and Housework: A Gynocentric Theory of Assortative Mating. *Journal of Marriage and Family*, 66: 1029–1033.

Putnam, R. D. (2000). *Bowling Alone*. New York: Simon and Schuster.

Pyszcynski, T., Solomon, S., and Greenberg, J. (2003). *In the Wake of 9/11: The Psychology of Terror*. Washington, DC: APA Publications.

Rainer, H., and Siedler, T. (2006). Does Democracy Foster Trust? (Working Paper 2006–31). Institute of Social and Economic Research, University of Essex, Colchester, England.

Reischauer, E. (1988). *The Japanese Today: Change and Continuity*. Cambridge, MA: Harvard University Press.

Remarque, E. M. ([1929]; 1996). *All Quiet on the Western Front*. New York: Fawcett Columbine.

Reniers, G. (2001). The Post-Migration Survival of Traditional Marriage Patterns: Consanguineous Marriages among Turks and Moroccans in Belgium. *Journal of Comparative Family Studies*, 32: 21–45.

Renton, A. M., Borisenko, K. K., Tichonova, L. I., and Akovian, V. A. (1999). The Control and Management of Sexually Transmitted Diseases: A Comparison of the Ukraine and the Russian Federation. *International Journal of STD and AIDS*, 10: 659–664.

Reykowski, J. (1994). Why Did the Collectivist State Fail? *Theory and Society*, 23: 233–252.

(2004). Unexpected Traps of the Democratic Transformation. *International Journal of Sociology*, 34: 35–47.

Rhodes, T., Ball, A., Stimson, G. V., Kobyshcha, Y., Fitch, C., Pokrvsky, V., Bezruchenko-Novach, M., Burrows, D., Renton, A., and Andrushchak, L. (1999). HIV Infection Associated with Drug Injecting in the Newly Independent States, Eastern Europe: The Social and Economic Context of Epidemics. *Addiction*, 94: 1323–1336.

Rhodes, T., Stimson, G. V., Crofts, N., Ball, A., Dehne, K., and Khodakevich, L. (1999). Drug Injecting, Rapid HIV Spread, and the "Risk Environment": Implications for Assessment and Response. *AIDS*, 13: S259–S269.

Rice, P. L. (1992). *Stress and Health*, 2nd ed. Pacific Grove, CA: Brooks/Cole.

Riley, M. W., Kahn, R., and Foner, A. (1994). *Age and Structural Lag: Society's Failure to Provide Meaningful Opportunities in Work, Family and Leisure*. New York: John Wiley and Sons.

Ritzer, G. (1993). *The McDonaldization of Society*. Thousand Oaks, CA: Pine Forge Press.

Roberts, J. N. (2004). What's "Social" about "Social Capital"? *British Journal of Politics and International Relations*, 6: 471–493.

Roberts, J. N., and Devine, F. (2004). Some Everyday Experiences of Voluntarism: Social Capital, Pleasure, and the Contingency of Participation. *Social Politics*, 11: 280–296.

Rohner, R. (1984). Toward a Conception of Culture for Cross-Cultural Psychology. *Journal of Cross-Cultural Psychology*, 15: 111–138.

Rose, R. (1995). New Russia Barometer IV. (Studies in Public Policy, No. 250). Glasgow: Centre for the Study of Public Policy, University of Strathclyde.

Rosenblatt, P. C., and Anderson, R. M. (1981). Human Sexuality in Cross-Cultural Perspective. In M. Cook, ed., *The Bases of Human Sexual Attraction*, pp. 215–250. London: Academic Press.

Rosenbrock, R. M. (2000). The Normalization of AIDS in Western European Countries. *Social Science and Medicine*, 50: 1607–1629.

Rosenfeld, M. J. (2002). Measures of Assimilation in the Marriage Market: Mexican Americans, 1970–1990. *Journal of Marriage and Family*, 64: 152–162.

Ross, M. W. (2005). Typing, Doing, and Being: Sexuality and the Internet. *The Journal of Sex Research*, 42: 342–352.

Rostgaard, T. (2004). Family Support Policy in Central and Eastern Europe: A Decade and a Half of Transition. UNESCO Education Sector, Early Childhood and Family Policy Series, 8, 2004. Retrieved at http://www.forumdafamilia.com/arquivo/familia/unescofamily04.pdf.

Roth, S., and Cohen, L. J. (1986). Approach, Avoidance, and Coping with Stress. *American Psychologist*, 41: 813–819.

Rothbaum, F., Pott, M., Azuma, H., Miyake, K., and Weisz, J. (2000). The Development of Close Relationships in Japan and the United States: Paths of Symbiotic Harmony and Generative Tension. *Child Development*, 71: 1121–1142.

Rothenbacher, F. (1998). Social Change in Europe and Its Impact on Family Structures. In J. Eekelaar and N. Thandabantu, eds., *The Changing Family: International Perspectives on the Family and Family Law*, pp. 3–31. Oxford: Hart.

Roy, P., and Hamilton, I. A. T. (2000). Intermarriage among Italians: Some Regional Variations in Australia. *Journal of Comparative Family Studies*, 31: 63–78.

Ruan, F., and Matsumura, M. (1991). *Sex in China: Studies in Sexology in Chinese Culture*. New York: Plenum Press.

Sarason, B. R., Sarason, I. G., and Gurung, R. A. R. (1997). Close Personal Relationships and Health Outcomes: A Key to the Role of Social Support. In S. W. Duck, ed., *Handbook of Personal Relationships: Theory, Research and Interventions*, 2nd ed., pp. 547–573. Chichester, England: John Wiley.

Sarason, I. G., Sarason, B. R., and Pierce, G. R. (1994). Social Support: Global and Relationship-Based Levels of Analysis. *Journal of Social and Personal Relationships*, 11: 295–312.

Sarnoff, I., and Sarnoff, S. (1989). *Love-Centered Marriage in a Self-Centered World*. New York: Hemisphere Publishing.

Saxena, F. C., Kulczycki, A., and Jurdi, R. (2004). Nuptiality Transition and Marriage Squeeze in Lebanon: Consequences of Sixteen Years of Civil War. *Journal of Comparative Family Studies*, 35: 241–258.

Schachter, S. (1959). *The Psychology of Affiliation*. Stanford, CA: Stanford University Press.

Scharf, T. (1995). The Social Integration of Elderly People in Rural Europe. In T. Scharf and G. C. Wenger, eds., *International Perspectives on Community Care for Older People*, pp. 95–121. Aldershot, England: Averbury.

Schmitz, P. G. (1994). Acculturation and Adaptation Processes among Immigrants to Germany. In A.-M. Bouvy, F. van de Vijver, P. Bowski, and P. Schmitz, eds., *Journeys into Cross-Cultural Psychology*, pp. 142–157. Lisse, The Netherlands: Swets and Zeitlinger.

Schvaneveldt, P. L. (2003). Mate Selection Preferences and Practices in Ecuador and Latin America. In R. R. Hamon and B. B. Ingoldsby, eds., *Mate Selection across Cultures*, pp. 43–59. Thousand Oaks, CA: Sage Publications.

Schvaneveldt, P. L., Kerpelman, J. L., and Schvaneveldt, J. D. (2005). Generational and Cultural Changes in Family Life in the United Arab Emirates. *Journal of Comparative Family Studies*, 36: 77–91.

Schwartz, S. H. (2004). Mapping and Interpreting Cultural Differences around the World. In H. Vinken, J. Soeters, and P. Ester, eds., Comparing Cultures: Dimensions of Culture in a Comparative Perspective, pp. 43–73. Leiden, The Netherlands: Brill.

(2006). What Explains Societal Differences in Culture? Invited paper presented at the eighteenth International Congress of IACCP, Isle of Spetses, Greece.

Schwartz, S. H., and Bardi, A. (1997). Influences of Adaptation to Communist Rule on Value Priorities in Eastern Europe. *Political Psychology*, 18: 385–410.

(2001). Value Hierarchies across Cultures. *Journal of Cross-Cultural Psychology*, 32: 268–290.

Schwartz, S. H., and Sagie, G. (2000). Value Consensus and Importance. *Journal of Cross-Cultural Psychology*, 31: 465–497.

Schwarzer, R., and Chung, R. (1996). Anticipating Stress in the Community: Worries about the Future of Hong Kong. *Anxiety, Stress and Coping*, 9: 163–178.

Schwarzer, R., Hahn, A., and Schröder, H. (1994). Social Integration and Social Support in a Life Crisis: Effects of Macro-social Change in East Germany. *American Journal of Community Psychology*, 22: 685–706.

Schwarzer, R., and Leppin, A. (1991). Social Support and Health: A Theoretical and Empirical Overview. *Journal of Social and Personal Relationships*, 8: 99–127.

Seccombe, R. (2002). "Beating the Odds" versus "Changing the Odds": Poverty, Resilience, and Family Policy. *Journal of Marriage and Family*, 64: 384–394.

Secondi, G. S. (2002). Biased Childhood Sex Ratios and the Economic Status of the Family in Rural China. *Journal of Comparative Family Studies*, 33: 215–234.

Segall, M. H., Dasen, P. R., Berry, J. W., and Poortinga, Y. H. (1990). *Human Behavior in Global Perspective: An Introduction to Cross-Cultural Psychology*. Boston: Allyn and Bacon.

Seltzer, J. A. (2004). Cohabitation in the United States and Britain: Demography, Kinship, and the Future. *Journal of Marriage and Family*, 66: 921–928.

Sered, S. S. (1990). Women, Religion, and Modernization: Tradition and Transformation amongst Elderly Jews in Israel. *American Anthropologist*, 92: 306–318.

Settles, B. H. (2001). Being at Home in a Global Society: A Model for Families' Mobility and Immigration Decisions. *Journal of Comparative Family Studies*, 32: 627–645.

(2001b). Conflicts between Family Strategies and State Policy in a Global Society. *Journal of Comparative Family Studies*, 32: 149–166.

Severy, L. J., Waszak, C., Badawi, I., and Kafafi, L. (2003). The Psychological Well-Being of Women in Menoufiya, Egypt. *American Psychologist*, 58: 218–223.

Sheela, J., and Audinarayana, N. (2003). Mate Selection and Female Age and Marriage: A Micro Level Investigation in Tamil Nadu, India. *Journal of Comparative Family Studies*, 34: 497–508.

Sheeran, P., Abraham, C., and Orbell, S. S. (1999). Psychosocial Correlates of Heterosexual Condom Use: A Meta-analysis. *Psychological Bulletin*, 125: 90–132.

Shlapentokh, V. (1984). *Love, Marriage and Friendship in the Soviet Union: Ideals and Practices*. New York: Praeger.

Shumway, D. R. (2003). *Modern Love: Romance, Intimacy, and the Marriage Crisis*. New York: New York University Press.

Sik, E., and Wellman, B. (1999). Network Capital in Capitalist, Communist, and Postcommunist Countries. In B. Wellman, ed., *Networks in the Global Village: Life in Contemporary Communities*, pp. 225–253. Boulder, CO: Westview Press.

Silbereisen, R. K., and Wiesner, M. (2002). Lessons from Research on the Consequences of German Unification: Continuity and Discontinuity of Self-Efficacy and the Timing of Psychosocial Transitions. *Applied Psychology: An International Review*, 51: 291–317.

Simpson, J. A. (1986). The Association between Romantic Love and Marriage. *Personality and Social Psychology Bulletin*, 12: 363–372.

Sinha, D. (1991). Rise in the Population of the Elderly, Familial Changes and Their Psychosocial Implications: The Scenario of the Developing Countries. *International Journal of Psychology*, 26: 633–647.

Smelser, N. J. (1959). *Social Change in the Industrial Revolution: An Application of Theory to the British Cotton Industry 1770–1840*. Chicago: University of Chicago Press.

Smit, R. (2001). The Impact of Labor Migration on African Families in South Africa: Yesterday and Today. *Journal of Comparative Family Studies*, 32: 533–548.

(2002). The Changing Role of the Husband/Father in the Dual-Earner Family in South Africa. *Journal of Comparative Family Studies*, 33: 401–415.

Smith, H. (1990). *The New Russians*. London: Hutchinson.

Smith, P. B., and Bond, M. H. (2003). Honoring Culture Scientifically When Doing Social Psychology. In M. A. Hogg and J. Cooper, eds., *Sage Handbook of Social Psychology*, pp. 43–64. Thousand Oaks, CA: Sage Publications.

Smith, P. B., Bond, M. H., and Kağitçibaşi, C. (2006). *Understanding Social Psychology across Cultures: Living and Working in a Changing World*. London: Sage Publications.

Smith, P. B., Dugan, S., and Trompenaars, F. (1996). National Culture and Managerial Values: A Dimensional Analysis across 43 Nations. *Journal of Cross-Cultural Psychology*, 27: 252–285.

Smock, P. J. (2004). The Wax and Wane of Marriage: Prospects for Marriage in the 21st Century. *Journal of Marriage and Family*, 66: 966–973.

Social Trends (2003). Social Trends 33, ed. by C. Summerfield and P. Babb. London: The Stationery Office. Retrieved from http://www.statistics.gov.uk.

Somasundaram, D. K. (1996). Post-Traumatic Responses to Aerial Bombing. *Social Science and Medicine*, 42: 1465–1472.

Sontag, S. (1989). *AIDS and Its Metaphors*. New York: Doubleday.

Sorokin, P. A. (1998). *On the Practice of Sociology*. Chicago: University of Chicago Press.

South, S. J., Haynie, D. L., and Bose, S. (2005). Residential Mobility and the Onset of Adolescent Sexual Activity. *Journal of Marriage and Family*, 67: 499–514.

South, S. J., Trent, K., and Shen, Y. (2001). Changing Partners: Toward a Macrostructural-Opportunity Theory of Marital Dissolution. *Journal of Marriage and Family*, 63: 743–754.

Spencer, H. (1892). *Sociology*. New York: Appleton.

(1897). *Principles of Sociology*. New York: Appleton.

Spengler, O. (1926). *The Decline of the West*. New York: Knopf.

Spicer, E. H. (1952). *Human Problems in Technological Change*. New York: Russell Sage Foundation.

Spjeldnæs, I., Peltze, K., and Sam, D. L. (2006). Continuity and Change in Reproductive Attitudes among Teenage Girls and Their Mothers and Maternal Grandmothers in South Africa. Paper presented at the eighteenth International Congress of the International Association of Cross-Cultural Psychology, Isle of Spetses, Greece.

Steward, J. H. (1955). *Theory of Culture Change: The Methodology of Multilinear Evolution*: Urbana: University of Illinois Press.

Stopes-Roe, M., and Cochrane, R. (1990). Support Networks of Asian and British Families: Comparisons between Ethnicities and between Generations. *Social Behaviour*, 5: 71–85.

Sugawara, I., and Akiyama, H. (2004). Friendship in Personal Network of Japanese Adults over the Life Course. Paper presented at the International Association for Relationship Research Conference, Madison, WI.

Suh, E., Diener, E., Oishi, S., and Triandis, H. (1998). The Shifting Basis of Life Satisfaction Judgements across Cultures: Emotions versus Norms. *Journal of Personality and Social Psychology*, 74: 482–493.

Sumbadze, N. (2006). Georgia. In J. Georgas, J. W. Berry, F. V. R. Van de Vijver, C. Kağitçibaşi, and Y. H. Poortinga, eds., *Families across Cultures: A 30-Nation Psychological Study*, pp. 319–326. Cambridge: Cambridge University Press.

Super, C. M., and Harkness, S. (1997). Modernization, Family Life, and Child Development in Kokwet. In T. S. Weisner, C. Bradley, and P. L. Kilbride, eds., *African Families and the Crisis of Social Change*, pp. 341–353. Westport, CT: Bergin and Garvey.

Svejnar, J. (2002). Transition Economies: Performance and Challenges. *Journal of Economic Perspectives*, 16: 3–28.

Svenkerud, P. J., Rao, N., and Rogers, E. M. (1999). Mass Media Effects through Interpersonal Communication: The Role of "Twende na Wakati" on the Adoption of HIV/AIDS Prevention in Tanzania. In W. N. Elwood, ed., *Power in the Blood: A Handbook on AIDS, Politics, and Communication*, pp. 243–253. Mahwah, NJ: Lawrence Erlbaum.

Sweeney, M. M., and Cancian, M. (2004). The Changing Importance of White Women's Economic Prospects for Assertive Mating. *Journal of Marriage and Family*, 66: 1015–1028.

Takyi, B. K. (2003). Tradition and Change in Family and Marital Processes. In R. R. Hamon and B. B. Ingoldsby, eds., *Mate Selection across Cultures*, pp. 79–94. Thousand Oaks, CA: Sage Publications.

Tannous, A. I. (1941). Social Change in an Arab Village. *American Sociological Review*, 6: 650–662.

Tashakorri, A., and Thompson, V. (1988). Cultural Change and Attitude Change: An Assessment of Post-Revolutionary Marriage and Family Attitudes in Iran. *Population Research and Policy Review*, 7: 3–27.

——— (1991). Social Change and Change in Intentions of Iranian Youth Regarding Education, Marriage and Careers. *International Journal of Psychology*, 26: 203–217.

Thornhill, N. W, and Thornhill, R. (1987). Evolutionary Theory and Rules of Mating and Marriage Pertaining to Relatives. In C. Crawford, M. Smith, and D. Krebs, eds., *Sociobiology and Psychology: Issues and Applications*, pp. 373–400. Hillsdale, NJ: Lawrence Erlbaum.

Thornton, A., and Young-Demarco, L. (2001). Four Decades of Trends in Attitudes toward Family Issues in the United States: The 1960s through the 1990s. *Journal of Marriage and Family*, 63: 1009–1037.

Ting-Toomey, S. (1991). Intimacy Expressions in Three Cultures: France, Japan, and the United States. *International Journal of Intercultural Relations*, 15: 29–46.

Toffler, A. (1970). *Future Shock*. New York: Random.

Tonkiss, F. (2004). Trust and Social Capital. Families and Social Capital (ESRC Research Group Working Papers, No. 7). London South Bank University. Retrieved from http://www.lsbu.ac.uk/families.

Tönnies, F. ([1887]; 1957). *Gemeinschaft und Gesellschaft [Community and Society]*. East Lansing: Michigan State University Press.

Tornstam, L. (1992). Loneliness in Marriage. *Journal of Social and Personal Relationships*, 9: 197–217.

Towianska, A., Rozlucka, E., and Dabrowski, J. (1992). Prevalence of HIV Anti-bodies in Maritime Workers and in Other Selected Population Groups in Poland. *Bulletin of the Institute of Maritime and Topical Medicine in Gdynia*, 43: 19–24.

Townsend, J. W. (2003). Reproductive Behavior in the Context of Global Population. *American Psychologist*, 58: 197–204.

Toynbee, A. J., and Caplan, J. (1972). *A Study of History*. Oxford: Oxford University Press.

Trappe, H., and Rosenfeld, R. A. (2000). How Do Children Matter? A Comparison of Gender Earnings Inequality for Young Adults in the Former East Germany and the Former West Germany. *Journal of Marriage and Family*, 62: 489–507.

Triandis, H. C. (1989). Self and Social Behavior in Differing Cultural Contexts. *Psychological Review*, 96: 269–289.

—— (1994). Theoretical and Methodological Approaches to the Study of Collectivism and Individualism. In U. Kim, H. C. Triandis, C. Kağitçibaşi, S.-C. Choi, and G. Yoon, eds., *Individualism and Collectivism: Theory, Method and Applications*, pp. 41–51. Thousand Oaks, CA: Sage Publications.

—— (2001). Individualism-Collectivism and Personality. *Journal of Personality*, 69: 907–924.

Triandis, H. C., Bontempo, R., and Villareal, M. J. (1988). Individualism and Collectivism: Cross-Cultural Perspectives on Self-in-Group Relationships. *Journal of Personality and Social Psychology*, 54: 323–338.

Turiel, E. (2002). *The Culture of Morality: Social Development, Context, and Conflict*. Cambridge: Cambridge University Press.

Tzeng, J. M. (2000). Ethnically Heterogamous Marriages: The Case of Asian Canadians. *Journal of Comparative Family Studies*, 31: 321–337.

Udry, J. R. (1981). Marital Alternatives and Marital Disruption. *Journal of Marriage and Family*, 43: 889–897.

UNAIDS (2002a). Global HIV/AIDS and STD Surveillance. Retrieved from http://www.unaids.org.

—— (2002b). *Response Analysis on HIV/AIDS in Georgia*. Tbilisi, Georgia. Retrieved from http://www.unaids.org.

—— (2006). 2006 AIDS Epidemic Update. Retrieved from http://www.unaids.org

Unger, J. (1993). Urban families in the Eighties: An analysis of Chinese surveys. In D. Davis & S. Harrell, eds. *Chinese Families in the Post-Mao Era*, pp. 25–49. Berkeley: University of California Press.

U.S. Census Bureau. *Your Gateway to Census 2000*. Retrieved from http://www.census.gov/main/www/cen2000.html.

Van de Vijver, F. J. R. (2004). A Cross-Cultural Analysis of the Family. Paper presented at the seventeenth International Congress for Cross-Cultural Psychology, Xi'an, China.

Van de Vijver, F. J. R., and Poortinga, Y. H. (1990). A Taxonomy of Cultural Differences. In F. J. R. van de Vijver and G. J. M. Hutschemaekers, eds., *The Investigation of Culture: Current Issues in Cultural Psychology*, pp. 191–214. Tilburg, The Netherlands: Tilburg University Press.

Van de Vliert, E. (2006). Autocratic Leadership around the Globe: Do Climate and Wealth Drive Leadership Culture? *Journal of Cross-Cultural Psychology*, 37: 42–59.

—— (2007). Climates Create Cultures. *Social and Personality Psychology Compass*, 1: 53–67.

Van Hemert, D. (2003). *Patterns of Cross-Cultural Differences in Psychology: A Meta-Analytic Approach*. Amsterdam: Dutch University Press.

Vannoy, D. (1998). The Patriarchal Legacy in Russian Marriages. Paper presented at the ninth International Conference on Personal Relationships, Saratoga Springs, NY.

Vannoy, D., and Cubbins, L. A. (2001). Relative Socio-economic Status of Spouses, Gender Attitudes, and Attributes, and Marital Quality Experienced by Couples in Metropolitan Moscow. *Journal of Comparative Family Studies*, 32: 195–217.

Vannoy, D., Rimashevskaya, N., Cubbins, L., Maysheva, M., Mesherkina, E., and Pisklakova, M. (1999). *Marriages in Russia: Couples during the Economic Transition*. Westport, CT: Praeger.

Vergin, N. (1985). Social Change and the Family in Turkey. *Current Anthropology*, 26: 571–574.

Verkasalo, M., Goodwin, R., and Bezmenova, I. (2006). Value Change Following a Major Terrorist Incident: Finnish Adolescent and Student Values before and after 11th September 2001. *Journal of Applied Social Psychology*, 36: 144–160.

Vernon, M. (2007). *The Philosophy of Friendship*. Basingstoke, England: Palgrave Macmillan.

Vincent, S. (2000). Flexible Families: Capitalist Development and Crisis in Rural Peru. *Journal of Comparative Family Studies*, 31: 155–170.

Wagels, K., and Roemhild, R. (1998). The German Way: Dissolving the Significance of Marriage. Paper presented at the fourteenth Congress of the International Association of Cross-Cultural Psychology, Western Washington University, Bellingham, WA.

Wagner, W. (1995). Description, Explanation and Method in Social Representation Research. *Papers on Social Representations*, 4: 156–176.

Waites, M. (2004). The Age of Consent and Sexual Consent. In M. Cowling and P. Reynolds, eds., *Making Sense of Sexual Consent*, pp. 73–92. Aldershot, England: Ashgate.

Walker, A. (2004). A Symposium on Marriage and Its Future. *Journal of Marriage and Family*, 66: 843–847.

Wan, C. K., Jaccard, J., and Ramey, S. L. (1996). The Relationship between Social Support and Life Satisfaction as a Function of Family Structure. *Journal of Marriage and Family*, 58: 502–513.

Wang, J. (2004). Study on Quality of Life in Chinese Rural Paid Blood Donors with HIV/AIDS. Paper presented at the seventeenth International Association for Cross-Cultural Psychology Conference, Xi'an, China.

Wang, R., Bianchi, S. M., and Raley, S. B. (2005). Teenagers' Internet Use and Family Rules: A Research Note. *Journal of Marriage and Family*, 67: 1249–1258.

Wapner, S., and Craig-Bray, L. (1992). Person-in-Environment: Theoretical and Methodological Approaches. *Environment and Behavior*, 24: 161–188.

Waskul, D. D. (2004). *Net SeXXX: Readings on Sex, Pornography, and the Internet*. New York: Peter Lang.

Waterman, A. S. (1981). Individualism and Psychological Independence. *American Psychologist*, 36: 762–773.

Watson, J. L. (1998). *Golden Arches East: McDonald's in East Asia*. Cambridge: Cambridge University Press.

Weber, M. ([1921]; 1968). *Economy and Society*. New York: Bedminster Press.
  (1958). *The Protestant Ethic and the Spirit of Capitalism*. New York: Charles Scribner.

Wellings, K., Collumbien, M., Slaymaker, E., Singh, S., Hodges, Z., Patel, D., and Najos, N. (2006). Sexual Behaviour in Context: A Global Perspective. *Lancet*, 368: 1706–1728.

Wellings, K., Fields, J., Johnson, A. M., and Wadsworth, J. (1994). *Sexual Behaviour in Britain*. London: Penguin.

Wellings, K., Nancharhal, K., Macdowall, W., McManus, S., Erens, B., Mercer, C. H., Johnson, A. M., Copas, A. J., Korovessis, C., Fenton, K. A., and Field, J. (2001). Sexual Behaviour in Britain: Early Heterosexual Experience. *Lancet*, 358: 1843–1850.

Wellman, B. (1985). Domestic Work, Paid Work and Network. In S. W. Duck and D. Perlman, eds., *Understanding Personal Relationships*, pp. 159–191. Beverly Hills, CA: Sage Publications.
  (1994). I Was a Teenage Network Analyst: The Route from the Bronx to the Information Highway. *Connections*, 17: 28–45.

Westermarck, E. (1922). *History of Human Marriage*. New York: Macmillan.

Whyte, M. K. (1992). Introduction: Rural Economic Reforms and Chinese Family Patterns. *China Quarterly*, 130: 317–322.

Whyte, M. K., and Parish, W. L. (1984). *Urban Life in Contemporary China*. Chicago: University of Chicago Press.

Wikan, U. (1996). *Tomorrow, God Willing: Self-Made Destinies in Cairo*. Chicago: University of Chicago Press.

Williams, D. (1990). Socio-economic Differential in Health: A Review and Redirection. *Social Psychology Quarterly*, 53: 81–99.

Williams, M., Chandler, J., Maconachie, M., Collett, T., and Dodgeon, B. (2005). Home Alone 1971–2001. Paper presented at the ESRC Seminar: Learning about the Past from the Present. London: South Bank University.

Wilson, S. M., Ngige, L. W., and Trollinger, L. J. (2003). Connecting Generations. In R. R. Hamon and B. B. Ingoldsby, eds., *Mate Selection across Cultures*, pp. 95–118. Thousand Oaks, CA: Sage Publications.

Wisendale, S. K. (2000). Family Policy in a Changing Vietnam. *Journal of Comparative Family Studies*, 31: 79–90.

Wong, O. M. H. (2003). Postponement or Abandonment of Marriage? Evidence from Hong Kong. *Journal of Comparative Family Studies*, 34: 531–554.

Xia, Y. R., and Zhou, Z. G. (2003). "The Transition of Courtship, Mate Selection, and Marriage in China." In R. R. Hamon and B. B. Ingoldsby, eds., *Mate Selection across Cultures*, pp. 231–246. Thousand Oaks, CA: Sage Publications.

Xu, A. Q. (2000). Standard of Spouse Selection: Reasons for Changes in the Past 50 Years. *Social Sciences Study*, 7: 18–30.

Xu, A. Q., Xie, X., Liu, W., Xia, Y., and Liu, D. (2007). Chinese Family Strengths and Resiliency. *Marriage and Family Review*, 41: 143–164.

Xu, X., and Whyte, M. K. (1990). Love Matches and Arranged Marriages: A Chinese Replication. *Journal of Marriage and Family*, 52: 709–722.

Yang, C.-F. (1988). Familism and Development: An Examination of the Role of Family in Contemporary China Mainland, Hong Kong and Taiwan. In D. Sinha and H. Kao, eds., *Social Values and Development: Asian Perspectives*, pp. 93–123. New Delhi: Sage Publications.

Yang, K. S. (1996). The Psychological Transformation of the Chinese People as a Result of Societal Modernization. In M. Bond, ed., *The Handbook of Chinese Psychology*, pp. 479–498. Hong Kong: Oxford University Press.

Yi, C. C., and Chien, W. Y. (2002). The Linkage between Work and Family: Females' Employment Patterns in Three Chinese Societies. *Journal of Comparative Family Studies*, 33: 451–474.

Yi, Z. (2001). A Demographic Analysis of Family Households in China, 1982–1995. *Journal of Comparative Family Studies*, 33: 15–33.

Young, M., and Willmott, P. (1957). *Family and Kinship in East London*. London: Routledge.

Yuchtman-Ya'ar, E. (2003). Value Priorities in Israeli Society: An Examination of Inglehart's Theory of Modernization and Cultural Variation. In R. Inglehart, ed., *Human Values and Social Change: Findings from the Values Surveys*, pp. 117–137. Leiden, The Netherlands: Brill.

Yun, H. A. (2004). Ideology and Changing Family Arrangements in Singapore. *Journal of Comparative Family Studies*, 35: 375–392.

Yurchisin, J., Watchravesringkan, K., and McCabe, D. B. (2005). An Exploration of Identity Re-creation in the Context of Internet Dating. *Social Behavior and Personality*, 33: 735–750.

Zontini, E. (2004). Italian Families and Social Capital: Rituals and the Provision of Care in British-Italian Transnational Families. Families and Social Capital ESRC Research Group, South Bank University, London. Retrieved from http://www.lsbu.ac.uk/families.

Zotovic, M. (2004). *Stres I Mentalno Zdravlje Dece: Studija Posledica Bombardovanja*. Belgrade: Zuduzbina Andrejevic.

Index

OTHER BOOKS IN THE SERIES (*continued from page iii*)

Growing Together: Personal Relationships Across the Life Span
  Frieder R. Lang and Karen L. Fingerman
Stability and Change in Relationships
  Anita L. Vangelisti, Harry T. Reis, and Mary Anne Fitzpatrick
Understanding Marriage: Developments in the Study of Couple Interaction
  Patricia Noller and Judith A. Feeney
Feeling Hurt in Close Relationships
  Anita Vangelisti